Taming Jaguar

Taming Jaguar

MIKE BARLOTTA

JASON WEISS

MANNING

Greenwich
(74° w. long.)

For electronic information and ordering of this and other Manning books, go to www.manning.com. The publisher offers discounts on this book when ordered in quantity. For more information, please contact:

Special Sales Department
Manning Publications Co.
32 Lafayette Place   Fax: (203) 661-9018
Greenwich, CT 06830   email: orders@manning.com

Ⲙ Manning Publications Co.   Copyeditor: Lori Jareo
   32 Lafayette Place   Typesetter: Denis Dalinnik
   Greenwich, CT 06830   Cover designer: Leslie Haimes

Printed in the United States of America
1 2 3 4 5 6 7 8 9 10 – VH – 03 02 01 00

To my wife Angela for her patience and love.
—Mike Barlotta

To my wife Meredith whom I'll love always and forever.
And to Mom and Dad—I told you that Apple IIc was an investment!
—Jason Weiss

brief contents

contents

2   *Designing components for the jungle*   *41*

5   *Factory objects 130*

preface

The application server market is a jungle in which several products and ideas abound. However, as in the jungle, only the strongest will survive. We believe that Jaguar CTS is the best application server on the market. We say that unabashedly and without restraint. Sybase has delivered a best-of-breed product that has delivered openness, scalablilty, and performance to the enterprise. Let the competition take note: Surviving in the jungle just got a bit tougher.

Since its initial introduction to the market, Jaguar CTS has become a proven technology platform capable of delivering powerful distributed applications. Teamed up with PowerDynamo, it is now known as Sybase Enterprise Application Server (EAServer), a platform that continues to provide a state-of-the-art, distributed architecture that companies are using as the cornerstone in their next-generation, Web-enabled applications. EAServer's robust feature set includes CORBA and J2EE (EJB, JSP, servlets) support, powerful declarative transaction capabilities and unmatched component support, as well as clustering to deliver a highly available and load balanced application. The features in EAServer have acted as a catalyst, taking customers' mission-critical applications to the next tier—the nth-tier.

The momentum that started with the release of EAServer 3.0 and the successful Build the Future tours has continued with the latest releases, EAServer 3.5 and 3.6, and the recent J2EE Whistle-stop Tour. With EAServer 3.6 (currently in beta), Jaguar CTS is a Java 2 Enterprise Edition (J2EE)-compliant application server, bringing many already supported features up-to-date with Sun's latest specifications. This book looks into how these powerful enterprise-level technologies can be taken advantage of on the Jaguar CTS platform.

Jaguar CTS is a large and complicated topic and encompasses many different technologies, some of them extremely new. *Taming Jaguar* is an advanced book that takes aim at covering new features related to J2EE and answering complex development and administration questions on the Jaguar CTS application server based on real-world experience from living and working with the product. *Taming Jaguar* is a guide to helping solve challenges in developing EAServer applications in both PowerBuilder and Java. But it is not a PowerBuilder book or a Java book; it is a Jaguar CTS book.

As managers, developers, and administrators, are you ready to begin taming this beast so that it can help run your enterprise or will you be overtaken by your competition? In the application server jungle, the lion is not king. The Jaguar is!

Intended audience

Make no doubt about it, this is an advanced book on EAServer. This book is not intended to teach a novice the basics required to become a Jaguar CTS developer. In many ways, this book is a sequel to the book *Jaguar Development with Power-Builder 7*. In writing *Taming Jaguar*, we did our best to minimize duplication of material between the two books. Although the book *Jaguar Development with Power-Builder 7* had as one of its objectives the transformation of client/server Power-Builder developers into Jaguar CTS component developers, it also presents EAServer clearly to those new to the technology. It clearly lays out the foundations required for understanding the Jaguar server, the component life cycle, and database connection caches, and walks you through developing your first Jaguar components. We consider the readers of this book to be beyond these learning stages and well beyond their first component deployment.

This book is aimed at advanced developers and administrators who have some experience with Jaguar CTS and little to no experience with PowerDynamo, the other half of EAServer. We have made the assumption that you are familiar and comfortable with PowerJ, PowerBuilder, and/or other development environments capable of authoring and deploying EAServer components. If you are new to EAServer, this book is probably not for you.

How this book is organized

We took a different approach with this book, presenting the information in a FAQ-styled format. This format was chosen so that readers could use this book as a reference and quickly find the information they need to solve their problems. The questions are grouped into chapters based on the theme of the questions.

Chapter 1: Becoming a Jaguar tamer

This chapter covers Jaguar administration techniques and considerations, including backups, as well as how to prepare a cluster of servers to implement load balancing and high availability.

Chapter 2: Designing components for the jungle

Designing a robust component is arguably more difficult than designing a traditional client application. This chapter covers crucial design techniques, stateful and stateless component design, and takes a detailed look at the effect of component property combinations such as bind thread, shared, and concurrent.

Chapter 3: Are these magic Beans?

An Enterprise Java Beans (EJB) primer using PowerJ and Jaguar. This chapter covers the basics behind the EJB specification and walks through creating and deploying an Entity Bean and a stateless Session Bean.

Chapter 4: Servicing the jungle

Jaguar services are a very powerful feature when integrated into the overall design of a distributed application. This chapter covers service component design and deployment issues.

Chapter 5: Factory objects

Factories are used by a client to create a remote instance of an object and get the required remote reference to use it. In this chapter we look at the less common PowerBuilder JaguarORB and CORBAObject, as well as discuss PowerJ's Initial-Context and CORBA ORB classes.

Chapter 6: Peering into the Jaguar interface repository

The Jaguar repository is the central nervous system of the server. This chapter details techniques that can be incorporated into any application, providing a look into Jaguar and its administrative capabilities. Also, we detail how to create a proprietary authentication service to validate client logon requests.

Chapter 7: Jaguar naming services

Jaguar naming services are largely responsible for Jaguar's ability to provide location transparency, high availability, and load balancing of client requests.

Understanding Jaguar's naming services is necessary to fully exploit Jaguar's advanced features.

Chapter 8: What to do when your Jaguar is caught in the Web

This chapter provides an overview on different architectural approaches that can be taken to access Jaguar CTS over the Web. The remainder of the chapter covers PowerDynamo basics.

Chapter 9: Jaguar and PowerDynamo

This chapter covers how PowerDynamo and Jaguar CTS can be integrated in detail using the java object in PowerDynamo. Special attention is given to dealing with Java–CORBA nuances.

Chapter 10: Jaguar and Java on the Web

This chapter explores extending Jaguar applications to the Web using Java applets and Java servlets. The basics behind both these technologies are explained along with several examples. In addition, we look ahead to Java Server Pages.

Appendix A: Jaguar data types
Appendix B: A look ahead at Jaguar 3.6
Appendix C: EAServer certification

Conventions

This book uses some conventions to bring important messages to the reader's attention or hammer home a certain point.

Command line examples and code listings are set in a fixed-pitch font. File names, new words, and emphasized words will be italicized.

Any warnings, tips, or notes associated with information being provided in this text will be pulled out and set apart in a Note, Tip, or Warning box. Please pay heed to these pull-outs, as they may contain additional, useful information, or warnings about exceptions to normal operations.

Watch for the new Report Cards, which are special sections set apart from the text that contain pros and cons of various technologies and designs.

Code samples

Since the jungle of enterprise computing is so diverse, we have developed a mix of HTML/DynaScript, Java, and PowerBuilder code examples. All of the code examples covered throughout the text as well as additional samples are available as downloadable source code on the book's web site, www.manning.com/barlotta3. Sybase's EAStudio 3.5 was used to write this book, which includes Jaguar CTS 3.5 and PowerDynamo 3.5. PowerJ 3.5 was used to create all of the Java examples shown in this book.

About the authors

The authors met at TechWave 1999 and found they shared interests in, among other things, Jaguar CTS. We shared tips and ideas through emails for several months until we came to the conclusion that an advanced book on these topics would benefit the user community.

Michael J. Barlotta is the director of technology for AEGIS Consulting. He is also the distributed technologies editor for the PowerBuilder Developer's Journal and the author of *Distributed Application Development with PowerBuilder 6* and *Jaguar Development with PowerBuilder 7*. He has mentored several clients on the Jaguar CTS product using PowerBuilder, PowerJ, and PowerDynamo and is the chief architect for the National Senior Olympics web site (www.nsga.com). Mike wrote chapters 1, 3, 8, 9, and 10 and also wrote the appendices. He may be contacted at mike.barlotta@aegisconsulting.com.

Jason R. Weiss is an independent software developer and a former certified PowerBuilder instructor, certified PowerBuilder developer, Microsoft Certified System Engineer, and Microsoft Certified Trainer. He routinely mentors enterprise clients on building distributed EAServer applications. Jason wrote chapters 2, 4, 5, 6, and 7, and he may be contacted at jweiss@wisemantechnologies.com.

acknowledgments

The authors would like to thank the following people for their contributions to this project:

- Jim O'Neill of Sybase Inc. for his contributions in reviewing the technical material and answering our questions whenever we were stuck. Jim took our calls and our emails and tirelessly answered them all. Thanks, Jim, we learned a lot.

- Mario Heggart, CEO of AEGIS Consulting for giving me (Mike) the time to do this project when he should have been making me earn my keep. Without Mario's dedication, I could not have done this project because I could not sacrifice any more time with my family or church to do another book.

- Dave Gilbert of Sybase Inc. for getting us in touch with the correct Sybase people when we needed answers to our questions.

- Marjan Brace and Ted Kennedy of Manning Publications for giving us the opportunity to write the book.

- Mary Piergies the production manager, the WordTech team of Lori Jareo and Kevin Walzer, Denis Dalinnik, and Dottie Marsico, who accepted the daunting task of producing this book in record time for TechWave 2000!

- To all the reviewers who made sure that this book was as technically correct and solid as possible, including: Tim Barlotta, Bill Buermeyer, Wendy Gereke, Dean Jones, Scott McReynolds, Jim O'Neill, John Olson, and Dave Wolf.

- And to the LORD, for bringing together such a talented and dedicated bunch of people who collectively made this book possible.

contacting the authors

We sincerely hope *Taming Jaguar* provides answers to those questions that have been troubling you and your development and/or production environment. If we have missed an area in which you have questions or problems, please let us know so we can try to help in the author online forum. If you have a valuable tip or technique that we may have overlooked, please provide us with some of your insight as well.

Writing on "bleeding-edge" technologies and evolving specifications in the fast-paced world of enterprise computing can be very exciting and is often a learning process for the authors as well as the readers. Trying to deliver this information in a way that is timely and user-friendly to developers is a tough job. In writing this book, every effort has been made to make sure that the material is error-free. However, errors are part of the game in writing about technology, and we the authors take the blame for any that appear in this book. As readers discover mistakes, we would very much like to be informed about them, preferably only once. The book's web site, www.manning.com/barlotta3, contains a listing of errata. In the event you come across a bug that has not been reported, please submit it using the author online forum.

The purchase of *Taming Jaguar* includes free access to the author online forum, where you can go to make comments about the book, ask technical questions, and receive help from the author and other Jaguar users. To access the forum, point your Web browser to www.manning.com/barlotta3.

All right. Enough talk. Now, let's go tame some jaguars!

1
Becoming
a Jaguar tamer

This chapter covers:
- Administrating Jaguar CTS
- Clustering servers in Jaguar CTS
- Synchronizing servers
- Implementing load balancing
- Implementing high availability
- Database caching tips

Jaguar Component Transaction Server (CTS) has many properties. While not as configurable as a modern Relational Database Management System (RDBMS), it can be tuned to operate optimally based on different application and operating scenarios. Jaguar servers are scalable and can be clustered together to provide load balancing and high availability to any application. This chapter will look at some issues involved with setting up and tuning Jaguar CTS from an administrator's point of view. The assumption this chapter makes is that the administrator is comfortable navigating through the Jaguar Manager interface and has some Jaguar experience.

1.1 *What should be done after installing Jaguar CTS?*

Jaguar CTS installation procedures vary from platform to platform. The particular nuances of installing Jaguar CTS on a particular platform are covered in the Sybase help. After installing Jaguar CTS there are several steps that need to be taken to prepare the application server for use. Here is a list of action items that need to be addressed by the administrator after installing Jaguar CTS, particularly for a production server.

1 Configure the listeners for network accessibility.

2 Change the jagadmin password. The default is blank, so for security reasons it is important to change the password.

3 Remove the packages containing the sample code shipped with the product.
   - SVU
   - SurfSideVideoPJ
   - SurfSideVideoPB

4 Remove the SurfSideVideoPJ/CleanupService component from the service property, com.sybase.jaguar.server.services. There have been documented problems with this service component in Jaguar 3.0x, and unless it is being used it will take up server resources.

5 Configure security options including roles, secure listeners, operating system authentication, and identities as needed.

6 Configure database connection caches based on application requirements.

7 Deploy the packages for the application.

One of the settings that will need to be changed on a production installation of the Jaguar CTS server is the maximum number of concurrent users that will be allowed. The maximum number of concurrent users allowed by default is only thirty. This can be changed on the Resources tab of the Server Properties dialog.

The administrator should enter the number of concurrent client connections required in the maximum client connections field, based on testing the application under production-level loads. Note that this field includes all non-HTTP (Hypertext Transfer Protocol) clients. The number of HTTP clients is controlled on the HTTP Config tab of the Server Properties dialog. The Message Pool size, Message Queue size, and Network buffer size options on the Resources tab are only used by Open Client applications.

NOTE   Jaguar CTS 3.0x supports the Windows NT 4, Solaris, HP-UX, and AIX operating system environments. Jaguar 3.5 supports the Windows NT 4 and Solaris operating system environments. Support for additional UNIX platforms including Linux, HP-UX, and AIX have been announced but there is no timetable on when they will be available. The Jaguar 3.5 Linux version is in beta at the time of this writing and does not support a PowerBuilder virtual machine (VM).

1.2   What is a logical server?

When Jaguar CTS is installed on a single physical machine, it is given a default logical server name of Jaguar. In most cases this is satisfactory for running the Jaguar CTS application server. Using the Jaguar Manager, however, you can create additional logical servers on a single machine. Each logical server is a separate instance of the Jaguar server running on the same physical machine. Each logical server shares the same repository directory but each logical server can set different server configuration properties and allow different packages, components, and database connection caches to be made available. Figure 1.1 illustrates a Jaguar Manager that is connected to Jaguar CTS with two logical servers, Jaguar and Jag2. Notice that each logical server has its own set of Listeners, Installed Connection Caches, Installed Packages, Installed Servlets, and Runtime Monitoring folders.

To create a new logical server, highlight the Servers folder and select File | New Server from the main menu or the popup menu. The New Server dialog will open. Enter a name for the new server. The server name cannot have any spaces and cannot exceed 255 characters. Click the Create New Server button. Configure the server properties and click OK.

Add the appropriate listeners for the new logical server. The logical server should have an IIOP (Internet Inter-ORB Protocol) connection. The IIOP connection is used by the Jaguar Manager administration tool and is required for clusters and synchronization. To add a listener, click the Listeners folder under the logical server name that you wish to configure. Select the New Listener... menu option as shown in figure 1.2. Enter the new listener name and configure the properties as

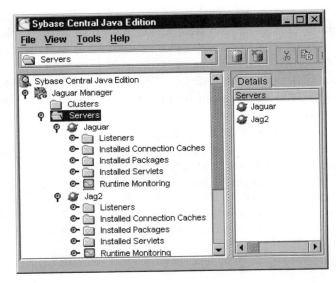

Figure 1.1
Logical servers in Jaguar CTS

shown in figure 1.3. Each logical server on the same physical machine should listen on different port numbers to avoid conflicts. Note that creating a separate logical server on the same machine is different from assigning two listeners on different ports to the same logical server. Each individual logical server will have its server properties configured the same way and offer the same packages and database caches on each listener, while two separate logical servers with different names can be configured differently and offer different packages and database caches.

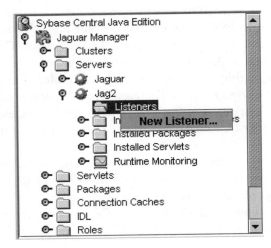

Figure 1.2
Adding a new listener

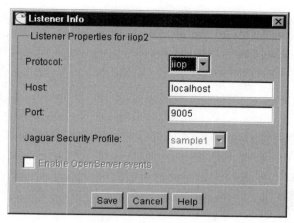

Figure 1.3
Listener properties

Each logical server must be started and stopped independently. To start the logical server on NT open a command prompt and type the following command from the %JAGUAR%\bin directory, assuming that Jag2 is the name of the logical server that you wish to start.

```
serverstart Jag2
```

NOTE   When running the serverstart.bat file, the default logical server that is started is Jaguar.

Each logical server should write to a different log file, especially if the Truncate Log On Startup option is enabled. If both servers write to the same log file, they will overwrite each other when they are started. In addition, if logical servers are writing to the same log file, it can be difficult to differentiate messages. To change the log file for the new logical server, click on the server name and select the Server Properties... option from the menu. Select the Log/Trace tab and change the log file name as shown in figure 1.4.

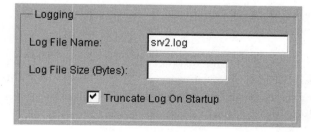

Figure 1.4
Changing the log file name

You can create logical servers to allow different clients to share a single Jaguar CTS installation on a single machine in an application hosting situation. Being able to run multiple applications on a single Jaguar CTS installation is a cost-effective way for an Application Service Provider (ASP) to handle numerous clients. By separating the applications, the ASP vendor can ensure that one client's packages and database connection caches are not going to be used by another client. This is similar to the Internet Service Provider (ISP) vendors that host several web sites on a single machine using virtual web sites. It can also be used to partition a large application. Partitioning an application is covered under load balancing.

WARNING	When hosting several different applications on the same installation of Jaguar CTS using logical servers, it is important to understand that anyone with a user account in the Admin Role can access and configure all logical servers on the machine. It is also possible for components from one client's application to read the Repository and lookup information on another client's application.

Once two or more logical servers are created, you can deploy packages of components to the Jaguar CTS application server. These packages are in the repository and appear under the Packages folder. Once packages are deployed to the machine, individual packages can be installed separately under each logical server. For example, on the Jaguar CTS server on hostA, we can deploy PackageA, PackageB, and PackageC. We can install PackageA under the default Jaguar server and PackageB under the new Jag2 server. Under this deployment configuration, any client accessing the logical server Jaguar can use components in PackageA, but not in PackageB and PackageC. Any client accessing the logical server Jag2 can use components in PackageB, but not in PackageA and PackageC. Even though a package is installed on the physical Jaguar CTS server machine and in the repository, the Jaguar server does not allow an instance of a component to be instantiated unless the package that the component is deployed with is installed on the logical server. This is illustrated in figure 1.5. A similar deployment configuration can also be done with database connection caches.

An administrator can configure the logical servers by connecting to the Jaguar CTS server through the Jaguar Manager. When using the Jaguar Manager, the administrator must connect to a particular instance of a logical server running on the physical machine by specifying the port number of the IIOP listener. Once connected, the administrator can configure the server properties or listeners of *any* of the logical servers as well as add and remove packages and connection caches. While an administrator can configure any logical server once they have logged into the

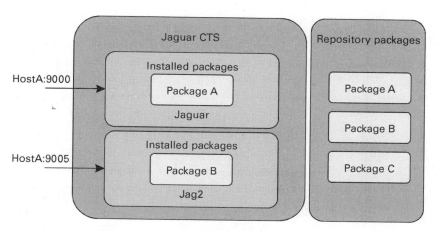

Figure 1.5 Deploying packages to different logical servers

Jaguar Manger, they still must connect to each logical server individually in order to start and stop the server through the Jaguar Manager. Even though the shutdown and start server menu option remains enabled for all logical servers in the manager interface, the Jaguar Manager shuts down and restarts only the server that it is connected to. In addition, the Jaguar Manager can Refresh and Set Ready only the logical server that it is connected to.

To delete a logical server, select the Servers folder, highlight the server you want to delete and choose the Delete Server menu option. Note that you cannot delete the logical server that you are connected to in the Jaguar Manager.

1.3 What is in the serverstart.bat file?

The serverstart.bat file is located in the %JAGUAR%\bin directory and is run from the command prompt. The serverstart.bat file is used to start and stop an instance of a Jaguar server in the console mode, and can also be used to start and stop the running of the Jaguar server as an NT service. This file also can be used to install and remove Jaguar CTS as an NT service. These concepts were introduced in the book *Jaguar Development with PowerBuilder 7*.

Running the serverstart.bat file has the following syntax:

```
serverstart [server_name [options] ]
```

The server_name is the name of the logical Jaguar server that needs to be acted upon. The default name is Jaguar if no server_name is specified. The default is to start the server in console mode unless another option is listed. The serverstart.bat file has several options that can be used when running it from the command line.

These options determine what action will be performed on the server. Table 1.1. lists the options that can be specified with the serverstart.bat file.

Table 1.1   serverstart.bat file options

Option	Description
-c	(default) runs the server in console mode.
-install	Installs the server as an NT service.
-remove	Removes the server from the NT service list.
-removeandinstall	Reinstalls the server as an NT service.
-start	Starts the NT service. The server must be installed as an NT service first.
-stop	Stops the NT service. The server must be installed as an NT service first.
-v	Lists the Jaguar version information.

When the batch file is executed and a logical server name is not specified, the default logical server "Jaguar" is started. The batch file defines environment variables whose values are limited in scope to the Jaguar server process, as opposed to the entire system. Some environment variables that are affected are PATH, CLASS-PATH, JAGUAR_JAVAVM, and JDK_LATEST.

The JAGUAR_JAVAVM environment variable determines which Java virtual machine (JVM) the Jaguar server will use. After connecting to Jaguar using the Jaguar Manager, the Java VM being used by Jaguar is listed under the com.sybase.jaguar.server.java.library property on the All Properties tab of the Server Properties dialog. The JVM is set in the serverstart.bat file and can also be set on the Java VM tab of the Server Properties dialog. The possible choices are Sun's JDK 1.1.x, JDK 1.2, and Microsoft's SDK 3.2. Note that changing the setting in the Jaguar Manager will not have any effect unless the server is stopped and restarted. In addition, starting the server with a batch file overrides this setting if the batch file sets the JAGUAR_JAVAVM environment variable.

When Jaguar CTS is installed, a batch file is provided to run the Jaguar server with one of the three Java virtual machines supported. Table 1.2 lists the version of JDK that is used by Jaguar when a certain batch file is utilized to start the server.

Table 1.2   Batch files and the Java VM

Java VM	JAGUAR_JAVAVM value	Batch file
Javasoft JDK 1.1.x	JAGUAR_JAVAVM=jdk11x	serverstart.bat
Javasoft JDK 1.2	JAGUAR_JAVAVM=jdk12	serverstart_jdk12.bat
Microsoft SDK 3.2	JAGUAR_JAVAVM=msvm	serverstart_msvm.bat

Let's create a batch file to run our new logical server Jag2 as a console. The StartJag2.bat file does *not* need to be created to start the Jag2 logical server, the original serverstart.bat file can be used by supplying the Jag2 name as an argument. This new file, however, can be placed on the desktop for easy access and can be used to change the environment variable values so that they are different from the ones used by the Jaguar logical server—like the version of the JDK, for example. First, create a file named StartJag2.bat. Then add the following code, which was copied from serverstart.bat. Note that the line that is commented out with the REM is the first line in serverstart.bat that was deleted, and all subsequent lines up to the error label. The lines in bold were then added to start the Jag2 logical server and display the appropriate title in the console.

```
@echo off
cls
SETLOCAL
if "%JAGUAR%" == "" goto setJaguar
:setJaguar
set JAGUAR=D:\Program Files\Sybase\Jaguar CTS 3.5
cd %JAGUAR%\bin
set SYBASE_SHARED=d:\Program Files\Sybase\Shared
set JDK_LATEST=d:\Program Files\Sybase\Shared\Sun\JDK118
set PATH=.;%JDK_LATEST%\bin;%JAGUAR%\dll;%PATH%;
set ADD_PATH=%JAGUAR%\cpplib;%JAGUAR%\bin;%SYBASE_SHARED%\Powerbuilder;
set PATH=%PATH%;%ADD_PATH%;
set CLASSPATH=.;%JAGUAR%\html\classes\powerjr.zip;%JDK_LATEST%\lib\classes.zip;
    %JAGUAR%\html\classes\ldap.jar;%JAGUAR%\html\classes\providerutil.jar;%JAG-
    UAR%\html\classes\jsdk.jar;%JAGUAR%\html\classes\datawindow.jar;%JAGUAR%\
    java\classes;%JAGUAR%\html\classes;%CLASSPATH%
set ENCINA_OTS_TK_SERVER_ARGS=serverName=JagSrv,restartString=JagOTSRe-
    start;JagOTSRestart.bak,logDevice=JagOTSLog.dev
set JAGUAR_JAVAVM=jdk11x

REM if "%2" == "" goto setdefaultoption
title Jaguar CTS (Jag2)
start "" /B /WAIT /min jagsrvagent.exe Jag2 -c
if errorlevel 1 goto error
goto end

:error
echo ****
echo An error occurred in operating the Jaguar server.
echo Please check the console and server log file.
echo ****
pause
goto end

:end
ENDLOCAL
```

1.4 How are packages moved from one Jaguar server to another?

As an application progresses from development to testing, and from testing to production, the Jaguar components need to be moved to different physical servers. Moving packages of components from one Jaguar server to another Jaguar server can be done in one of four ways.

1 Deploy the components from the appropriate IDE (Integrated Developer's Environment).

2 Export the package from one server and import it into another.

3 Synchronize using the "by server" option.

4 Synchronize the cluster.

Before moving the components to another Jaguar server, it may be necessary to configure security, database connection caches, and other environmental variables in order to get the server up and running. This is required if either of the first two options is used to move the components because they will not replicate these settings.

Moving components from one Jaguar server environment to another using a development IDE like PowerBuilder or PowerJ is not recommended, especially in testing and production environments. In a typical development environment, developers may not have Admin rights to testing or production machines, so they will not be able to deploy the components. Most administrators will be unfamiliar with the particular tools and code used to develop an application. Additionally, all the other options presented here ensure that all the components and their properties are correctly duplicated from one machine to another, which is not necessarily the case when using the development tools. Each of the remaining options is covered in more detail in this chapter.

REPORT CARD
Deploy with IDE

Pros	▪ Developers may deploy packages easily.
Cons	▪ Developers are required to have Admin rights to the server. ▪ IDE moves over only packages and components. Connection caches and other server properties are not moved. ▪ Some component properties may be lost during deployment unless the IDE allows all Jaguar component properties to be manipulated. ▪ Some component properties may be incorrectly copied to the new environment as they may have been changed in development.

Cons	▪ IDE is a labor-intensive method of deploying packages and components to many servers, because it requires a separate manual process to connect to each Jaguar server through the IDE.

Note that in evaluating the deployment of packages and components to a Jaguar server using an IDE, we are considering the movement of components from development servers to testing servers, from testing servers to production servers, and/or from one production server to another production server. Note that while an application is being developed, using the IDE to deploy packages and components to development servers is still recommended.

1.5 How are packages imported and exported between Jaguar servers?

Jaguar CTS has a built-in facility to export packages into a Java archive (JAR) file. This JAR file can be copied to another machine to be imported into the Jaguar CTS server. This technique is an excellent way for developers to send their application packages so they can be loaded onto a Jaguar server to which they do not have network access, like an application service provider hosting their application.

To export the package, log into the Jaguar Manager and expand the Packages folder. Select the package that needs to be moved to another Jaguar server. Right click with the mouse to access the popup menu. Choose the Export Package option. The Export dialog will open as illustrated in figure 1.6. Enter the path where the JAR file will be created. Also select whether the JAR file should be exported as a Jaguar JAR file or as an Enterprise Java Beans (EJB) JAR file.

After exporting the packages that need to be moved, use the Jaguar Manager to log into the Jaguar server that needs to have the packages imported. Remove the package(s) that you are importing to the Jaguar server if they already exist. They are located under the Packages folder. Select the Installed Packages folder under the logical server name that the package is being imported under (typically Jaguar), and right click with the mouse to access the popup menu. Choose the Import option. The Import dialog will open as illustrated in figure 1.7. Enter the path to the JAR file that was created above, and select whether the JAR file should be imported as a Jaguar JAR file or as an EJB JAR file. This option must match the option used to export the JAR file. Once the packages are imported and installed on the Jaguar CTS server, they can be accessed by client applications. It is important to note that any server properties, security settings, and database connection caches must be set up in a separate step as required by the packages and components.

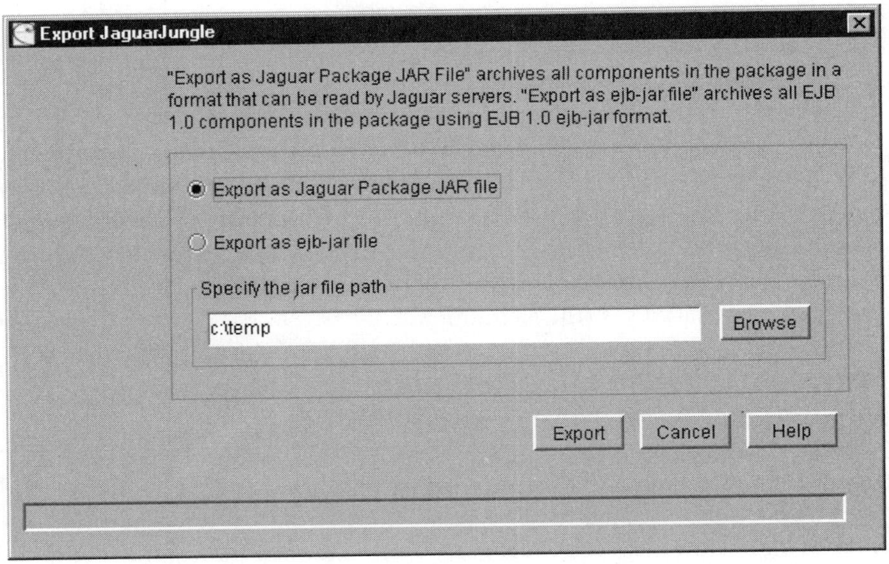

CHAPTER 1
Becoming a Jaguar tamer

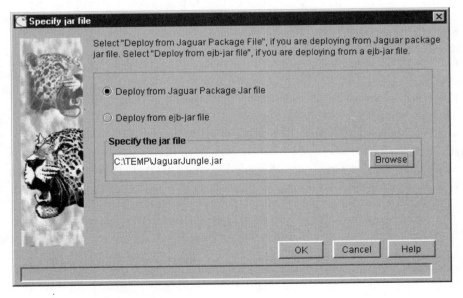

Figure 1.6   Export dialog

Figure 1.7   Import dialog

REPORT CARD
JAR file

Pros	■ The JAR file is an easy way to move packages without setting up a cluster. ■ This method is an ideal way to move packages between Jaguar servers that are not networked together.
Cons	■ A separate export and import is required for each package. ■ This method does not include any other information like server properties or connection caches. ■ The JAR file is labor intensive to deploy to many servers, because it requires a separate connection to each server through the Jaguar Manager.

1.6   How can a Jaguar server be backed up?

When dealing with enterprise systems, backing up data in a database is a common practice. It stands to reason that backing up the application server ought to be a good idea as well. Backing up a Jaguar CTS server can be looked at from several directions. Here is a list of some of them:

1   Use version control software and back up the source code. This allows the application to be redeployed should there be a need.

2   Export the JAR files for all of the packages containing components. Store these on a backup medium. This allows the application to be imported should there be a need.

3   When a cluster is used to deploy the application, each Jaguar server can act as a backup because they all have the application files installed. Synchronization can be used to restore a machine in the cluster when there is a problem. This technique requires at least one server in the cluster to have the deployed application intact.

4   Backing up a Jaguar installation can also be done by copying the entire directory structure starting with the %JAGUAR% directory and including all the subdirectories to a backup medium. This is an excellent way to back up the entire Jaguar server environment, not just the deployed application components. One important point when backing up Jaguar using this technique is that the files will have various locks on them while the server is running so Jaguar CTS needs to be stopped before backing up these directories.

| TIP | Regardless of how a Jaguar CTS server is backed up, we recommend that version control software always be used to back up different versions of the application source code. |

1.7 What is a cluster?

A cluster is a group of application servers that share replicated repository information and work together as a single logical server. The primary purpose of the Jaguar cluster is to provide load balancing and high availability, both of which are covered in this chapter.

When designing and configuring a Jaguar cluster, each cluster requires:

- A primary server
- A name server
- Member servers
- The same logical server name on primary and member servers

The primary server contains the master copy of the repository for all the servers in the cluster. It also contains the list of all the servers in the cluster. Each member server in the cluster must share a logical server name with the primary server. In the installation of Jaguar CTS, each server is set up with a default logical server named Jaguar, and as long is this is not changed, there is no problem. The primary server replicates its repository via synchronization to all the other servers in the cluster. Each logical server (i.e., Jaguar) on a member server shares configuration information, packages of components, connection caches, and servlets with the logical server that has the same name on the primary server. Each primary server and member server can participate in only one cluster.

The Jaguar cluster is integrated with the Jaguar naming service and requires a name server. Any Jaguar server can be turned into a name server by enabling the Naming Server option. The name server maps the component name to an object reference that stores its physical location. This allows the name server to direct client requests for a particular component based on the name to the proper server in the cluster. All the primary and member servers in a cluster register the names and object references of their components with each name server in the cluster. This process is known as binding. A name server can also act as a primary server or a member server in the cluster. Figure 1.8 illustrates a cluster of Jaguar servers, designating the roles of each.

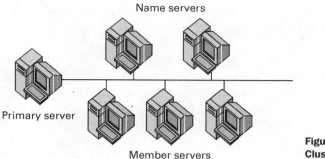

Name servers

Primary server

Member servers

**Figure 1.8
Cluster overview**

TIP   A name server can service more than one cluster if it is not used as a primary or member server.

1.8   *How do I create a cluster?*

There are some preparatory steps that must be taken on each server to create a cluster of Jaguar servers. First, each machine that will be added to the cluster must have
Jaguar CTS installed—with the same software version and level of patches. Once the
Jaguar software is installed on each machine, use the Jaguar Manager to configure
the listeners. You must make sure to set the host names so that each Jaguar CTS
server is network accessible. At least one listener must be set up to use IIOP to allow
synchronization to take place. In addition, an Admin account must be used to perform synchronization between servers in the cluster. During synchronization, the
primary server logs into each server and replicates the repository. It is recommended that a single Admin account and password be duplicated on each server to
allow synchronization to be performed against all the servers in the cluster at once.
If using the jagadmin account to synchronize the cluster, coordinate the jagadmin
password so that each server in the cluster uses the same one. If using a separate
account other than jagadmin, add the new account to the Admin role on each
server. If the servers in a cluster do not share a common account and password with
Admin rights, synchronization of the cluster must be performed from the primary
server on a server-by-server basis using each server's unique Admin login.

TIP   When using Operating System Authentication in a cluster, each machine
should have access to the same set of users.

If the default logical server *Jaguar* is not being used, then define a logical server on each machine that matches a logical server name set up in the repository of the primary server.

All the machines in the cluster should be considered equals, running the same Jaguar software versions and patches. They also should run the same operating system with the same service packs and patches installed. Allowable differences between machines include CPU speed and number, plus the memory and disk space available. Another allowable difference is whether the Name Server option is enabled. Of course, the primary server designation will be set only for one server. The Packages and Connection caches installed on each server should be the same on each machine unless the application is being partitioned (see Load balancing).

Once all the machines are set up, connect to the primary server using Jaguar Manager and highlight the Clusters folder. Select File | New Cluster from the main menu or popup menu. The New Cluster dialog will open. Enter the name of the new cluster and click the Create New Cluster button. The Cluster Properties dialog pictured in figure 1.9 will open. The primary server field will default to the Uniform Resource Locator (URL) of the server that you are currently connected to, and it cannot be edited. This is why an administrator must connect to the primary server when creating the cluster.

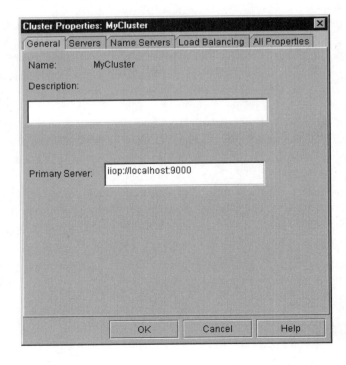

Figure 1.9
Cluster Properties: General tab

To add additional member servers to the cluster click on the Servers tab. Click on the Add button and type the IIOP address in URL format for each member server as shown in figure 1.10. Once this is complete, add the name server(s) to the cluster. Before a Jaguar CTS server can be added to a cluster as a name server it needs to be configured to act as a name server as described in chapter 7. Once Jaguar CTS is acting as a name server it can be added to the cluster. To add a name server to the cluster click on the Name Servers tab on the Cluster Properties dialog. Click on the Add button and type the IIOP address in URL format of the name server. Once all the member and name servers are added to the cluster click OK to save the cluster. Once the cluster is created the primary server can be used to synchronize the repository with the member servers.

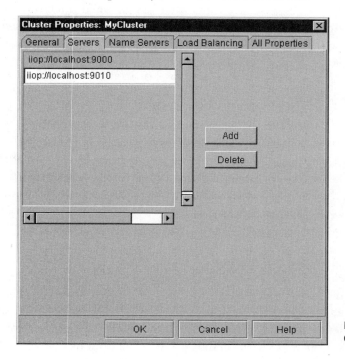

Figure 1.10
Cluster Properties: Servers tab

1.9   *What is synchronization?*

Synchronization allows the administrator to replicate the repository of the primary server to one or more of the member servers in a cluster. Once a cluster has been set up, all configuration changes and component deployments should be made to the primary server. Changes made to the primary server are propagated to the member servers through synchronization. When synchronizing the cluster, the primary server replicates the appropriate files and settings based on the level of synchronization and the options selected. It applies the changes to each member server one at a time in turn. So using the picture in figure 1.11 as an example, the primary server will first replicate the appropriate changes to the repository on ServerA, followed by ServerB, and then ServerC.

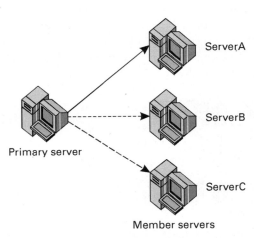

ServerA

ServerB

Primary server

ServerC

Member servers

Figure 1.11   Synchronization overview

To synchronize a cluster of servers, connect to the primary server using Jaguar Manager. You can synchronize a cluster of servers at the cluster, server, package, or component level depending on what has changed since the last synchronization operation. Synchronizing at the different levels will affect what is actually replicated to the servers in the cluster. For example, synchronizing at the package level allows only that package to be replicated. If the package is the only item that has changed on the primary server, this is a quick way to propagate only that change. In addition, synchronization can be done outside a cluster by specifying the IIOP address in URL format of each server that should be synchronized with the current server. This technique is known as synchronization "by server." For the rest of this discussion, we will be synchronizing a cluster unless otherwise noted.

After creating a cluster for the first time, it is essential to synchronize the servers in the cluster at the cluster level as illustrated in figure 1.12. This ensures that database connection caches, server properties, and security settings are copied to each machine. To perform the synchronization operation, click on the cluster, server, package, or component icon and select the File | Synchronize menu option. The Synchronize dialog will open as shown in figure 1.13. The options that are available will depend on whether the cluster, server, package, or component level was selected.

In the Connect section of the dialog, supply the username and password that will be used to log on to each Jaguar server in the cluster. This user should be duplicated on all the servers in the cluster and included in the Admin role. Otherwise, synchronization using the Cluster option will not be possible. In the Targets portion, choose the Cluster option and select the cluster name from the drop down list. The Cluster target should only be chosen when connected to the primary

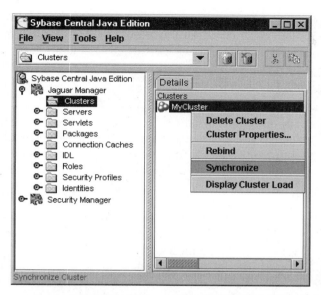

Figure 1.12
Synchronize the cluster menu option

Figure 1.13
Synchronize the Cluster dialog

server in the cluster and the changes need to be replicated to all the servers in the cluster. The only time a synchronization operation should be done from a member server instead of the primary server is in the rare case where a new primary server is being designated. Specify the synchronization options and click the Start Sync button to synchronize the cluster.

TIP   If another account other than jagadmin is used to connect to servers in the cluster, it is suggested that operating system authentication be enabled to require that a password be entered to perform the synchronization.

1.9.1 *Package synchronization*

Package synchronization is performed whenever the synchronize menu option is chosen from a particular package. It is also done when the synchronize menu option is selected at the server or the cluster level and the All Package Files option is enabled. When the All Package Files option is enabled, it specifies that *all of the packages* deployed to the Jaguar server be sent to the member servers in the cluster. However, only the packages that are installed for each logical server on the primary server will be installed to the corresponding logical server that is found on the member server as shown in figure 1.14. The items sent during a package synchronization include package properties and all of the files sent during a component synchronization (see below) for each of the components in the package. Other files that need to be included with the synchronization are specified in a comma-separated list in the com.sybase.jaguar.package.files property. Synchronizing at the package level is similar to exporting a package with a JAR file.

1.9.2 *Component synchronization*

Component synchronization is done whenever the synchronize menu option is chosen from a particular component in a package or from the package itself. It is also done when the synchronize menu option is selected at the server or the cluster level and the All Package Files option is enabled. The items that are synchronized include Interface Definitions Language (IDL), component properties, and the implementation files. Implementation files depend on the component implementation language and include DLL, PBD, and CLASS files. For example, a Jaguar component written in Java has a component property (com.sybase.jaguar.component.java.class) that specifies the implementation file for the Java component. The class file specified in this property along with any additional class files specified in the component property com.sybase.jaguar.component.java.classes are included in the synchronization. Other files that need to be included with the component during synchronization are specified in a comma-separated list in the com.sybase.jaguar.component.files property.

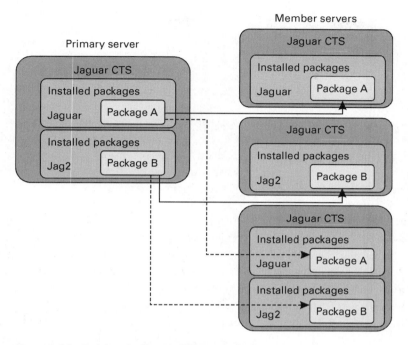

Figure 1.14 Synchronization to different logical servers

1.9.3 *Servlet synchronization*

Servlet synchronization is performed when the All Servlet Files option is enabled during a Cluster- or Server- level synchronization. For each servlet installed on the Jaguar server, all of the servlet properties and the servlet class are copied to each member server.

WARNING   When trying to replicate servlets in a cluster using Jaguar 3.5 running on Windows NT 4, only the servlet properties are copied. The servlet class files are not sent to the member servers! When the member servers are started, they will report errors stating that the servlet class was not found.

1.9.4 *All Cluster Files synchronization*

When the All Cluster Files option is selected, all of the properties needed to replicate the repository are synchronized. This includes the server properties, the %JAGUAR%/Repository/Security directory, and the afconfig.dat file, which stores role, and database connection cache definitions.

WARNING When trying to synchronize using the All Cluster Files option in a cluster using Jaguar 3.5 running on Windows NT 4, the roles and the database connection caches are not sent to the member servers!

1.9.5 *Remaining cluster options*

When a synchronization operation is performed, one of the options is to create a new cluster version number by enabling the New Version option as pictured in figure 1.8. The cluster version number is used by the servers in the cluster to determine whether or not they should join the cluster when they startup. How a server handles a version mismatch is based on the cluster startup option selected. The version number is useful only in a cluster.

A synchronization operation in a cluster can be performed only from the primary server. However, in cases where the primary server is down and cannot be restarted, an administrator can connect to another Jaguar server within the cluster and designate it as the new primary server by enabling the New Primary option. The server that will be designated as the new primary server should have all of the latest information, property settings, and packages before performing the synchronization.

The Verbose, Refresh, and Restart options are available for all levels of synchronization. The Verbose option writes detailed synchronization messages to the log file of the primary server. The Refresh option specifies that a refresh be performed at the end of synchronization. This will ensure that each member server flushes instance pools and database connection caches so that the new items are used. The Restart option tells the member servers to restart after the synchronization operation completes. The "then wait" option allows a time-out to be specified so that when a member server does not restart, the synchronization operation moves to the next server. Using either the refresh or the restart option is recommended with each synchronization operation.

WARNING When trying to replicate using Jaguar 3.5 running on Windows NT 4, the "then wait" feature does not become enabled even after clicking on the Restart option.

After a synchronization operation is finished executing, it is recommended that a rebind of the cluster is performed to refresh the name servers. This step is not required if the Restart option was selected because each member server will perform a bind with the name servers in the cluster on start up.

When moving packages and components from the development environment to the testing environment, or from the testing environment to the production environment, it is probably easier to use the Synchronize by Server option. The strategy here is to synch the primary server in the test cluster with the primary server in the production cluster and then synchronize the production cluster from the primary server. This prevents an administrator from having to put test and production servers in the same cluster to propagate changes.

REPORT CARD
Synchronization - Cluster

Pros	▪ This method is the easiest way to move the complete server installation or just parts (such as single package or component) to another Jaguar server, especially when dealing with a large number of servers.
Cons	▪ This method requires setting up and maintaining a cluster.

1.10 *What does rebinding a cluster do?*

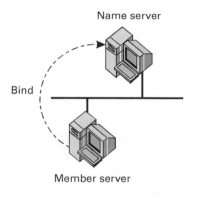

Name server

Bind

Member server

Figure 1.15   Binding components to a name server

Binding is performed when a server maps the component name to an object reference and registers this with the name server. This action is performed for all the components that a Jaguar server has installed, as illustrated in figure 1.15. The name server adds the new bindings to its namespace, which makes the components on a particular server available to clients. When rebinding is done on a cluster, all the servers in the cluster bind their component names to object references and register them with each name server in the cluster. Rebinding of the cluster should be done after a synchronization operation is performed to ensure that new packages and components are available to the cluster. To rebind the cluster, highlight the name of the cluster and select File | Rebind from the menu as shown in figure 1.16.

TIP	A Jaguar server in a cluster performs a bind operation with each name server in the cluster on startup. Likewise, a name server in a cluster will automatically poll all the member servers when it is restarted and cause them to perform a bind operation.

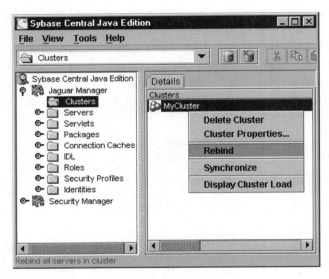

Figure 1.16 Rebind the cluster

1.11 *What are the cluster startup options?*

When a Jaguar server is part of a cluster, it tries to determine if it is "synched-up" with the other members of the cluster during startup. How the Jaguar server attempts to determine if it is "synched-up" is based on the cluster version numbers and the value of the com.sybase.jaguar.cluster.startup cluster property that can be edited on the All Properties tab of the Cluster Properties dialog. The com.sybase.jaguar.cluster.startup property has three valid values:

- check_primary
- check_servers
- disable_check

The check_primary value is the default value. The Jaguar server in the cluster will check the cluster version on the primary server. If the primary server has a different cluster version, the server will remain in Admin mode. If the primary server has the same cluster version number, the server will join the cluster and be in the Ready mode. When the primary server is not available, the server continues to check for the primary server in a loop, making it inaccessible.

When the check_servers value is set, the Jaguar server in the cluster will check the cluster version with all the servers in the cluster. If any server has a higher cluster version, the server will remain in Admin mode. If there is a discrepancy in cluster version number, but none of the version numbers are higher, then the server will use the algorithm specified in the Jaguar documentation to determine its Startup mode. The algorithm is as follows:

"Let M be the number of cluster members (including the primary), and let N equal to M/2 (integer division). If at least N other servers are available and have the same cluster version number, this server joins the cluster and is ready to accept client connections."

If none of the servers has a higher cluster version but less than *N* servers are available, the server continues to perform this check in a loop—making it inaccessible. The advantage to using the check_servers option is it allows a Jaguar server to join a cluster when the primary server is not available.

When the disable_check option is set, no checking is performed when the Jaguar server starts up. It immediately joins the cluster in the Ready mode, barring any other problems.

TIP   Using disable_check is not recommended because it can result in several Jaguar servers in a cluster running different versions of components at the same time. The authors recommend using check_servers to ensure that the cluster can continue serving requests even when the primary server has a problem.

1.12   *What are the Admin and Ready modes?*

A Jaguar server can be in one of two modes, Admin or Ready. Actually a Jaguar server can be in four modes if you count Starting up and Shutdown. A Jaguar server is in the Admin mode when it is running, but it is accepting only connections from the Jaguar Manager. A Jaguar server that is up and running, and accepting connections from the Jaguar Manager and clients, is considered in the Ready mode. The Ready mode is the "everything is running normally" mode for Jaguar.

A Jaguar server will usually be put into the Admin mode when there is a problem starting the server because of a cluster version mismatch. Other problems on startup can also cause the server to be put in the Admin mode. The Admin mode is useful because it lets problems with the Jaguar server be corrected through the Jaguar Manager. It also allows a synchronization operation to be performed on it. A Jaguar server in the Admin mode can be forced into the Ready mode using the Set Ready menu option in the Jaguar Manager.

1.13   *Can synchronization be done outside a cluster?*

Synchronization is a powerful way to replicate information between servers in a cluster. However, server properties, package, component, and servlets, as well as cluster files (database connection caches, roles, and so on) can all be replicated to another Jaguar server outside a cluster. The only requirement is that the Jaguar servers that are involved are to be accessible over the network.

To synchronize non-clustered servers, connect to the Jaguar server that has the files that need to be moved to another Jaguar server. Choose the level that needs to be synchronized and select the Synchronize option from the popup menu. This could be done at the server, package, and component levels. The Synchronize Server dialog as pictured in figure 1.17 will open. Under the Connect section of the dialog, specify the username and password that will be used to log on to the server or servers listed in the Target portion of the dialog. Under the Target section of the dialog, select the Servers option and list the IIOP address in URL format of each server that will be synchronized. Additional servers can be added by separating the URL addresses with a comma. Note that all the servers need to have the same Admin username and password specified in the Connect section for this to work. Under the Options section, specify what part of the repository to replicate. See section 1.9, "What is Synchronization?", for more details on these options.

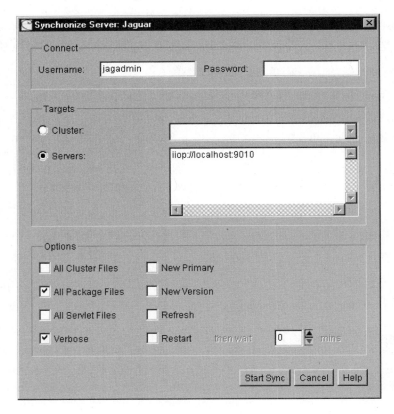

Figure 1.17
Synchronize by Server

Synchronization outside a cluster may be useful when moving packages and components from the development environment to the testing environment, or from the testing environment to the production environment. The strategy here is to synch the primary server in the test cluster with the primary server in the production cluster and then synchronize the production cluster from the primary server. This prevents an administrator from having to put test and production servers in the same cluster to propagate changes.

REPORT CARD
Synchronization — By Server

Pros	■ Synchronization by server is the easiest way to move the complete server installation or just parts (single package or component) to another Jaguar server. ■ It does not require a cluster.
Cons	■ This method requires network connectivity to other servers. ■ This method is not as easy as a cluster with a shared Admin account to replicate the repository to several servers.

1.14 How is a server added to a cluster?

In order to add a server to a cluster, highlight the cluster name in the Jaguar Manager under the Clusters folder. Choose the File | Cluster Properties... menu option to open the Cluster Properties dialog. To add a member server to the cluster, select the Servers tab, click the Add button, and add the IIOP URL for the new member server. If you are adding a name server to the cluster, select the Name Servers tab, click the Add button, and add the IIOP URL for the new name server.

When a member server has been added to the cluster, synchronize the new server with the primary server. After adding a member server or a name server, perform a rebind on the cluster. The Rebind option refreshes all of the name servers within the cluster so that they are aware of the new member server(s).

1.15 How is a server removed from a cluster?

In order to remove a server from a cluster, highlight the cluster name in the Jaguar Manager under the Clusters folder. Choose the File | Cluster Properties... menu option to open the Cluster Properties dialog. Select the Servers tab to remove a member server from the cluster. If a name server is being removed from the cluster, select the Name Servers tab. Highlight the server that needs to be deleted and click the Delete button.

Once the server has been removed from the cluster, connect to the deleted server and remove the cluster name from com.sybase.jaguar.server.cluster property and remove all the addresses of the name servers from the com.sybase.jaguar.server.nameservice, except the actual server being removed from the cluster. Both properties are under the All Properties tab on the Server Properties dialog. After the server has been removed from the cluster, we also need to refresh the name servers so that they no longer report that components are available on the member server that has been removed. This is accomplished by performing a Rebind on the cluster.

1.16 How is a cluster deleted?

To delete an existing cluster, connect to the primary server. Highlight the cluster that you want to delete under the Clusters folder and select the Delete Cluster menu option. After deleting the cluster, remove the cluster name from the property com.sybase.jaguar.server.cluster and remove the addresses of the name servers from the property com.sybase.jaguar.server.nameservice. Both properties are under the All Properties tab on the Server Properties dialog. You will also have to connect to each server that was part of the cluster and remove the cluster name from the property com.sybase.jaguar.server.cluster and remove the name servers from the property com.sybase.jaguar.server.nameservice to avoid having each server attempt to reestablish a connection with the cluster when they are restarted.

1.17 What is load balancing?

In an enterprise application, maintaining optimal and consistent performance at all times is important even under heavy loads. However, this can be difficult to handle especially on the Internet because it may be difficult to determine when peak traffic will occur or how many users will be on the system at one time. Enterprise applications also need to be scalable. Scalability is the ability of an application to meet increased demands (more users) while maintaining a consistent level of performance under the stress of a production environment. A system built using a multitier architecture should be able to grow with the business and handle increasing workloads without having to be rewritten by adding more hardware either to a single machine or by adding additional machines.

Jaguar delivers scalability in two ways. First, it maximizes the use of resources on any one server, allowing a single server to support significant loads. Jaguar does this by pooling threads, database connections, and component instances. In addition, an application built using stateless components can also improve the resource consumption on the server and increase the scalability. Secondly, Jaguar, like all multitiered architectures, address scalability through load balancing. Load balancing allows an application to service more requests and achieve consistent levels of performance by dispersing the client requests across multiple machines, allowing the horsepower and resources of several servers to act like a single logical server. This is illustrated in figure 1.18.

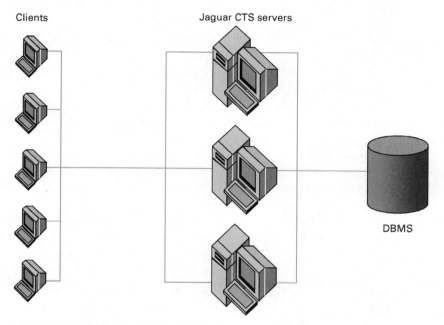

Figure 1.18   Load balancing overview

Load balancing in Jaguar CTS is implemented through a cluster, allowing an application to share the workload across multiple servers. In order for load balancing to work, the components need to be deployed onto each server in the cluster. Replicating components in the middle tier across several servers allows client requests to be routed to the server with the least processing demands places on it. The ability to add additional servers to the middle tier enables an application to grow as the demands increase—without sacrificing performance. Setting up load balancing in Jaguar CTS requires the following steps:

1 Create a cluster.

2 Add member and name servers to the cluster.

3 Synchronize the cluster.

4 Restart the member servers.

Once a cluster is set up and synchronized, Jaguar will handle load balancing automatically.

1.18   *How does Jaguar handle load balancing?*

Load balancing in Jaguar CTS relies on the Naming Service. Clients attempting to access components in a clustered Jaguar environment should use the Naming Service, either implicitly or explicitly, to find and create components. The name servers implement the Naming Service. The Jaguar Naming Service can be accessed through the CORBA CosNaming API, the Java Naming and Directory Interface (JNDI), or the Jaguar SessionManager interface. The CosNaming and SessionManager interfaces require CORBA stubs on the client. JNDI requires EJB stubs on the client. The Naming Service chapter, Factory chapter, and EJB chapter address these in more detail.

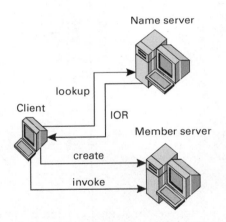

Figure 1.19   How the Naming Service works

When the client accesses the Naming Service, no matter what API it uses, it needs to resolve the name of the component. The name server takes a client request for a component by name and looks it up in the name space, which lists all the servers that can provide an instance of the object. The name server returns this list of servers in an Interoperable Object Reference (IOR) to the client. The client uses the IOR from the name server to get a remote object reference to the object on the Jaguar server as shown in figure 1.19.

The IOR returned by the name server is actually an IOR to a Factory object. The Factory object is used to create a remote object reference (component IOR) for the particular component that the client is interested in. The Factory IOR contains zero or more profiles depending on how many servers can handle creating an instance of the requested object as illustrated in figure 1.20. Each profile contains information on the server location (host name and port) as well as the location of the object on the Jaguar server. The location of the object on the server is known as an object key, which is a binary value that is used by the server. The object key is passed with each request from the client to the Jaguar server to let Jaguar know which object is being operated on.

The profiles are stored in an array as part of the IOR. The array of profiles in the IOR is returned in a different order by the naming server in response to a client's

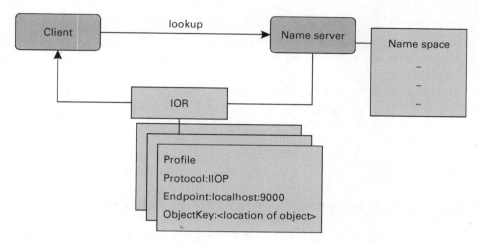

Figure 1.20   Load balancing using IOR

request, based on the load balancing distribution policy that is set up. The client uses the create method on the Factory object to get a component IOR, which allows it to actually call methods on the component. The Factory object uses the first profile in the array to get a component IOR and creates the object instance on the server specified in that profile. If for some reason the server specified in the first profile should not be able to provide the service because the Jaguar server is no longer available, the next profile in the list is attempted. The component IOR returned by the create method contains only one profile, which is for the server that the component was created on. Because the component IOR only has one profile, all the requests to that component are directed to the same Jaguar server.

Because the name server returns a randomized list of the profiles with the Factory IOR and the client chooses the server it will use to satisfy the request based on the order in which the profiles are presented, we can see that load balancing is tightly integrated with the Naming Service. The Java code sample below illustrates how the SessionManager interface can be used to interact with the Naming Service and get a remote object reference to a Jaguar component. The lookup method on the session object uses the Naming Service to get the Factory object but hides the details of this from the client.

```
// Example using SessionManger interface
import SessionManager.*;

String myURL = "iiop://name_server_host:9000";

// initialize the ORB
java.util.Properties props = new Properties();
```

```
props.put("org.omg.CORBA.ORBClass","com.sybase.CORBA.ORB");
org.omg.CORBA.ORB orb = ORB.init((String[]) null, props);
// get the SessionManager/Manager Factory object using CosNaming
org.omg.CORBA.Object ior = orb.string_to_object(myURL);
Manager manager = ManagerHelper.narrow(ior);

// create session on Jaguar & get SessionManager/Session object
Session session = manager.createSession("jagadmin", "");

// get the Factory object for component
// and use Factory to get object reference
org.omg.CORBA.Object factObj = session.lookup("SVU/SVULogin");
Factory factory = FactoryHelper.narrow(factObj);
org.omg.CORBA.Object myObj = factory.create();
SVULogin = SVULoginHelper.narrow(myObj);
```

1.19 How is load balancing configured on Jaguar?

The name server is the heart of load balancing in Jaguar CTS. It uses the load balancing distribution policy set up on Jaguar to return profiles in an IOR in a different order to each client request to balance the load. In this section, we will look at the four different load balancing policies that Jaguar implements.

The four load balancing policies that Jaguar supports are:

- Random
- Round-robin
- Weighted
- Adaptive

1.19.1 Random and round-robin

In a cluster that has similar physical machines, the random and round-robin policies are ideal because the incoming client requests are handed out evenly (as evenly as possible) to all participating Jaguar servers. The random policy, which was the only policy available before Jaguar 3.5, will randomize the profiles returned in an IOR by the name server. Using the round-robin policy, the name server will pass out the server profiles in such a way that it starts at the top of the list of servers and works its way to the bottom and then starts handing them out from the top again. For example, given Jaguar servers A, B, and C, which all support the same object, the first request for the object will be given the profiles as A, B, and C. The second request for the object will be given the profiles as B, C, and A, and the third as C, A, and B and so on.

1.19.2 Weighted

The weighted policy is ideal for clusters that contain a mix of higher and lower powered machines. The weighted policy allows an administrator to assign a weight to each server in the cluster. Larger numbers indicate more powerful servers that can handle a larger load, so the name server will push more requests to them.

1.19.3 Adaptive

The adaptive policy is also a good choice for clusters that have machines of varying power and capability. The adaptive policy disperses profiles based on runtime statistics and load metrics compensating for servers that are overworked by directing requests to other servers. While this policy is great for balancing a load based on both machine capability and usage, it does require more overhead to use because the Jaguar servers are gathering load metrics at different intervals.

1.19.4 Setting the load balancing policy

Load balancing depends on a cluster of Jaguar servers. To set up load balancing policies, highlight the cluster name and select the File | Cluster Properties menu option. When the Cluster Properties dialog opens, select the Load Balancing tab as shown in figure 1.21.

In order to select a load balancing policy, you must enable dynamic load balancing. Once this is done, the rest of the dialog becomes enabled. The policy drop down list box lists the four policies that Jaguar supports. If the random or round-robin policies are selected, the rest of the options are not used. When the weighted policy is selected, the Weights button is enabled. Clicking the Weights button will open a dialog that lists each server in the cluster and allows a weight to be assigned to it. The possible weight range is 1 to n, where n is the value set in the maximum weight field, which determines the maximum weight that can be entered for any server in the cluster.

The adaptive policy relies on load metrics to determine how to direct requests. The load metrics measure system statistics and the load of each server in the cluster and generate a numerical weighted value for each server based on the data. This weight is used similar to the weighted policy to direct requests to the servers that can handle the most work and are underused. In the adaptive policy, however, the weight for each server changes at runtime based on the updated load metrics.

The different intervals are used by the adaptive policy to generate new load metrics and are measured in minutes, except for the sample interval, which is measured in seconds. Each Jaguar server has a load collector. The system load metrics for a Jaguar server are collected at each sample interval by the load collector. As each broadcast interval elapses, the data collected is sent to each member server in the

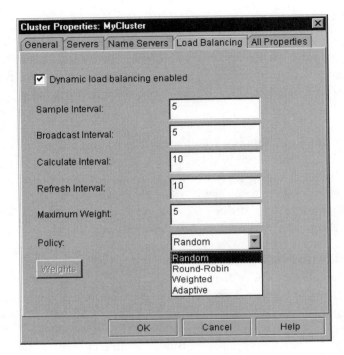

Figure 1.21
Configuring load balancing
for a cluster

cluster. As each calculate interval passes, the name servers calculate a new weight for each server and store them in a list. This list is called a normalized load list (NLL). As the refresh interval elapses, the name server updates the NLL it was using to direct requests with the newly calculated one. The refresh interval should be equal to or greater than the calculate interval.

1.20 *What is partitioning and how does it affect load balancing?*

When setting up basic load balancing, each server in the cluster contains the same packages, components, servlets, and connection caches as every other server. Setting up a cluster so that each server is an exact duplicate of another server, at least as far as the software and components that are installed on each, is the easiest way to implement load balancing. That, however, may not be the best setup for all situations. You can divide a cluster into partitions or subgroups of servers so that each server in a partition contains the same set of packages, components, servlets, and connection caches as another server. However, servers in different partitions will vary as to the components that they support.

Partitions are set up by creating different logical server names on the primary server and installing the subset of components to each logical server as appropriate. Each member server in the cluster is given one or more logical server names that correspond with the subset of components that it will support. The synchronization routine will replicate the repository correctly based on the logical server names as covered in the section 1.9, "What is synchronization?". Also see section 1.2, "What is a logical server?" for details on setting up a logical server. Partitioning an application into different sets of components is often useful to separate CPU-intensive operations from database-intensive operations so that the CPU-intensive components can be placed on higher powered machines with more processors. This allows them to take advantage of the extra processing power while the database components can be placed on smaller machines where they will not need the CPU power as much.

1.21 How can a Jaguar application be made highly available?

When building enterprise applications, it is important that the application is both reliable and available 24×7. Setting up a clustered environment for load balancing can also provide high availability in a multitiered Jaguar application. By replicating components onto several application servers that are clustered together, we can ensure that even if one server goes down there are additional servers ready to take over until that server can be brought back up. In fact, by using a cluster of Jaguar servers, an application will always be accessible unless all the name servers, all the member servers, or both, are down.

In order to guarantee high availability in an application, there must be a duplication of all parts of the application. To set up a cluster of Jaguar servers that will ensure high availability, there should be at least two name servers and at least two member servers on separate physical machines. The member servers should each contain all the packages, components, and servlets that make up the application. The name servers can act as member servers as well and still provide high availability. To set up the application so that there is not any single point of failure, the cluster startup property should be set to the value check_servers so that the cluster can operate without the primary server.

The name server and the load balancing mechanism described above are used to distribute requests to the appropriate Jaguar CTS servers. When a Jaguar server in a cluster goes down, it is up to the name servers to detect this situation and stop passing out profiles in the IOR specifying this server to clients. In addition, Jaguar must handle any clients that were being serviced by the downed server by rerouting them to another Jaguar server in the cluster transparently. The Jaguar CTS server will automatically handle rerouting a session when a Jaguar server goes down so that the client application is unaware of the situation. Nevertheless, a developer will need to take the appropriate measures to ensure that components can handle this as well.

1.22 How do name servers detect when a Jaguar server goes down?

The name servers in a cluster can check whether the primary or member servers are accepting requests by periodically pinging them. This is called *heartbeat detection* in Jaguar CTS. During heartbeat detection, the name server sends a request to each server in the cluster and waits for the server to respond. If a server does not respond, the name server stops returning profiles to client requests that specify that server. This causes all requests to be rerouted only to servers that can handle the request and are up and running. During the next pinging cycle, the name server can detect when a server comes back on line and start sending requests to that server again automatically.

To enable heartbeat detection, log into the Jaguar server using the Jaguar Manager and open the Server Properties dialog. Select the Naming Service tab as shown in figure 1.22. Make sure the Jaguar server is enabled as a Naming Server and check the Enable Heartbeat option. The heartbeat frequency is the number of seconds the name server will wait between pinging the servers in the cluster. The default is 120 seconds.

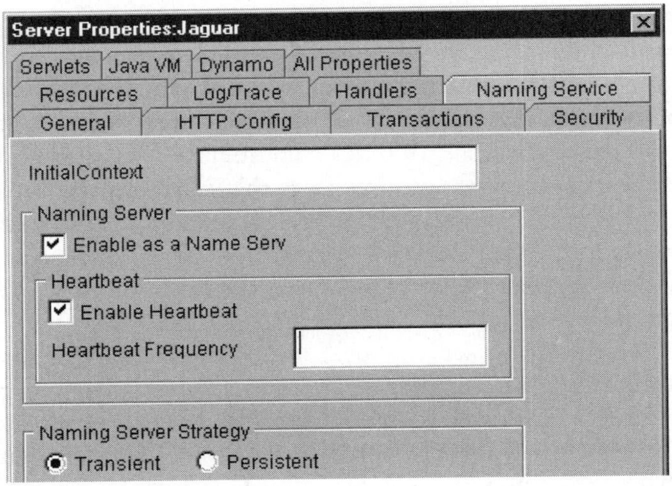

Figure 1.22
Enabling heartbeat detection

1.23 How do client applications access Jaguar for high availability?

To guarantee high availability, clients should specify more than one Jaguar server URL address when they attempt any actions. The list of addresses should be separated by a semi-colon as shown below:

```
iiop://Jaguar1:9000;iiop://Jaguar2:9000
```

This ensures that when the first server specified in the list fails that the client Object Request Broker (ORB) will use one of the other profiles to try the request again, completely transparent to the client application. The list of URL addresses should contain the list of the member servers when using the location property of the PowerBuilder connection object, when specifying the URL for the Session-Manager::Manager object, or when specifying the URL for the InitialContext Provider property when using JNDI. The list of URL addresses should contain the list of the name servers when using the NameServiceURL property of the ORB when using CosNaming.

1.24 How is automatic failover handled by Jaguar?

When a client application is using a component on a server and that particular server fails, Jaguar can transparently move the client session from the failed Jaguar server to another server in the cluster. However, Jaguar cannot provide transparent failover for the client's object reference to the component unless the component supports automatic failover. When automatic failover is enabled, Jaguar will make sure the client object reference remains valid and point it to another server capable of handling the component. If the component does not support automatic failover and a server goes down, the client application must create a new instance of that component to get a new object reference and continue processing.

A Jaguar component can support automatic failover by enabling the Automatic Failover option on the Transactions tab of the Component Properties dialog. However, as a general guideline, only components that have AutoDemarcation/Deactivation enabled (in other words, stateless components) should be considered as capable of truly supporting automatic failover. Any component that retains state in server memory between method calls will lose this information when the component fails over to another Jaguar server. Stateful components that store state in a persistent storage that is accessible from all the servers in the cluster, such as a database, are also candidates for automatic failover.

WARNING　Supporting automatic failover can result in a duplicate INSERT. When a server crashes after a transaction when an INSERT is committed but before the reply to the client request is sent out, the Jaguar server detects the problem and the component call fails over to another server where the method is called again. This results in a second INSERT. To avoid this problem, code INSERT logic in a two-step process, GetID which returns a new ID for the row; and InsertID, which performs the actual INSERT with the number returned by the call to GetID. Using this technique, the INSERT function relies on another function call to generate the ID. Because the INSERT is already committed in this scenario, a second call to the method due to a failover would attempt to INSERT with the same ID and fail.

1.25　How is a cluster monitored?

Jaguar Manager provides a useful monitoring tool that lets an administrator keep track of all the servers in a cluster, watch the load balancing to ensure that all servers are used adequately, and determine which servers are available and which are down. To view the cluster load from Jaguar Manager, highlight the cluster name and select File | Display Cluster Load. A window with a graph measuring the load on each server will open. A list of each server in the cluster is also included, specifying which servers are in Admin or Ready mode and which version of the cluster they are running.

1.26　How can I have more than one Jaguar server installed on a single machine?

Creating another installation of Jaguar CTS on a machine already installed with the Jaguar software is a very easy process. Here are the steps:

1　Stop the Jaguar CTS server.

2　Copy the entire %JAGUAR% directory to a new location.

3　Change the serverstart.bat file for the "new" installation as described below.

4　Start the "new" Jaguar CTS installation. Log into the Jaguar Manager just as you would with the original installation and change the listeners so they do not conflict with the original installation.

5　Stop the "new" Jaguar CTS installation so that the listener changes take effect.

6　Start both Jaguar CTS servers.

The serverstart.bat file is located in the %JAGUAR%\bin directory. When changing the serverstart.bat file for the "new" installation, locate the %JAGUAR% assignment line. It should look something like this:

```
set JAGUAR=D:\Program Files\Sybase\Jaguar CTS 3.5
```

Change it to point to the new Jaguar directory location:

```
set JAGUAR=E:\Jaguar CTS 3.5
```

In order to differentiate between the two Jaguar servers when they are running, it is a good idea to change the title bar of the console. To do this, locate all the title commands inside the batch file and change them to something like this:

```
title JagCTS2 %1
```

While this may not be a common occurrence on a production installation of Jaguar CTS, it does allow a developer to test clustering, load balancing, and high availability on a single machine.

1.27 *What is a database sanity check?*

Jaguar CTS uses database connection pooling to cache database connections. This increases the scalability of an application by maximizing server resources on both the Jaguar server and the database server. Getting a connection to a database is an expensive and resource-consuming process. Database connection caching allows a single connection to the database to be shared by several different client sessions on the Jaguar server. This is possible by recapturing database connections when they are idle. This is managed by Jaguar CTS.

One of the options on the database connection cache is the sanity check. When this option is enabled, the Jaguar server will check on the state of the database connection before it is pulled out of the cache and given to a client by pinging the database that the connection is connected to. If the connection is invalid, the connection is dropped and a new connection is established.

The sanity check ping is performed by sending an SQL statement to the database. This SQL statement is specified in the property com.sybase.jaguar.conncache.check. The default SQL statement is listed below:

```
select 1
```

Jaguar checks the SQLState returned by running the default sanity check SQL statement and drops the connection if it returns an 8XXX value. If this SQL statement is not supported by the database used by the connection cache (like Oracle), it can be modified. Once it is modified, any exception is considered a bad connection and is dropped. The SQL statement that can be used with an Oracle DBMS is listed below:

```
select 1 from dual
```

The Jaguar properties of a database connection cache cannot be set through the Jaguar Manager because there is not an All Properties tab on the Connection Cache Properties dialog. In order to modify the properties of a database connection cache, a property file will need to be manually created. In the %JAGUAR%\Repository\ConnCache directory, create an ASCII text file. The file name should match the name of the database connection cache with the extension ".props". So, for example, the database connection cache MyCache would have a property file named MyCache.props. Once the file is created, properties for the cache can be added, modified, and deleted. To change the sanity check SQL, add the com.sybase.jaguar.conncache.check property as follows:

```
com.sybase.jaguar.conncache.check=SELECT 1 FROM DUAL
```

NOTE   To learn more about database connection caches and how to set them up, check out *Jaguar Development with PowerBuilder7,* published by Manning Publications Co.

1.28 What is JagRepair?

JagRepair is a special Jaguar server that allows an administrator to repair configuration errors that prevent the server from successfully starting up. The JagRepair server can be started so that the administrator can log into Jaguar CTS using the Jaguar Manager and correct the errors. To start the JagRepair server, type the following command at the command prompt:

```
serverstart JagRepair
```

Once the server starts up (in Admin mode), use the Jaguar Manager to connect to the server. Use the jagadmin user account and the host name localhost on port 9000.

Designing components
for the jungle

This chapter covers:

- Jungle Safari Shipping Company case study
- Stateful versus stateless review
- Building stateless components
- Overview of different component properties

In talking with many of you, we frequently field inquiries regarding stateful versus stateless component design, with many of you saying that you have only a few dozen users. Stateless component design is quintessential in developing robust, scalable, distributed applications. Sure, you may have only a few users, but how are you planning on taking advantage of Jaguar's clustering capabilities with that stateful design? How are you going to scale when the user base grows from dozens to hundreds or thousands? Although Jaguar 3.5 introduced the ability to provide stateful failover, this feature is enabled only for components developed in Java (the failover algorithm uses Java serialization) and not other languages. The U.S. Navy has a saying that holds true in virtually every aspect of life. The saying is affectionately known as the seven Ps (for this book, the fifth *P* was modified):

Proper prior planning prevents pathetically poor performances.

In this chapter, we are going to look at writing good, clean component designs. We will discuss different design techniques and discuss the pros and cons of each technique. Both stateful and stateless approaches will be described, although the conversation will lean toward stateless techniques. We will end the chapter discussing the Memento design pattern.

2.1   What is the Jungle Safari Shipping Company?

Throughout *Taming Jaguar*, we will work with a fictitious company named the Jungle Safari Shipping Company. Safari Shipping runs a profitable business picking up large packages and delivering them deep into the heavily populated Jaguar jungle.

Lately, Safari has come under immense pressure from customers to provide a more real-time, accurate picture of the shipping status of a package. After evaluating vendors, Safari has decided to leverage its existing PowerBuilder experience. The company also feels that it has seen the future and that future is J2EE, so the company wants to use this project to begin to make the move over to PowerJ.

Safari runs a lean operation, and as such doesn't require a large complex data model to implement its application (after all, we only have so many pages!). Figure 2.1 shows the tables used by the Safari Online Shipping (SOS) web site. To briefly cover the data model, customers are assigned a userID and password that grants them access to the web site to view the shipping status of their packages. Customers have the ability to indicate their notification preference (email, fax, and so on) in the notify_type column of the package table. When populated, the system will automatically send out a detailed delivery report, including the delivery date and signature, via the appropriate medium.

Safari's software must be able to take its delivery details and disseminate that information via various broadcast mediums. These targeted broadcasts are to the company's most important asset, its loyal customer base. Safari routinely picks up the package

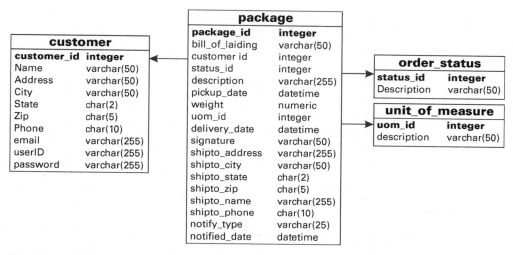

Figure 2.1 This diagram shows the Jungle Safari Shipping Company data model.

from the customer and brings it to its shipping hub (sometimes even via riverboat on the Amazon). Once the package is at the hub, workers use a PowerBuilder application to enter the details of package.

Later, customers who desire delivery notification will have the ability to log on to the SOS web site and view a list of all the packages they have shipped. There, the customer can inspect the details of a package and optionally request delivery notification through one of the available notification types. Initially, Safari has identified that the broadcast notification service will include email, fax, and pager.

As stated earlier, Safari's dedicated team of information technology (IT) staff and professional consultants has made the decision to use Sybase tools, including Jaguar CTS, and will be using both PowerJ and PowerBuilder for component development.

The IT team has decided to use PowerBuilder to develop the fax component, while PowerJ will be used for the email and paging. There is a rumor around the office that in the near future the company may wish to add support for another broadcast medium: synthesized voice (for voice mail messages).

Throughout *Taming Jaguar,* we will focus on component design principles and techniques to help Safari Shipping provide a powerful notification interface for its shipping business to make customers happier.

2.2 What are the different Jaguar component types?

Jaguar provides three distinctly different component types. Each component type is designed for a different purpose and each has its own set of strengths and weaknesses.

The actual implementation and instantiation of a component inside of Jaguar is directly related to the associated component properties for each type. We will look at these properties shortly, but first, let's review the three types in table 2.1:

Table 2.1   Jaguar component types

Standard	A standard component represents the most common type of Jaguar component. These components usually contain the implementations of traditional business logic routines, including calculations, and can participate in Jaguar-controlled database transactions. Jaguar will typically (depending on the component properties) create multiple instances of a standard component in response to simultaneous client requests for the same component.
Shared	Jaguar will create only a single instance of a shared component regardless of the number of clients or components requesting the shared component. A common use of a shared component is to establish a data cache that provides access to commonly requested data. This technique eliminates repetitively querying a database, and can be initially populated and periodically refreshed through a service component.
Service	Service components are designed to run in the background under the control of the Jaguar CTS server. They perform background and batch processing that is not invoked by a client application. Services can be used to purge stale data from a database, or process requests from a queue (which may be implemented as a shared component). We cover services in chapter 4.

2.3   *What's on a Component Properties Instances tab page?*

A component has a multitude of properties, but the discussion here focuses on the properties found on the Instances tab page on the Component Properties dialog. These properties play a crucial role in Jaguar's approach to instantiation and access to a component. Each of these properties will be discussed below in detail in table 2.2, outlining what each is individually as well as how each property relates to the others and the net effect of the combination of properties on the component. The component properties dialog, shown in figure 2.2, is accessed inside Jaguar Manager through the right mouse button menu on a component.

Table 2.2   Properties found on the Instances tab page

Reentrant	The reentrant property is applicable only if the component is an Enterprise Java Bean. The EJB specification explicitly prohibits the use of reentrant code, or what is more commonly referred to as a loopback, which is covered in chapter 3.
Transient	This is another property specific to EJB components. It indicates that the object is valid only for the life of the client session, and is one of the properties used in defining what type of bean the component is (entity, stateful session, or stateless session).
Stateless	If the stateless property is checked, Jaguar doesn't fire the `activate!` or `deactivate!` methods of a component. The intent here is to provide a small performance boost. Theoretically, if the component is stateless, there isn't any stateful data that needs to be initialized. Although this property was an addition in Jaguar 3.5 specifically for an EJB component, the effect is the same on all components.

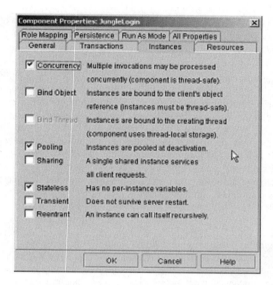

Figure 2.2
Properties found on the Instances tab page

Stateless (continued)	Checking the stateless property does not automatically enable Automatic Demarcation/ Deactivation, nor does it necessarily deactivate the component instance after a method call.
Pooling	When pooling is turned on, Jaguar indefinitely postpones the physical destruction of the component instance. Pooling is another property that enhances overall component performance when turned on because Jaguar doesn't waste time instantiating and destroying resources after each client has finished working with a component. Also, when turned on, Jaguar does not invoke the `canReuse()` function or the `canbepooled!` event. This event (or method) fires on a component only when pooling is set to false, providing the developer an opportunity to control if a component should or should not be pooled. Pooling of a stateful SessionBean is illegal.
Bind object	Bind object is a feature unique to EAServer at this time; this feature is not currently implemented by any of the component models presently supported in EAServer. In effect, it will permit multiple clients to call the same component instance via different containers (Jaguar Servers). This is different from a shared object that is tied to a single container. The idea is that such a component would serve as a storage component for persistent data across the cluster, and the container's transactional services ensure the data is in effect replicated to each instance on each container.
Bind thread	By turning on bind thread, you are indicating that any method calls on the component must use the same thread Jaguar used to create the instance of the component because data is stored inside of that thread using thread local storage (TLS). This property is extremely critical for PowerBuilder and COM components deployed to a Windows NT machine. If the component is deployed to a Jaguar server running on any flavor of UNIX, then this property is ignored, even if the component was developed inside of PowerBuilder. In the Windows environment, PowerBuilder's nonvisual DataStore actually uses internal resources that uses Windows' TLS. However, the need for enabling bind thread is applicable only if the DataStore is stored in an instance variable and is not destroyed between method calls.

Bind thread (continued)	In other words, if you use local variables, you can safely leave bind thread turned off. Non-Windows PowerBuilder virtual machines were written in such a fashion that there is no reliance on TLS. COM objects rely on TLS.
Sharing and Concurrency	These two properties are easiest to explain when they are discussed together. This is due to the inherent dependencies upon one another and the vast implementation difference between the combinations of the two settings. Sharing dictates the number of component instances Jaguar can create. Whenever sharing is turned on, Jaguar can create only a single instance of a component class. Concurrency determines if clients can simultaneously invoke method calls on the same instance. When concurrency is enabled, Jaguar allows the methods of a single instance to run in separate threads, and therefore to be accessed by more than one client at a time. It is worth noting that the EJB specification explicitly restricts the ability of a single instance to simultaneously service requests from multiple clients. For each scenario we are about to discuss, assume two clients attempting to interact with the same component class simultaneously.

Concurrency: off
Sharing: off
If you have both concurrency and sharing turned off, Jaguar will create multiple instances of a component class for multiple clients. However, only one instance of the component class can be active at any point in time, and Jaguar will block the creation of additional components if one of the instances is presently active because concurrency is turned off. For example, `methodA()` from Client 1 will be executed in Instance 1, and `methodA()` from Client 2 will be executed in Instance 2. But Client 2, however, will have to wait until the method call on Instance 1 finishes before its method call on Instance 2 is started.

Concurrency: on
Sharing: off
If you have concurrency turned on and sharing turned off, and the clients are both attempting to execute methods at the same time on the component class, Jaguar will create multiple instances of the component and will execute each method in parallel, or concurrently, on separate threads in separate instances.

Concurrency: on
Sharing: on
If you have both concurrency and sharing turned on, Jaguar will create only a single instance of a component class, which both clients will execute against, and there is the potential for multiple clients to be working with this single instance at any given point in time. PowerBuilder doesn't support this combination because a PowerBuilder component is not thread-safe.

Concurrency: off
Sharing: on
If you have concurrency turned off and sharing turned on, Jaguar will create a single instance, against which both clients will execute. At any given moment in time, however, only one client may be actively working inside of the component, period. All other requests are queued and executed serially. |
| | **WARNING:**   **PowerBuilder Developers**: PowerBuilder components cannot support multiple methods inside of the same component executing in parallel because PowerBuilder components are not thread-safe. |

Sharing and Concurrency (continued)		For this reason, PowerBuilder components should leave concurrency turned off when sharing is turned on! Our discussion of sharing and concurrency wouldn't be complete if we didn't discuss the role of bind thread in conjunction with these two properties. If sharing and bind thread are turned on, this forces Jaguar to invalidate the concurrency option regardless of the actual setting because the component is forced to remain associated with the thread that created it. With sharing turned on (resulting in at most a single instance), it is illogical and not possible to have multiple threads executing in parallel against the component.

2.4 What is the difference between stateful and stateless?

Stateful and *stateless* are terms that refer to the lifetime or duration of a component after a method invocation is made from a client connection and the execution of that method has finished. *Stateful components* have the ability to utilize instance variables to store persistent, client-specific data in between method invocations. These components are dedicated to a single client session.

NOTE   Stateful components can be pooled after they are deactivated, so an instance can service several client sessions, especially in the case where early deactivation/transaction committed takes place.

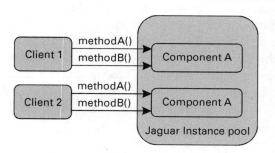

Figure 2.3   This illustration shows two clients invoking methods in a stateful environment.

Unfortunately, time elapses between method calls from the client to the server, and during this time the server is using resources (memory) to maintain the component's state. This approach doesn't scale well as the number of concurrent users increases. In figure 2.3, we see two clients connecting to an instance of Jaguar Component A. Each client then invokes `methodA()`. After the call to `methodA`, the client is waiting for the user to acknowledge and respond to the return value before invoking `methodB()`. Pay particular attention to the fact that for each client, both methods are guaranteed to execute against the same instance inside Jaguar, and that the component will remain dedicated to the client session that connected to it. This is good in a stateful component because we may have stored state in `methodA` that we will use in our subsequent call to `methodB`. However, these instances remain bound to the client session regardless of the amount of time a user takes to respond, not to exceed the timeout property of the component (timeout=0 means indefinitely).

Stateful designs require the server to maintain resources for a component even though the associated client may not be actively involved with that component. It is because of this requirement that a stateful design does not scale well when the server is faced with a large increase in the number of client connections. However, a stateful component's unique ability to retain instance data between method calls does provide advantages in certain business rule implementations, and although we will emphasize a stateless design, our intent is not to stereotype all stateful components as a bad design. In fact, some business process implementations are cleaner using a stateful design.

A *stateless component* does not have the ability to use instance variables to maintain client-specific data between method invocations. This does not mean that stateless components are not allowed to use instance variables. In fact, there are a large number of production-level stateless components the authors have seen that successfully use instance variables. Storing a component reference is one example of a stateless component using an instance variable. The overhead required to look up the component would only occur once, and each method execution on the stateless component can reuse the instance. This technique results in a slight performance gain on the component. The instance variable is instantiated in the constructor! event of the component and reset in the destructor! event of the component by the developer. As another example, a component can partition redundant logic inside of private or protected methods that are invoked from the public method. This keeps the method signatures of the private and protected methods small because they have access to the instance variables. Remember, this approach assumes the instance variable stores either non-client-specific data or data that is reset in the deactivate! event. In the event a developer uses this type of logic with DataStores or COM objects, it is suggested that the component set its bind thread property to true. As discussed previously in this chapter, if it is not set, unexpected results may occur because future method invocations may be running on a different thread—a thread that is unable to access data stored through the use of TLS.

If the state of the instance variables needs to persist between component method calls, prior to resetting the instance variables, their values need to be stored somewhere else besides inside the component. In fact, it is very common for a stateless component to persist in its state somewhere external to Jaguar, like a database or a flat file. In figure 2.4, we see the same two clients from earlier invoking the same methods. The client still presents the return value from methodA() to the user in between method invocations and waits for the user to respond before invoking the second method, but this time Jaguar does not hold onto the component instance between the calls, and of course does not maintain any state values either.

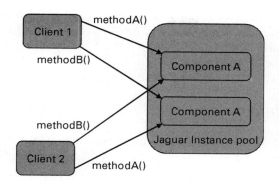

Figure 2.4 This diagram illustrates two clients invoking methods in a stateless environment.

In fact, if the components are multithreaded and not shared (concurrency=true, sharing=false), Client 1 and Client 2 could theoretically be invoking `methodA()` and `methodB()` on different component instances at the same time, but in different threads. Given these settings, a stateless design allows Jaguar to better manage incoming client method requests. Jaguar is now in a position to determine that it does not even need to create another instance of the component to satisfy the requests from a new client. Instead, if it can, it will just grab an available thread from Jaguar's thread pool and associate that thread with the requested method, conserving valuable system resources.

The concern may arise that if it is possible to invoke only a single method, why go through the trouble of using instance variables and persisting state? This is actually an easy question to answer. A stateless component is bound to a single client only during the execution of a single *public* method. At the conclusion of the public method, the component is released, and typically put back into the instance pool for the next client who requests the component. Notice the emphasis here on public method. A component's class can support public, private, and protected methods, regardless of the development language. It is extremely common for developers to partition their script, pulling out recurring code and placing it into a function to conserve the object's footprint in memory.

A stateless component will live only for the life of the single public method invocation; however, to stress a point made earlier, that public method may invoke other private or protected methods that reference and utilize component instance variables. This is one reason why developers may use instance variables inside of a stateless component. In this case, however, developers must pay particular attention to the component properties, discussed earlier in the chapter, if any of the instance variables are instantiated and populated in the `constructor!` event of the component.

NOTE   Although there is no requirement to reset the instance variable data to default values during the execution of the `deactivate!` event, it is strongly recommended that developers form the habit of initializing their instance variables in the `activate!` event or clearing their variables in the `deactivate!` event. If a developer does not clear these values, the next client will inherit the value of the instance variables, and obviously this could lead to undesirable results and a difficult situation to debug. The Jaguar component life cycle is not covered in this book. For more background information on the Jaguar component life cycle and how it impacts component state and its transactions, see chapter 8, "The Jaguar Component Life Cycle," in *Jaguar Development with PowerBuilder 7*.

2.5   *Is my component stateful or stateless?*

Typically, a state*ful* component will set the Automatic Demarcation/Deactivation property to false, set the transaction property appropriately, set the instance timeout property greater than zero, and create a method (such as of_destroy()) to allow clients to deactivate the component. Figure 2.5 shows the Transactions tab page of the Component Properties dialog.

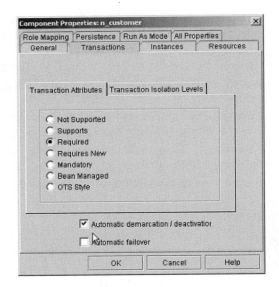

Figure 2.5
This screen capture shows the Transactions Properties tab page from inside Jaguar Manager. This component is stateless because Automatic Demarcation/ Deactivation is enabled.

Stateful components may opt to leave the component's timeout property set to zero. The importance of setting this timeout property cannot be stressed enough though. Zero indicates infinity, which means that the component will never deactivate itself unless it is explicitly asked to by the client. In the event the client inadvertently forgets to deactivate the component, the timeout property would kick in (if set above zero) and deactivate the component automatically, firing the deactivate! event in the process. If the timeout property is not set, clients forgetting to deactivate a component through setComplete() / completeWork() or set-

`Abort()` / `rollbackWork()` force a significant waste of server resources, potentially bringing the Jaguar server to its knees over a period of time.

A state*less* component is much simpler to define compared to a state*ful* component. The only required setting needed to create a stateless component is Automatic Demarcation/Deactivation. When this property is turned on, the component is stateless. Period. Figure 2.5 shows the `SurfSideVideoPB/n_customer` component, included with Jaguar as a sample. Notice that Automatic Demarcation/Deactivation is selected, making the component stateless.

It is worth mentioning that with the advent of EAServer 3.5, Sybase introduced a new component property called `com.sybase.jaguar.component.stateless`. In the `SurfSideVideoPB/n_customer` pictured in figure 2.5, this property is set to false, yet the component is still stateless because of the demarcation setting. Turning this stateless property on causes the `activate!` and `deactivate!` events (and the corresponding Java method equivalents) in components to cease firing. However, using the stateless property by itself will not cause the component to become automatically deactivated after a method call.

2.6   *How do I build a stateful component?*

There are logically three different approaches developers can take when building a stateful component. In each of three approaches, Automatic Demarcation/Deactivation is turned off. The primary difference between the approaches is the way the component interacts with Jaguar-controlled database transactions. The different transactional abilities of a component are pictured in figure 2.5.

The first approach we will look at results in a stateful component with the Jaguar transaction attribute of Not Supported. In this scenario, the component is still capable of working against a database, including updating data, but the component does not participate in any of Jaguar's transactions. In other words, the complete transaction logic is controlled by the developer, and Jaguar will never issue a `commit` or `rollback` command to the database on behalf of the developer. It is the sole responsibility of the developer to ensure that the component completes its database transaction properly. An important note is that a component that uses Not Supported cannot share its transaction with another Jaguar component.

Another common approach used to build a stateful component is known as *early deactivation*. A stateful component using early deactivation sets its Jaguar transaction attribute to either Required or Requires New. For example, let's assume that our component has four `setxxxxx()` methods and a method called `completeUpdate(Boolean)`. The client will invoke each of the set methods, in a logical order for the business rule being implemented. After all the necessary data has been passed to the component, the client invokes the `completeUpdate()` method to save the data to the database. After running the appropriate SQL, the component will `call setComplete() / completeWork()` or `setAbort() / rollbackWork()` to vote on the transaction based on error processing and business logic. Jaguar will use the vote to commit or rollback the transaction. It is important to note that the component will be deactivated from the client session, and all the state stored in memory is lost. This is why the term early deactivation is used, as Jaguar will deactivate the component but not the client.

The final stateful component design approach is a hybrid. In this example, we have a pure stateful component with the same set of methods described above, but the Jaguar transaction attribute is typically set to Not Supported. In the hybrid approach, the various set methods are invoked as they were before, and then when the `completeUpdate()` method call is made, it makes a call to another component, usually stateless, to handle the transaction processing, passing in all the instance data the component collected. In this case, the management of the transaction is deferred to the component receiving the call from our stateful component so that the stateful component remains activated to the client session.

2.7   *How do I build a stateless component?*

After reviewing stateful versus stateless components, and how to build a stateful component, the next step is to discuss how to build a stateless component. Building a stateless component is actually very easy. The real dilemma is how to maintain any stateful information between method calls. This is a very broad issue, and there are probably as many answers as there are consulting firms in a large city. For the rest of this chapter, we will be looking at different design techniques that can be applied to create a stateless component and manage its instance data. The following statement serves as a synopsis of our problem:

Instance variable information generated in a stateless component during a method invocation is lost at the conclusion of the method. Obviously, this information may be needed in future method invocations. Our goal in the remainder of this chapter is to provide insight into how a developer can manage this information between method invocations.

We will be reviewing a number of possibilities for designing and managing stateless components. These suggestions will attempt to point out both positive and negative characteristics of the approach.

- Client caching design
- Database caching design
- Flat-file caching design
- Shared component caching design

2.7.1 *The client caching design*

The theory behind the client caching design is extremely straightforward and very easy to implement. Clients already have to maintain a variable for the Jaguar component proxy, so it would not be too much trouble to add a few more variables on the client and maintain our state information on the client. At first glance, this seems like a very acceptable approach.

When applying a client caching design, the function signature (the method name, the data types of its parameters, and the return value) is extended to include a number of pass-by-reference parameters. These parameters provide state initialization at the beginning of the method invocation and then are written to (assigned) before the end of the method's invocation to be returned to the client for storage until future use. A more extensive state requires a larger number of required method parameters.

Unfortunately, if we step back and think about this approach, we begin to realize that it violates a major rule of object-oriented and component development: encapsulation. To simplify, *encapsulation* is information hiding or the idea of limiting the access to all of the internal details of an object to the outside world. Violating this rule dispenses with object maintainability, not to mention data integrity, in a traditional two-tier Client/Server application, and even more so in an *n*-tier, distributed application.

When another variable needs to be added and managed, an application needs to be rebuilt on both the server as well as the client, and this needs to happen simultaneously. In other words, you don't have the luxury of updating the server component on Monday and the client on Tuesday. This means application downtime and goes against our goal of achieving a highly available application. Because there may be thousands of clients spread across the globe, we are now looking at a major dilemma.

All in all, this technique is good for getting your feet wet in a simple research and development application, but not suggested for a large scale, mission critical production application where the goal is to be highly available.

NOTE   The nature of a thin-web client does alleviate some of the problems associated with deploying a change to the server and client because the client application is still technically stored on a server and downloaded each time it is used. Web clients typically use client caching of state in a unique way. They use a cookie that stores state in name/value pairs in a file which is passed back and forth between the web client and the web server.

REPORT CARD
Client caching design

Pros	■ This design is easy to understand and initially implement.
Cons	■ Larger function signatures are required in order to include extra state information.
	■ Encapsulation is violated.
	■ Network traffic is increased, which may require you to increase your network bandwidth.

2.7.2 *The database caching design*

The database caching design is an above-average design that typically represents the most realistic solution. The primary benefit of using the database to store a component's state lies in the fact that the component is most likely already interacting with the database, so there is little to no effort required to get to the database. Unfortunately, many database administrators do not like the idea of transient data being stored inside the database and there are technical drawbacks to implementing the database caching design. Some databases, such as Oracle, do not support temporary tables to the extent that other vendors do. This results in a potentially large number of permanent tables holding temporary data. Also, because there is a high volume of interaction with these persistent-temporary tables, it is possible on a poorly tuned server to lead to a bottleneck in application performance.

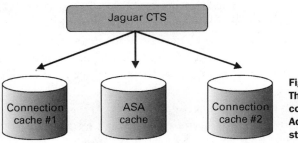

Figure 2.6
This illustration shows a sample connection cache design. It uses Adaptive Server Anywhere to store stateful data between method calls.

Another technical drawback is that relational databases traditionally cannot map persistent object data in a straightforward manner. Objects, by nature, can be quite complex. Mapping the instance data in the object to a single row in a table may not be straightforward or desirable. In fact, this is where object-oriented databases (OODBMS) tend to shine due to their unique ability to store an instance of an object as easily as if it were only a couple of text fields.

No where is it written that the Jaguar server is allowed to work only with a single connection cache. Utilize a different database engine or instance for storing the primary business data—the stuff that needs to be backed up on a routine basis and represents the mission critical information than you do to manage your state. Figure 2.6 shows an architecture with an instance of Adaptive Server Anywhere used to manage the stateful session data and two additional databases located elsewhere for the application's persistent data.

One of Jaguar's strongest features is its ability to provide a Highly Available/ Load Balanced implementation. These capabilities can be exploited only in a clustered environment, which involves two or more Jaguar servers working together to eliminate a single point of failure (we discussed setting up and administering a Jaguar cluster in chapter 1). Compared to all of the stateless component instance data caching techniques this chapter will look at, this is the most realistic option available because it ensures that state information will be available to the component regardless of the physical Jaguar server on which the component is executing. By using a database caching technique, new Jaguar servers can be added to the cluster, increasing the application's scalability, without any extra work by the administrator or the developer.

One of the concerns that ultimately comes up after the decision is reached to use the database caching design is that of how the data should be indexed. This dilemma is quickly solved, courtesy of Jaguar. When a client establishes a connection with the Jaguar server, Jaguar is responsible for authenticating the users (making sure the users are who they say they are). After authentication occurs, Jaguar assigns a session ID to the client session. The session ID is statistically guaranteed to be unique—even across different Jaguar servers. Without going into much more detail, this session ID can be conceptually thought of as akin to DCE's universally unique identifier (UUID), or for Microsoft users, the globally unique identifier (GUID). Combine the session ID with the property name, and you have a primary key. This technique works well when the client uses a persistent connection. However, when a client does not rely on a persistent connection (such as Web / PowerDynamo), and uses Jaguar connection pooling, this technique is not viable, and another arbitrary session ID generation algorithm should be employed. For example, a simple implementation could generate a random number and concatenate the login ID of the user.

One final note about utilizing the database to store stateful data from stateless components is that it will be necessary to design a mechanism that will automatically purge out data after it is no longer needed. One approach is to have the stateless component have a method that the client can call letting the component know that the state can be flushed. A better approach is to use a Jaguar service object that deletes data based on the value of a last modified time stamp and determines if a predefined time duration has elapsed in which the data could safely be deleted.

At the end of this chapter, we will be discussing the Memento design pattern and use it to implement the database caching design we have discussed here.

REPORT CARD
Database caching design

Pros	■ Many components already have connectivity to the database, so little to no extra programming required.
	■ This design can easily be implemented in a secondary database cache against an Adaptive Server Anywhere or similar database located directly on the Jaguar server.
	■ This design adapts to a Jaguar cluster without any component coding changes.
	■ Jaguar may provide a primary key in many situations—the session ID.
Cons	■ A good database server with multiple disk controllers is required to keep bottlenecks to a minimum.
	■ There are possible political implications due to storage of temporary data in permanent tables (on some database systems).
	■ Network traffic increases, but usually traffic is on a higher bandwidth backbone than client connections.
	■ Persistent component data may be difficult to map into a relational schema.

2.7.3 *The flat-file caching design*

Utilizing a flat-file caching design is really a step backward and is ill-advised. Yes, file access is second nature for most programmers, making this approach very easy to understand and code. But as Jaguar component developers, we need to look at the big picture. First of all, you the developer would have to write all the management routines, including the file layout design (such as .ini, comma-delimited, or tab-delimited). This isn't that large of an obstacle to overcome, but think about this next point. How are you going to coordinate file access between components requesting data simultaneously, assuming you used a single file to manage the component's state? Some of you may have responded by saying we'll just use multiple files, one for each user.

Using files to store stateful data between method invocations is probably acceptable in a design that will use only a single Jaguar server. However, most designs are going to want to take advantage of Jaguar's advanced capabilities. For anyone who wants to design a system capable of exploiting all of Jaguar's capabilities, we recommend using a database caching design over a flat-file design. To oversimplify, a database is specifically designed to handle concurrent access and remove platform-specific file access issues. In addition, Jaguar clusters can point to a single database to gain access to pertinent stateful data, which is much simpler than maintaining multiple files across multiple machines.

Okay, so you've decided against our recommendation and are going to use a flat-file caching design anyway. Let's see what advice we can offer. First of all, to eliminate file access problems, it is probably very wise to implement one file per user. In this way, multiple instances of a component can be simultaneously reading and writing to their stateful files. Given this, we need to look for a way to generate a unique file name and probably pass it back to the client, where it must be cached for future method calls. So what are our options for generating a unique file name, and more importantly, where would we store these files?

If Windows NT servers are used exclusively, then you could utilize a couple of well-documented Win32 API calls from kernel32.dll, `GetTempFileName()` and `GetTempDirectory()`.

```
DWORD GetTempPath(
   DWORD nBufferLength,      // size of buffer
   LPTSTR lpBuffer          // path buffer
);

UINT GetTempFileName(
   LPCTSTR lpPathName        // directory name
   LPCTSTR lpPrefixString    // file name prefix
   UINT uUnique             // integer
   LPTSTR lpTempFileName     // file name buffer
);
```

If you are unsure about locking the component onto Windows NT, then there is another option available. As we did above in the database caching design, we could utilize the session ID assigned to the user as the file name. With this approach, there would be no need to pass anything back to the client for caching. In fact, this approach encapsulates your storage design from the client, making it superior to the two aforementioned Win32 methods.

If the component were developed in Java, developers have another option available to them known as *object serialization*. Object serialization is a topic in and of itself. To simplify, object serialization converts a Java object into a bit-blob. Once in this form, it can be sent anywhere, including into a file. When the object is needed again, the bit-blob is deserialized back into a Java object. Java handles most of the details of this object-to-blob conversion for you, and in fact, every EJB component supports the `java.lang.Serializable` interface as part of the EJB specification.

One final note about utilizing a number of flat files to store stateful data from stateless components: It will be necessary to design a mechanism that will automatically purge out old files after they are no longer needed. Regardless of which type of flat-file storage implementation is used, the best approach would be to design a simple Jaguar service that runs as frequently as necessary. Inside of this service, take a snapshot of all the files in the directory that contains the stateful files. Filter out files that should be deleted by looking at their last modified time stamp and determining if enough time has passed in which the file could safely be deleted. The window that dictates if a file should be considered active or not is arbitrary based on your application requirements.

REPORT CARD
Flat-file caching design

Pros	▪ Network bandwidth does not increase.
	▪ Operating systems supported by Jaguar CTS have easy-to-use file routines.
	▪ Jaguar provides a unique filename for non-web clients—the session ID.
Cons	▪ Jaguar's automatic failover abilities on stateless components are compromised.
	▪ A single file design introduces a bottleneck into the system whereby a client's component instance is waiting in a queue for file access to read/write data.
	▪ The developer must design a system to purge out the files after so many minutes.

2.7.4 *Shared component caching design*

Depending upon the language used to implement a shared component, the capabilities of the shared component will differ (PowerBuilder components are not multi-thread capable). The purpose of this section is to discuss the design of your shared component to handle caching of stateful data, so we will not be getting into the technical differences here between shared objects written in PowerBuilder or Java. Review component properties earlier in this chapter, and see chapter 4 for more details on actually implementing a shared component.

Regardless of which language you are using to implement the shared component, if the purpose of the shared component is to cache data, the internal design of the component will probably be the same—name/value pairs associated with a key (necessary to differentiate between different users). We recommend using the session ID as the primary key, either the Jaguar session ID for persistently connected clients or your own arbitrary session ID for clients using pooled Jaguar connections. These keys could be stored inside of a Java hash table, a DataStore, or even in the database using a small table with three columns combining the database caching design with the shared component design, for example:

Proptable
Session_id
var_name
var_value

NOTE   Although this is a shared component, the `activate!` and `deactivate!` events will fire each time a client establishes a connection to the shared object written in PowerBuilder. Therefore, the initialization of the DataStore should take place in the `constructor!` event and destruction (`DESTROY lds_myDataStore`) should take place in the `destructor!` event; bind thread and sharing properties should be set to true, and concurrency should be set to false. If you are looking for a good example of using a shared component from PowerBuilder, see the section entitled "Shared components" (8.7.1) of chapter 8 in *Jaguar Development with PowerBuilder 7*.

One clear advantage shared components have over everything else we have discussed up until this point is that the entire object is already instantiated and stored in RAM. Accessing memory is always going to outperform a database (even local) or file access. Also, DataStores and hash tables have native functionality, such as the `datastore.Find()` method, which makes locating a particular name/value pair very simple and very fast.

One problem with this technique, which is difficult to overcome, is the limited ability to propagate the shared component's stateful data across multiple Jaguar servers in a clustered environment. A common argument is that "we'll only deploy the shared component on a single server, so it won't be necessary to propagate the values between the different servers." This is a short-sighted design because the system cannot take advantage of load balancing or high availability. Combining this solution with the database technique helps solve this problem.

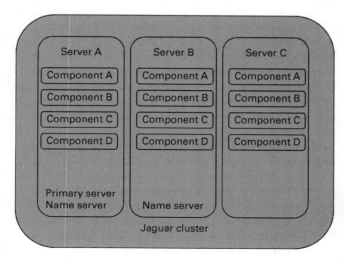

Figure 2.7
This illustration highlights component distribution across a single Jaguar cluster.

Deploying a component, regardless of type, to only a single Jaguar server immediately creates a single point of failure. When designing and implementing an application that must be highly available, it is particularly important to avoid single points of failure. As a Jaguar cluster implements multiple name servers, so too should your design implement a component across multiple servers, as viewed in figure 2.7. In this way, if the server should encounter a catastrophic event, another server can take over the workload, albeit at a performance penalty.

REPORT CARD
Shared component caching design

Pros	• Network traffic does not increase. • This design can leverage a cache with the session ID as the primary key to store and look up name/value pairs.
Cons	• Jaguar's automatic failover abilities are potentially compromised on components required to communicate with a shared object designed to run on a single server (single point of failure). • Atomic operations are potentially enforced against the shared object (if developed in PowerBuilder), resulting in a first in, first out (FIFO) queue and a bottleneck in the system.

2.8   *What is the Memento design pattern?*

Throughout the book we will refer to design patterns. The purpose of this book is not to regurgitate material from patterns books, such as *Design Patterns* by Gamma et. al. However, we would like to point out various design patterns that fit certain situations in an effort to help you develop better component designs.

We've just finished discussing different approaches for storing the internal state of a stateless object. There is a behavioral pattern known as the *Memento design pattern*. This design pattern is intended to store an object's internal state so that the object can restore this state at some later point in time. One of the primary benefits of the Memento design pattern is that it accomplishes its task without violating encapsulation. For instance, the client caching design discussed earlier in the chapter revealed that the client would be responsible for storing and managing a stateless component's state, thereby violating encapsulation and making maintenance down the road a near impossibility.

The Memento design pattern is documented as a stand-alone object that is responsible for saving the state of a requestor object. Ideally, the memento object itself would be stateless and rely on one of the different designs we looked at previously in this chapter to cache state like a database. In the `activate!` event of our stateless component, we would restore the component's state by connecting to this memento class and invoking a method (let's name it `getState()`), and pass it in our primary key (probably the session ID and the name of the component). In the `deactivate!` event, this same stateless component would again connect to the memento class and invoke a similar method which would store the state (let's name it `setState()`), and pass it in our primary key. Obviously, we need to work with more than just the primary key—specifically we need to read and write the instance data.

The instance data of each component is most likely going to vary, both in number and in style. The decision to implement a single memento class that works with objects across the board versus a memento class for each component is a difficult one to make. It is recommended to utilize a single memento class that works across the board. This forces a neutral design and allows for future growth with no extra programming required. It also keeps the number of components to a minimum.

To eliminate the data-type issues, we recommend that the data type of each instance variable be encapsulated away from the memento class. This can be accomplished by casting everything to a string. Although this puts pressure on the stateless component in the `activate!`/`deactivate!` events to perform data conversion, it keeps the Memento design pattern very simple. For instance, consider this possible function signature for `getState()` and `setState()`:

```
int getState( string sessionID, &
              string componentName, &
              ref string argNames[], &
              ref string argValues[] )

int setState( string sessionID, &
              string componentName, &
              string argNames[], &
              string argValues[] )
```

The session ID and the component name together represent the primary key for storing the name/value pairs. During the `deactivate!` event, the stateless component would connect to the memento class, cast all of its internal instance variables to a string array, and invoke the `setState()` method. Internally, the `setState()` method may be implemented similar to the following high-level algorithm:

```
DELETE from the db all outdated data tied to the
session ID / component name

FOR EACH argument
    INSERT a row into the database
    with the name/value pair
NEXT

RETURN a SUCCESS or FAILURE result
```

When the stateless component runs the `activate!` event, it can restore its state by connecting to the memento class and invoking the `getState()` method, and cast the values back to the appropriate data type for each of its instance variables. Internally, the getState() method may be implemented similar to the following high-level algorithm:

```
SELECT from the database all data associated
with the Session ID and the componentName

Enumerate the name/value pairs into the reference
arrays provided by the requestor

RETURN the number of name/value pairs
```

There are a couple of miscellaneous notes about implementing this memento class. First and foremost, use a DataStore instead of embedded SQL when performing the INSERT into the database. This should yield better performance and cleaner code inside of the get method. In the set method, use an embedded SQL DELETE statement so that we don't waste network bandwidth retrieving the old values that are no longer of any use.

Because the memento class is itself stateless and easily pooled, go ahead and define an instance variable to hold your memento class. Create the instance of the memento class in the constructor! event and destroy it in the destructor! event. Using this technique, the activate! and deactivate! events can get down to business immediately retrieving and storing data, respectively. This type of design does require an additional step. Over time, data in this table may become stale for a number of reasons, including client session time out and unexpected system failure (such as sudden power loss). It is necessary to periodically clean out this data, and in chapter 4 we will demonstrate Jaguar services—perfect for doing this type of work.

Using a memento class is a great approach for managing stateful data in a stateless world. It is a fully documented design pattern, exposes only two straightforward get and set methods, and encapsulates the storage mechanism from every component. This encapsulation affords developers the ability to switch between most of the different caching mechanisms described earlier in this chapter without having to recompile and redeploy each and every component. In other words, developers could choose to start out using a flat-file caching mechanism and switch to a database caching technique later simply by rewriting the memento class get and set methods and redeploying the object.

Are these magic Beans? 3

This chapter covers:

- Overview of EJB
- Developing EJB components in PowerJ
- Accessing EJB components versus CORBA components
- EJB and PowerBuilder

The EJB specification has really taken off as far as popularity goes, so much so that EJB support in application servers has become a necessity instead of a feature. Part of that is due to the major push by the industry to adopt J2EE or Java 2 Enterprise Edition. J2EE builds on the Java 2 Standard Edition, which defines the core Java API. J2EE defines standards related to Java and distributed enterprise applications and addresses many of the low-level complexities involved with building a distributed application. Some of the APIs addressed by J2EE include leading-edge technologies and the hottest industry trends including Enterprise Java Beans (EJB) 1.1, Servlets 2.2, Java Server Pages (JSP) 1.1 and related technologies like JNDI and Java RMI-IIOP. In this chapter we will focus on Enterprise Java Beans.

3.1   *What is EJB?*

Enterprise Java Beans is a Java specification for a server-side component model. It establishes a framework in which Java components can be built and defines the interaction between the EJB server or container and the component itself. EJB is a specification put forth by Sun, which was developed in conjunction with its partners, including Sybase. The EJB API is contained in the javax.ejb package. However, it is only an API and a specification and it relies on different vendors to implement the technology in their application servers in conformance with the specification to work.

FYI   The latest information on the EJB specification, including EJB 1.1 and the EJB 2.0 draft, can be found on the Sun Microsystems Web site: http://java.sun.com/products/ejb/docs.html

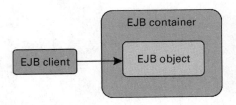

Figure 3.1   A high-level look at EJB

The EJB object runs in an EJB container as pictured in figure 3.1. The EJB container is the vendor-specific implementation of the EJB specification. The EJB container provides a context for the EJB object to run in that is well-defined and allows an EJB object to be portable between different application servers. The EJB container is also responsible for managing features such as the life cycle of an object instance, transaction management, resource pooling, and the naming service for the EJB object. How these features are implemented will be vendor-specific but they must be made accessible through the EJB API.

The strength behind the EJB specification is that it promotes portability of components between different application servers and builds upon existing technologies, including Java RMI, JNDI, CORBA, and Java itself. The power of EJB goes beyond just its portability. The EJB specification also moves low-level features such as transaction management, resource pooling, life cycle management, and security away from the component and into the EJB container. This means that an EJB developer does not have to worry about writing code to handle these functions. Instead the EJB component has deployment and runtime properties, known as declarative properties, which tell the EJB container how to manage the instance of the EJB object. For example, the declarative properties tell the EJB container what type of Bean it is, how the Bean wants transaction contexts to be managed, if the Bean instance should be pooled, and whether or not it is stateless or stateful. The declarative properties can be altered after deployment through the application server without changing code or recompiling the Java class. An example of a declarative property is the Pooling property of a Jaguar component, which tells the Jaguar server whether the instance of the component should be pooled or destroyed when a client has finished using it. This property can be enabled or disabled through the Jaguar Manager by an administrator without redeploying the component. Jaguar CTS provides some level of declarative property functionality for all of the component types that it supports, but these capabilities have been enhanced to embrace the EJB specification. Table 3.1 lists the level of support for Enterprise Java Beans in Jaguar CTS.

Table 3.1 Jaguar support for EJB

Jaguar release	EJB support
Jaguar CTS 3.0x	EJB 0.4
Jaguar CTS 3.5	EJB 1.0
Jaguar CTS 3.6	EJB 1.1

Before looking at the EJB component in any more detail, it is important to understand some of the technologies that help define Enterprise Java Beans. The first important thing to understand about the EJB specification is that it is designed around Java Remote Method Invocation (RMI). In fact, EJB is really just a framework built on top of Java RMI. However, by combining Java RMI with the CORBA IIOP protocol, and incorporating the JNDI and JTA technology, EJB becomes a powerful distributed component model.

3.1.1 What is Java RMI?

Java RMI is a native Java API for creating distributed applications. Java RMI provides the capability to write remote Java objects and clients that can access them. The Java RMI classes are located in the java.rmi package. Java RMI is an easy way to build distributed Java applications. Unfortunately, Java RMI only allows clients and server-side objects to be written in Java. Like most distributed technologies including CORBA, Java RMI uses a client stub and server skeleton architecture that are used to handle invoking methods on remote objects, marshaling of data, and network communications. Java RMI also defines its own network protocol JRMP and has its own naming service called the RMI registry. The RMI registry binds object names to remote objects, allowing client applications to perform lookups and get remote object references. The RMI registry is accessible through the java.rmi.Naming class as well as the JNDI classes that are in the javax.naming package.

Java RMI objects consist of a remote interface and a Java class. The methods for a Java RMI object are defined on the remote interface, which *extends* the java.rmi.Remote interface. The Java class *implements* the remote interface. All methods in the remote interface must throw java.rmi.RemoteException and can use only primitive Java data types (int, short, etc.) or Java classes that implement the java.io.Serializable interface.

The Java class that *implements* the remote interface *extends* a particular Java class or interface depending on whether it is a nonpersistent Java RMI object (java.rmi.server.UnicastRemoteObject), a persistent Java RMI object (java.rmi.activation.Activatable), a Java RMI-IIOP object (java.rmi.PortableRemoteObject), or an Enterprise Java Bean (javax.ejb.EnterpriseBean).

3.1.2 *What is JTA?*

The Java Transaction API (JTA) is a Java API used to manage transactions. The JTA classes are located in the javax.transaction package. The JTA class, UserTransaction, allows an EJB component to mark transaction boundaries and commit or roll back transactions outside of a container-managed transaction. Only EJB components that have a transactional property of TX_BEAN_MANAGED can use the UserTransaction class. The javax.transaction.UserTransaction class is similar to the Jaguar InstanceContext class in the com.sybase.jaguar.beans.enterprise package and should be used in its place. The InstanceContext class is part of the now obsolete EJB 0.4 specification implementation in Jaguar CTS.

3.1.3 *What is JNDI?*

Java Naming and Directory Interface (JNDI) is a Java API used to access different naming and directory services. The JNDI classes are located in the javax.naming package. The Java classes that implement the JNDI API rely on other classes, known as the Service Provide Interface (SPI), to provide the actual Java class implementations so that JNDI works with a particular Naming Service. This is similar to JDBC, where the Java classes and interfaces defined in the java.sql package rely on the implementation of the Java classes provided by the JDBC driver to access a particular database. JNDI works with several Naming Services including LDAP, the RMI registry, and the CORBA Naming Service. JNDI is used by EJB clients to find the home interface for a particular EJB object (more on this soon).

3.1.4 What is CORBA?

Common Object Request Broker Architecture (CORBA) is a specification defining a distributed object communication infrastructure or object bus made up of Object Request Brokers (ORB) and describes how objects and methods can be called over a network. CORBA is defined by the Object Management Group (OMG), which is a consortium made up of members and vendors in the software industry. CORBA is a specification, and like EJB, relies on vendor implementation and conformance to standards to create actual working products. One of the strengths of CORBA is the fact that it is language neutral, allowing components and clients written in different languages to interoperate. This is accomplished through client-side stubs and server-side skeletons, which are used to mask language differences, handle invoking methods on remote objects over a network, and provide data marshaling. CORBA stubs and server-side skeletons are generated using the IDL for a particular component. The Interface Definition Language (IDL) is a language-neutral way of describing an object and the methods it implements. IDL defines the data types that CORBA can pass over a network. The OMG has produced IDL mappings for different languages, including Java. The IDL-to-Java mapping defines how the IDL data types correspond to the Java data types detailing which data types can be used in a Java class to implement a CORBA object.

CORBA also addresses the issue of interoperability between ORBs with the Internet Inter-ORB Protocol (IIOP) definition. IIOP is a TCP/IP-based object-network protocol, which ensures that any CORBA ORB can access any another CORBA ORB and use the components installed on it even if they are both written by a different vendor. For example, components running in Jaguar CTS can access components running on BEA Weblogic. CORBA does not, however, address portability of components between ORBs written by different vendors, so while Jaguar components can *access* Weblogic components, Jaguar components cannot be *deployed* and run on the Weblogic server. CORBA also does not define how components should be built or provide a framework for building them, although some vendors have attempted to provide this.

CORBA also defines a Naming Service, which allows clients to look up CORBA components on the network using the CosNaming API. The Java classes that implement CORBA are found in the org.omg.CORBA and the org.omg.CosNaming packages. For more information on CORBA or the OMG, point your browser to www.omg.org.

3.1.5 *How do Java RMI, CORBA, and EJB come together?*

EJB fills in the gaps of the CORBA specification and provides a framework and server-side component model that addresses portability—something CORBA currently lacks. An EJB component can run on *any* application server that supports the EJB specification. Although EJB provides a portable server-side component model, it needs an open-object communication infrastructure to pass messages over a network and allow it to integrate with other existing distributed enterprise applications. CORBA provides just that with IIOP. IIOP has a large base of support, because most application servers today are CORBA/IIOP-compliant and many applications have been written using CORBA objects.

Java RMI has been implemented over the CORBA/IIOP protocol and is known as Java RMI-IIOP. This replaces JRMP with IIOP, allowing Java RMI objects and Enterprise Java Beans to be accessed from non-Java clients. Java RMI-IIOP also allows a Java RMI and an EJB component to access CORBA components written in languages other than Java using Java RMI. The Java RMI-IIOP objects rely on JNDI to work with the CORBA Naming Service to find CORBA components.

NOTE   EJB 1.0 uses Java RMI to define its remote interfaces. This allows many data types that CORBA/IIOP cannot support to be used. The EJB 1.1 specification requires EJB interfaces to adhere to the Java RMI-IIOP data types, ensuring that the data can be passed over IIOP.

CORBA IDL is more restrictive in the data types it supports than Java RMI is. In order to run Java RMI over IIOP, some changes needed to be made. The CORBA IDL to Java mapping put forth by the OMG already addressed mapping CORBA IDL data types to Java language constructs, allowing Java to interact with other CORBA objects. The Helper and Holder classes generated with Java stubs are part of these mappings to handle narrowing classes and passing data types by reference. Placing Java RMI over IIOP required restricting the parameters and return types of Java RMI to be compliant with CORBA IDL and mapping RMI constructs to CORBA. This strict subset of Java RMI is known as RMI/IDL. The EJB 1.1 specification requires an EJB component to use only Java RMI-IIOP data types. While EJB relies on CORBA and the application server to handle the low-level nuances of transporting Java RMI object messages over the network using the IIOP protocol, it does not use the same CORBA stubs to implement its component model. In addition, EJB breaks the language neutrality aspect of the CORBA specification. So while EJB relies on many of the existing CORBA technologies, it is not a CORBA component model.

The Java language (or, is it a platform now) supports portability of software between operating systems and hardware platforms. Platform independence is achieved through the Java Virtual Machine (JVM). EJB promotes portability of components between competing application servers providing implementation independence. The industry is very excited to have achieved operating system and application server independence, which breaks away from "vendor lock in." Of course, when using EJB, there is no language independence, but the industry and Sun don't seem to have a problem with the Java language becoming the new de facto standard upon which the industry will depend. Maybe that's because "vendor lock in" is also pronounced "Microsoft Windows."

Evaluating the EJB component model can be difficult because many factors are involved when building a distributed enterprise application. Our report card looks at Enterprise Java Beans at a broad level, so some of the "pros and cons" may not be a factor in your decision-making process.

REPORT CARD
EJB

Pros	<ul><li>EJB defines a component model that is portable between application servers.</li><li>Declarative properties allow EJB components to be configured at runtime.</li><li>EJB uses existing CORBA/IIOP infrastructure.</li></ul>
Cons	<ul><li>EJB is limited to the Java language.</li><li>EJB is a new and unproven technology.</li><li>EJB is an evolving technology that leads to incompatibilities between EJBs written to different levels of the specification.</li><li>Use of proprietary extensions by EJB server vendors may limit portability of EJB components.</li><li>Clients need to use a different API to access an EJB component than they do for a CORBA component.</li></ul>

3.2   *What is an EJB component?*

An EJB component is a server-side component that runs in an EJB container. The container is the environment that interacts with the EJB component on behalf of an application server. The container manages the life cycle of an EJB instance and its transactional state based on the type of Bean it is and the property settings of the component.

An EJB is made up of two interfaces and a Bean class—at least as far as a developer and a client application are concerned. As we will see, there are many other parts of an EJB component that are hidden by the application server (EJB container). An EJB component has two interfaces: a Home interface and a Remote interface. The Home interface *extends* the EJBHome interface in the javax.ejb package and defines methods that control the life cycle of the Bean, including finding, creating, and destroying it. The Home interface and EJBHome object are similar to a CORBA factory object. The Remote interface *extends* the EJBObject interface in the javax.ejb package and is customized by a developer to define the methods that are exposed to client applications. The methods of the Remote interface are the ones developers will write to implement business functionality and clients will invoke. The Bean class is the Java class that maintains any object state in instance variables and implements the business methods on the Remote interface. Both the EJBObject and EJBHome interfaces extend the java.rmi.Remote interface as shown in figure 3.2, which illustrates that EJB has its roots in Java RMI. The remote interface of an EJB component and the Java class that implements the EJB component functionality are similar to the remote interface and the Java class that implements the Java RMI object.

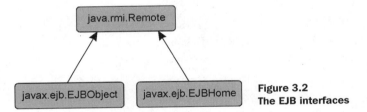

Figure 3.2
The EJB interfaces

The EJB container uses the Home interface and Remote interface to generate the client-side stubs and the server-side implementations of the EJBHome and EJBObject for a particular Bean class. The methods on the Home interface are implemented by the EJBHome object, which is generated by the application server when the EJB is deployed. The EJBHome object helps the container manage the Bean life cycle and acts like a factory object for the client, providing a way to get a remote object reference to the remote interface of an EJBObject. The methods on the Remote interface are implemented by the EJBObject object. The EJBObject is also generated by the application server when the EJB is deployed and wraps the Bean class. The EJBObject works with the container to handle transactions, pooling, security, and other application server services. The EJBHome and EJBObject objects are specific to the vendor implementation of the EJB specification.

The Bean class does not actually "implement" the Remote interface as a Java developer may expect; however, it does need to provide a method with a signature that matches each of the methods defined in the Remote interface. The Bean class also provides some methods that are invoked by the EJBHome object to notify the Bean when certain events occur, like when it is created, activated, deactivated (or passivated), and removed. The Bean class does not have to do anything special in the methods that the Home interface uses to notify it about particular events other than to provide method signatures for them. The methods on the Home interface that must be implemented by the Bean class are determined by the type of Bean, Entity, or Session (more on that soon).

The parts that make up an EJB component are listed in table 3.2. Figure 3.3 illustrates how these parts work together. From the picture, notice that the Home and Remote interfaces are implemented by the EJBHome and EJBObject objects respectively, and that the client-side stubs are generated from these objects so that the client application never has direct access to the Bean class. This is also true for cases when an EJB component accesses another EJB component.

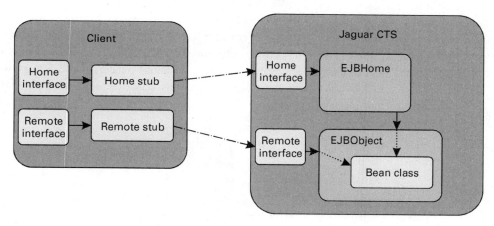

Figure 3.3   The parts of an EJB component

Table 3.2   Parts of an EJB component

Parts of an EJB	Description
Home interface	Defines methods that control the life cycle of the Bean.
Remote interface	Defines methods that are exposed to client applications.
Bean class	The Java class that implements the EJB component with methods corresponding to the Home and Remote interfaces.
EJBObject	Generated by the EJB server during deployment, it implements the Remote interface and wraps the Bean class.

EJBHome	Generated by the EJB server during deployment, it implements the Home interface and helps the container manage the Bean life cycle.
Home stub	Client-side representation of the Home interface (EJBHome) generated by the EJB server.
Remote stub	Client-side representation of the Remote interface (EJBObject) generated by the EJB server.

NOTE   We highly recommend the book *Enterprise JavaBeans*, 2nd edition, published by O'Reilly. This will give you a better overall understanding of Enterprise Java Beans and different design considerations. In addition, check out the EJB specification itself at the following URL: www.javasoft.com/products/ejb/docs.html

The Home interface is used by the client application to get a stub (or remote object reference) to the Remote interface. The reference to the Remote interface that is returned by the Home interface is used to invoke methods on the Bean class through the EJBObject. The stub (remote object reference) to the Remote interface sends the method call and data over the wire using Java RMI. The EJBObject responds to the request from the client and passes the call to the actual Bean class as illustrated in figure 3.4. The EJBObject handles many aspects of how the Bean class is operated on before and after the method is invoked based on the EJB properties. This includes getting an instance from a pool, managing the transactional state, and determining the security context.

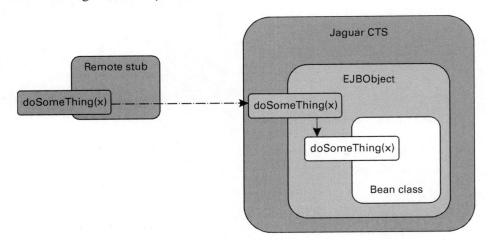

Figure 3.4   Calling an EJB method

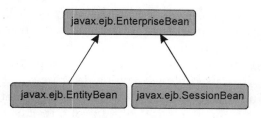

Figure 3.5   EJB Bean types

How an EJB is handled is not only based on its properties but also on its type. There are two types of EJB components, Entity Beans and Session Beans. An Entity Bean represents a single entity of persistent data, usually a single row in a table of a database. A Session Bean represents operations or tasks that are performed on data. The type of Bean is determined when the EJB component is being designed and developed. The Bean class *implements* either the EntityBean or the SessionBean interface. Both of these interfaces extend the EnterpriseBean interface as shown in figure 3.5. The EnterpriseBean interface is the primary interface for all EJB components.

3.3   *What is an Entity Bean?*

An Entity Bean is an EJB component that models persistent data and wraps a single entity of data, usually a row of data in a table on a relational database. The persistent data, however, does not have to be stored in a database, as anything that persists the state can be used. Entity Beans represent concrete entities like customers, packages, tickets, and products. An instance of an Entity Bean is used to provide consistent access to the data for a particular entity. They also contain validation rules and secure the data. An Entity Bean never represents a list of data, tasks, or a business process—that is what Session Beans are used for. For example, the Safari Shipping Company deals with packages, lots of packages. An Entity Bean represents a single package. Operations that are performed on the package, for example finding a package or changing its status as it is shipped to its destination are handled in Session Beans.

NOTE   An EJB container does not have to support the Entity Bean in the EJB 1.0 specification; however, this becomes a requirement in the EJB 1.1 spec. Jaguar CTS 3.5 supports the Entity Bean in its implementation of EJB 1.0.

Entity Beans deal with persistent storage. Persistent storage means that the data is long lasting and should be available beyond the life of the object, client session, or server. The data in an Entity Bean is kept in a persistent storage facility, usually a database. The management of the data can be container-managed or Bean-managed. When data is managed by the container, the retrieval of data and the INSERTS, UPDATES, and DELETES are handled automatically by the EJB container. This alleviates the developer from having to manage database connectivity or write SQL statements within the Bean. Container-managed persistence requires a mapping of instance variables (data members) on the Entity Bean object to columns in a database. How this is handled depends on the vendor. When persistent data is Bean-managed, the Entity Bean takes care of its state by acquiring database connections and issuing SQL statements. A Bean-managed Entity Bean can still take advantage of database connection caches and the container managed transactions. However, it needs to provide logic and SQL statements to query and update an entity.

NOTE   An Entity Bean that uses Bean-managed persistence must use the Jaguar Transaction Manager to manage the commit or roll back of transactions because an Entity Bean cannot use Bean-managed transactions. Using Bean-managed persistence is *not* the same as Bean-managed transactions (TX_BEAN_MANAGED), which are covered later.

The Entity Bean instance is not handled like any other Jaguar component or CORBA object. We will describe how the Entity Bean should appear to act to a client according to the EJB specification. It is important to note that the specification allows vendors to implement an Entity Bean differently within the container as long as the implementation does not alter how the Entity Bean is defined. An Entity Bean instance that represents a single entity is like a shared object. The Entity Bean class itself can have multiple instances in memory, but only one instance of an Entity Bean for a given primary key (more on this soon) is ever instantiated. Therefore, an Entity Bean that represents a single row of data in a database needs to be shared by all EJB clients, including other EJB components that need access to the data. This means the Entity Bean must allow concurrent access. The EJB container manages concurrent access to a Bean class instance, which allows multiple remote references to the EJBObject to be given to clients as illustrated in figure 3.6. This allows the component instance to be shared by many users.

Although an Entity Bean instance can have more than one remote object reference to it, the EJB container ensures that only one client can access the Bean class instance at a time. So once a method is being executed on an Entity Bean for a client, no other client can invoke a method on the Bean class until that method has finished running. This prevents the developer from having to worry about writing thread-safe code. Long-running methods, however, can cause bottlenecks in an application if several clients are attempting to access the same entity at once.

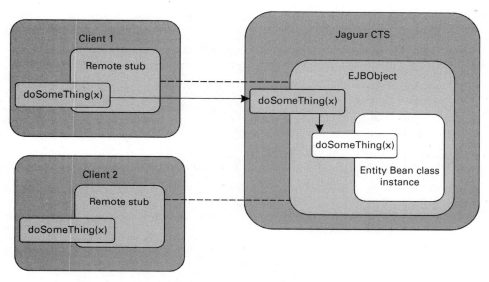

Figure 3.6   Concurrent access to an Entity Bean is managed by the EJB container

FYI   The EJB specification defines the client-view of the Entity Bean in such a way that it appears that only one instance of an Entity Bean has access to the data for a particular entity and is shared by multiple clients. As long as access to the data is synchronized and the data-integrity of the entity is ensured, the vendor has leeway into how the actual component instance is handled in the container. Jaguar CTS actually allows several instances of an Entity Bean to represent a single entity, that is, to have the same primary key. The database locking and transactional capabilities are relied on to ensure that the data is synchronized and transactions are not violated when multiple clients access several Entity Bean instances representing the same entity. The Jaguar CTS implementation handles an Entity Bean instance like a standard, stateless component.

When designing Beans, it is important to understand that reentrance of an EJB component is prohibited by default in the specification. Reentrance is also called a loopback. A loopback is when an EJB component instance is reentered after it calls a method on another Bean. For example a method, doSomeThing, on EJB A is invoked which in turn calls a method, doProcess, on EJB B. The method on EJB B follows this with a call to a method, doSomeThingElse, on EJB A. It is this third method call back to EJB A that creates a loopback to the original calling object. All of the methods are called while the original method doSomeThing is running as shown in figure 3.7. In figure 3.7, the remote interface stubs for the internal calls are not shown to help simplify the picture and illustrate the loopback. Loopbacks in an Entity Bean are not allowed by default, but this can be changed by enabling the Reentrant property on the Instance tab of the Component Properties dialog.

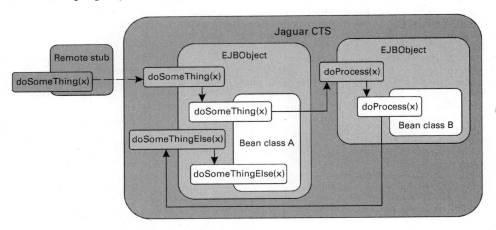

Figure 3.7   The loopback in an EJB component

When we described an EJB component, we said it was made up of a Home interface, a Remote interface, and a Bean class. An Entity Bean has one more piece, and that is the primary key class. Each Entity Bean class has an associated primary key class that can be used to look for a particular instance of an Entity Bean. This primary key allows each instance of an Entity Bean to be uniquely identified and is usually the primary key for a row in a table in a database that the Entity Bean models. It is this primary key that allows the Bean class to associate itself with a particular unique entity. Once the instance of an Entity Bean takes on the identity of a particular entity, it remains bound to that entity for as long as that entity exists. At least this is the idea. In practice, an EJB container can passivate and pool instances to maximize the use of resources. We will look at passivation later. The primary key is used by the container to help other clients find the instance of an Entity Bean that represents the data they want to work with. Remember, in principle, if two or more clients want to work with the same piece of data, they will share a single instance of the Entity Bean, even if the implementation by the vendor does not physically handle the object instances this way.

An Entity Bean implements the javax.ejb.EntityBean interface. This provides several methods, which are used by the container to control the life cycle of the Bean class and manage its state. When the container interacts with the Entity Bean through the EJBHome or EJBObject, methods are called on the Bean class as listed in table 3.3.

Table 3.3   Entity Bean methods

Entity Bean method	Description
setEntityContext	Called by container after the instance is created and before ejbCreate.
create	Called by client to get a remote reference to a new Entity Bean; delegates the call to the ejbCreate method.
ejbCreate	Called by container when create method is called on EJBHome object and INSERTS a new row into the database.
ejbPostCreate	Called by container after the ejbCreate method; the call is made on the newly assigned EJBObject and Bean class.
remove	Called by client to remove an Entity Bean; delegates the call to the ejbRemove method.
ejbRemove	Called by container when remove method is called on EJBHome/EJBObject object and DELETES the row from the database.
unsetEntityContext	Called by container before the instance is destroyed and after ejbRemove.
ejbActivate	Called by container when instance is activated. When the instance is activated, ejbLoad is called after the call to ejbActivate.
ejbPassivate	Called by container when instance is passivated. When the instance is passivated, ejbStore is called prior to the call to ejbPassivate.
ejbStore	**Called by container to store data in the database via an** UPDATE.
ejbLoad	Called by container to retrieve/refresh data from the database.
findXXX	Called by client to get a remote reference to an existing Entity Bean; delegates the call to the ejbFindXXX method.
ejbFindXXX	Called by container when findXXX method is called on EJBHome object; determines if a row exists in the database based on the find criteria.

The Home interface of an Entity Bean is used to create a new entity and therefore a new Entity Bean instance. It is also used to find an Entity Bean that represents an existing entity and to remove an Entity Bean instance along with the entity it represents. When createXXX, findXXX, and remove methods are invoked against the Home interface and the EJBHome object, the container delegates the call to the Bean class's appropriate ejbXXX method. For example when the findByPrimaryKey method is invoked on the EJBHome object, the container calls the ejbFindByPrimaryKey method on the Bean class.

Finder methods (findXXX) are very important parts of an Entity Bean. A client must be able to find an Entity Bean instance that represents data it is interested in using and get a remote reference to it. The client does so using the findXXX methods defined on the Home interface. An Entity Bean can have any number of findXXX methods defined on the Home interface for various types of searches. Each must have a corresponding ejbFindXXX method on the Bean class with the same method signature. One of the findXXX methods that *must* be defined on the Entity Bean is the findByPrimaryKey method. This method must be implemented on the Bean class as ejbFindByPrimaryKey and allows searches to be made with the primary key value itself.

The findXXX methods on the Home interface must be declared so that they return a remote reference to the Entity Bean's Remote interface (EJBObject) or a collection (java.util.Collection) of them if more than one Entity Bean instance satisfies the search criteria. The EJB container manages the remote reference that is returned by the findXXX method. The EJB container returns the remote reference to an Entity Bean based on the return value of the ejbFindXXX method. The ejbFindXXX method on the Bean class should perform any queries or searches to determine if the entity that is being requested by the client exists. If the entity exists, the method should return the primary key class with the primary key value of the entity or a collection (java.util.Collection) of them if more than one Entity Bean instance satisfies the search criteria. The primary key class and value are used by the container to look for an instance of an Entity Bean that is mapped to that particular primary key so that the proper remote reference can be returned to the client. If an instance of the Entity Bean for a given primary key is not found, an available instance of the Entity Bean class is taken from the pool and assigned the primary key. This is illustrated in figure 3.8. In the figure, the client has gotten a Home interface to the Entity Bean. The client is looking to access the data for entity B and uses the appropriate findXXX method on the Home interface to find it. The container grabs an available Entity Bean instance and runs the ejbFindXXX method. The ejbFindXXX method runs a query and determines that entity B exists. It returns a primary key class with the primary key for entity B. The container takes the result, finds the instance of the Entity Bean for entity B, and returns the remote reference to that EJBObject.

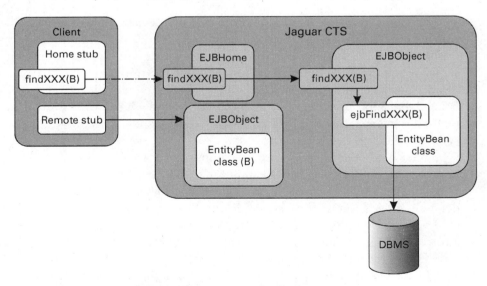

Figure 3.8   Using the findXXX method to get a remote reference

Another way the client can get a remote reference to an Entity Bean is to use the createXXX methods on the Home interface and EJBHome object. When a client wants to create a new entity—for example, a new package is dropped off at Safari Shipping and needs to be delivered—the createXXX method is invoked. The createXXX method has the same purpose as the findXXX method, and that is to return a remote reference of an Entity Bean to the client. The findXXX method, however, is used to access an existing entity and the createXXX method is used to create a new entity. Like the findXXX methods, there can be several create methods on an Entity Bean that accept different types and numbers of arguments. When the createXXX method is invoked, the container takes an available Entity Bean instance from the pool and associates it with an EJBObject. Next the corresponding ejbCreateXXX method on the Bean class is executed.

Each createXXX method on the Home interface must be declared to return a reference to the remote interface (EJBObject) for the Entity Bean. Each createXXX method also needs a corresponding ejbCreateXXX method on the Bean class itself. It is the responsibility of the ejbCreateXXX method on the Bean class to INSERT a new row into the database, creating the new entity. The ejbCreateXXX method must also return the primary key class with the primary key value of the newly created entity. The primary key that is returned by the ejbCreateXXX method is used by the container to associate the EJBObject and Bean class to the new entity so it can be found on subsequent findXXX calls.

Once the client—which can be another EJB component—has a remote reference to the Entity Bean instance, it can call any of the methods in the Remote interface.

TIP   An ejbFindXXX method should not load the data for the entity it is looking for into its instance variables because it may not actually represent the entity itself. It may just be being used to determine if a particular entity exists and what its primary key is.

Now that we understand how a client typically acquires a remote reference to an Entity Bean, let's look at the rest of the ejbXXX methods. It is important to point out that an Entity Bean reference can be obtained by calling a business method as well. The next important concept to understand about an Entity Bean is that when the state is updated or refreshed, it is controlled by the container. An Entity Bean should not have custom methods to handle retrieval of data, or INSERTS, UPDATES, and DELETES. Instead, a developer should use the methods defined by the EJB specification to handle these tasks as listed in table 3.4.

Table 3.4 What to code in an EntityBean method

Entity Bean method	Description
ejbLoad	Query database to load instance data.
ejbCreate	Insert a new row into the database.
ejbStore	Update a row in the database.
ejbRemove	Delete a row from the database.
ejbFindByPrimaryKey	Query database to determine if the primary key is valid.

The container will handle calls to the ejbStore and ejbLoad methods as they cannot be called directly by the client. When the ejbLoad and ejbStore methods are actually called by the EJB container varies depending on the vendor implementation. The ejbLoad method is used to retrieve state from a persistent storage and can be called by the container at any time. It is usually called by the container after activation, or a remote reference to the Bean class is handed out. The ejbStore method is used to save state to persistent storage and can be called by the container at any time. It is usually called by the container before a Bean class is passivated.

The EJB container creates several pooled instances of the Entity Bean class using the default constructor. These pooled instances are not associated with an EJBObject or an entity at this time. The Entity Bean classes in the pool remain inactive until they are requested. Entity Bean classes in the pool are requested when the container needs to associate a Bean instance to an EJBObject in response to a create request or a successful find request in which there is no instance currently representing the entity that was searched for. A pooled instance can also be used to execute a findXXX method for a client request and returned to the pool without being associated to an EJBObject. This is the case when an instance of an Entity Bean is already available for the entity that was recently searched for in the findXXX method.

As additional unique entities are requested, more and more instances of Entity Beans are required that take up memory and resources. An EJB container can reclaim instances of Entity Bean instances by passivating them. When an instance of the Bean class is passivated, it is disassociated from the EJBObject and the entity it represents. It is then used to satisfy another request or is placed in the pool. The client reference to an Entity Bean that is passivated is not affected. The remote reference still represents an Entity Bean that represents the entity it found or created. Calls to methods using the remote reference will result in an instance in the pool being activated that is associated with an EJBObject and having its state restored to the correct entity. The instance that actually services the request may be different than the one that was used before passivation; however, all of this is transparent to the client.

The ejbLoad method should use the getPrimaryKey method on the EntityContext object to get the primary key class and value instead of a value stored in an instance variable, because a particular instance of an Entity Bean can be reused to service different requests after being passivated and activated. The ejbStore method can use the primary key value stored in an instance variable, assuming it was restored in the ejbLoad method, or it can use the EntityContext object.

The create and remove methods are very different from their counterparts on Session Beans. The create, as we saw, will INSERT a new entity into the database and return a remote reference to the new Entity Bean. A remove will disassociate the Entity Bean instance from the EJBObject, invalidate the client reference, and DELETE the entity that the Entity Bean instance represents!

NOTE   PowerJ 3.5 supports the creation of only EJB 1.0 targets. Developers are no longer encouraged to create EJB 0.4/CORBA targets in PowerJ using the com.sybase.jaguar.beans.enterprise.ServerBean interface. Existing PowerJ components that use this interface can be edited and deployed in PowerJ 3.5, but they will not be supported in a later release of PowerJ and should be converted to EJB 1.0. Jaguar 3.5 still supports EJB 0.4 components but Sybase has not commented on its future support in later releases of Jaguar CTS.

3.4   How do I build an Entity Bean in PowerJ?

Our Jungle Safari Shipping Company has several excellent candidates that can be represented by an Entity Bean. We will look at the package entity and build our Entity Bean in PowerJ 3.5. To create an Enterprise Java Bean, you must create a new target. The New dialog shown in figure 3.9 will open. Select the EJB 1.0 Component and click the OK button.

The EJB Wizard will prompt the developer for the type of Bean they wish to build as pictured in figure 3.10. Choose the Entity Bean. We will be covering the Session Bean later in this chapter. The next dialog will ask for the target name and location as shown in figure 3.11.

The Java Package dialog is shown in figure 3.12. The Java package is used to group similar classes together. It also is usually a company's domain name in reverse. We will specify the com.safari package for the Jungle Safari Shipping Company. We will call our Entity Bean the PackageBean.

An Entity Bean's primary key class is very important in enabling a client to locate an instance of an Entity Bean. The primary key must be a serializable Java class; that is, a Java class that implements the java.io.Serializable interface. PowerJ

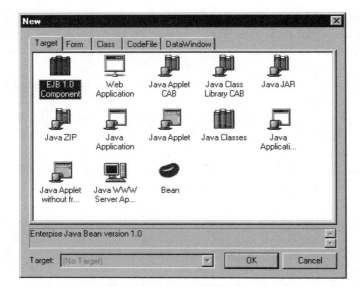

Figure 3.9
An EJB 1.0 target

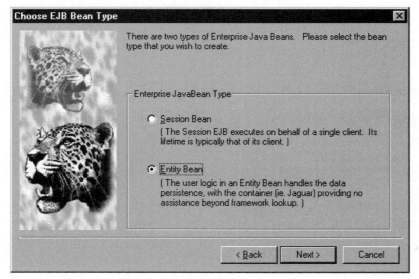

Figure 3.10   Building an Entity Bean

allows us to specify a custom Java class for our primary key now, even though we have not created it yet. The primary key Java class name must include the Java package in which the class is located. We will put our primary key Java class in the com.safari package.

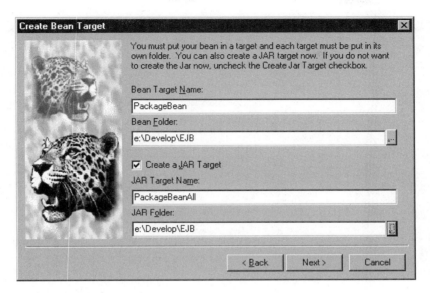

Figure 3.11   The target name and location

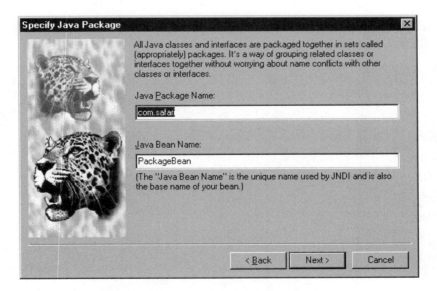

Figure 3.12   Define the Java package and Bean name

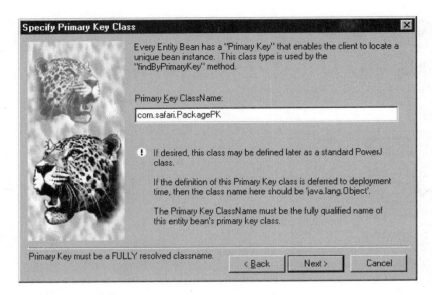

Figure 3.13   The Primary Key class

The dialog pictured in figure 3.14 asks for the name of the remote interface. We will call our remote interface PackageBeanRemote.

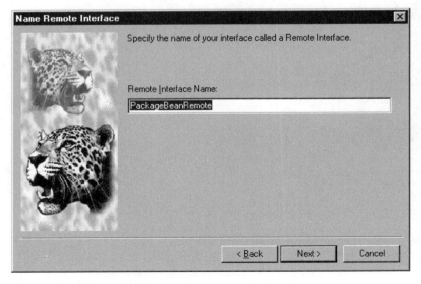

Figure 3.14   The Remote interface name

EJB transaction support is a big part of the EJB specification and will determine how the container manages the Bean instance. We will cover EJB transactions later in this chapter. For now we will have our Entity Bean execute all its methods in a transaction managed by the EJB container by setting the transaction support to Required as shown in figure 3.15.

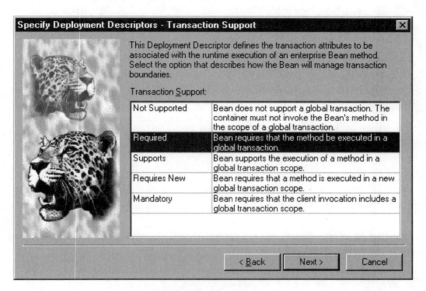

Figure 3.15   EJB Transaction support

One of the benefits of developing an EJB for Jaguar CTS in PowerJ is the ability to automatically deploy the component when we are finished developing it. Figure 3.16 allows us to specify the Jaguar server and the Jaguar package that we will deploy our EJB component to.

After generating the Entity Bean, we need to create the primary key class. The primary key class of the Entity Bean must be a public Java class that implements java.io.Serializable. It must also have a default constructor method that has no arguments. To create a primary key class in PowerJ, create a new class under the target PackageBean. When the New dialog opens, choose the Class tab and select the Standard Class icon.

On the Class Wizard dialog, specify the name of the primary key class as shown in figure 3.17. The package and class names should match the names of the package and primary key class defined in the Entity Bean (see figure 3.13). After finishing with the dialog, click the Next button. This will open the next Class Wizard dialog where the interfaces that the Java class implements are defined. Type the

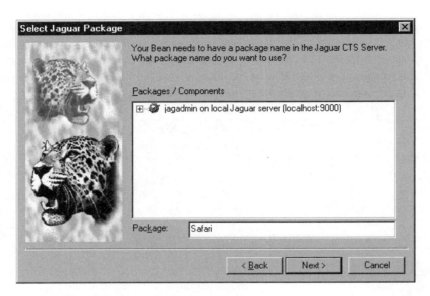

Figure 3.16   Deploying the EJB to Jaguar CTS

java.io.Serializable class. After the interface is added, click on the Finish button to generate the Java class.

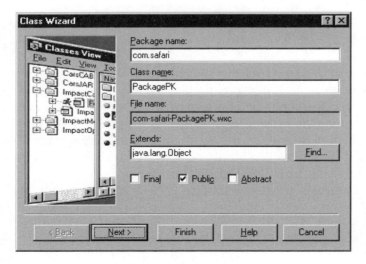

**Figure 3.17
Creating the Primary
Key class for an Entity**

Before building our Entity Bean, we will finish writing our primary key class. First we need to add an instance variable to the Java class that will hold the value of the primary key.

```
public String Package_Key;
```

Next we need to add two public methods named PackagePK. These are the constructor methods for the Java class. One should have no arguments and set the instance variable to null. The other method should accept a String argument and initialize the instance variable with it. The code for the primary key class PackagePK is listed below:

```
package com.safari;

public class PackagePK
extends java.lang.Object
 implements java.io.Serializable
{
      public void PackagePK()
    {
        Package_Key = null;
    }

    public void PackagePK(String PackageID)
    {
        Package_Key = PackageID;
    }

    public String Package_Key;
}
```

Now that the primary key class is finished, we can tackle our Entity Bean. As figure 3.18 shows, there are quite a few files that were generated by PowerJ. These files represent the Home and Remote interfaces and the Bean class implementation. The Entity Bean class implementation is the class named com.safari.PackageBean-Bean. The Home interface is named com.safari.PackageBeanHome and the remote interface is named com.safari.PackageBeanRemote. The com.safari.PackagePK is the Java class that we created to represent the primary key. The PackageBeanAll (Java JAR) target was generated by PowerJ as well. It builds the EJB JAR file that needs to be deployed. It also keeps track of the Jaguar server and package that we want to deploy our EJB to.

The first method we want to take notice of is the setEntityContext method on the PackageBeanBean class. This method is generated for us by PowerJ. The setEntityContext method is used by the container to pass in an EntityContext object. The EntityContext object can be used to get information on the EJB server as well as look up the primary key for an Entity Bean (getPrimaryKey) or vote to roll back a transaction (setRollbackOnly). The Bean class must store the EntityContext object reference in an instance variable in the setEntityContext method if it wants to be able to use it later, which was also done automatically for us by PowerJ.

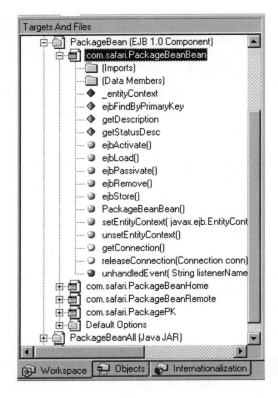

Figure 3.18
The Entity Bean files in PowerJ

```
public void setEntityContext( javax.ejb.EntityContext parm0 ) throws
  java.rmi.RemoteException
{
        this._entityContext = parm0;     // generated helper code
}
```

Our Entity Bean will use Bean-managed persistence so we will need to handle getting database connections and issuing SQL statements. In order to take advantage of the Jaguar Transaction Manager, we must use database connection caches set up in Jaguar. The EJB specification does not specify an interface to acquire database connections from the EJB container. As a result, we will use the com.sybase.jaguar.jcm package to access connection caches on Jaguar. On the PackageBeanBean class, we will need to import the following packages:

```
import java.sql.*;
import com.sybase.jaguar.server.*;
import com.sybase.jaguar.jcm.*;
```

. The Bean class will need an instance variable in which to store the Jaguar connection cache name. This cache name can be stored in a component property and read using the Jaguar::Repository interface as described in chapter 5. In our example we will simply hard-code the value.

```
String JagCache = "Safari_JDBC";
```

The Jaguar server will need to have a connection cache configured through the Jaguar Manager to connect to the proper database using JDBC drivers. The connection cache must also enable connection cache by name access to work in our example.

Next, define a protected user function for the class named getConnection. This method will encapsulate the logic needed to get a database connection cache using the connection cache name and return a java.sql.Connection object. The code sample is listed below:

```
protected Connection getConnection()throws SQLException
{
    JCMCache _cache = null;
    Connection conn = null;
    try {
        // Get a JDBCconnection cache handle
        //from JaguarConnection Manager.
        _cache = JCM.getCacheByName(JagCache);
        if (_cache == null) {
            Jaguar.writeLog(true, "getConnection:Could not access
connection cache by name (" + JagCache + ").");
        }

        // get JDBC Connection class
        conn = _cache.getConnection(JCMCache.JCM_FORCE);
        if (conn == null) {
            Jaguar.writeLog(true, "getConnection:Could not get a
connection from cache (" + JagCache + ").");
        }
    }
    catch (com.sybase.jaguar.util.JException je) {
        throw new SQLException("getConnection:Error getting
Connection from cache");
    }

    return conn;
}
```

Our Bean class will need to return the database connection back to the cache when it is finished. We will define another protected user function, releaseConnection, to accomplish this. The function will accept a java.sql.Connection object and use the JCMCache object to release it. The code sample is listed below:

```
protected void releaseConnection(Connection conn)
throws SQLException
{
    JCMCache _cache = null;
```

```
      if (conn != null) {
         try {
            _cache = JCM.getCacheByName(JagCache);
            if (_cache == null) {
               Jaguar.writeLog(true, "releaseConnection:Could not
access connection cache by name (" + JagCache + ").");
            }

            _cache.releaseConnection(conn);
         }
         catch (com.sybase.jaguar.util.JException je) {
            throw new SQLException("releaseConnection:Error
releasing Jaguar Connection to cache");
         }
      }
   }
```

Once database connectivity and the connection cache are set up, we can look at implementing the rest of the Entity Bean. In addition to any custom methods we want to implement on our Entity Bean, the following methods need to be handled to fully implement out Package Entity Bean:

- ejbFindByPrimaryKey
- ejbLoad
- ejbStore
- ejbCreate
- ejbRemove

We will examine only the ejbFindByPrimaryKey and the ejbLoad methods in this chapter. To see the remaining methods, download the code samples provided with the book.

The ejbFindByPrimaryKey method accepts a primary key object, the one we defined earlier, and uses the value to determine if the entity requested exists. To check for the entity, our method will get a Jaguar connection cache using the getConnection method and execute the following SQL statement:

```
SELECT package_id
  FROM package
WHERE pagkage_id = <primary key value>
```

If the result set returned from this SQL statement has a row, then the method should return the primary key class indicating that the entity exists. The container handles the rest of the work, determining if the entity already has an Entity Bean instance associated to it and returning the remote reference to the Remote interface. Once the SQL statement is finished, we clean up our objects and return the database connection using the releaseConnection method. The code for the ejbFindByPrimaryKey method is listed below:

```
public com.safari.PackagePK ejbFindByPrimaryKey
( com.safari.PackagePK primkey )
throws java.rmi.RemoteException, javax.ejb.FinderException
{

    Connection conn = null;
    Statement stmt  = null;
    ResultSet rs= null;

    // Get a JDBC connection cache handle
    // from Jaguar Connection Manager.
    try {
      // get JDBC Connection class
      conn = getConnection();

      // Create a Statement instance
      //and send query
      stmt = conn.createStatement();
      stmt.execute("SELECT package_id FROM package WHERE
package_id=" + primkey.Package_Key);

        // get result set
        rs = stmt.getResultSet();

        if (!rs.next()) {
          // result set has no rows
          // ObjectNotFoundException is descended
          //from FinderException
          throw new javax.ejb.ObjectNotFoundException("No Package
 found for Package ID:" + primkey.Package_Key);
        }
    }
    catch (com.sybase.jaguar.util.JException je) {
      throw new java.rmi.RemoteException("", je);
    }
    catch (SQLException se) {
      throw new java.rmi.RemoteException("", se);
    }
    finally {
      try {
        if (rs   != null) rs.close();
        if (stmt != null) stmt.close();
        if (conn != null) this.releaseConnection(conn);
      }
      catch (SQLException se) {
        throw new java.rmi.RemoteException("", se);
      }
    }

    return primkey;
}
```

The ejbLoad method is responsible for retrieving the data for the entity that the Entity Bean class represents. In order to do that, we will need the primary key value. The EJBObject that wraps our Entity Bean instance knows the primary key value that can be accessed through the getPrimaryKey method of the EntityContext object as shown in the code sample below:

```
// Get Primary Key
myPK = (PackagePK)_entityContext.getPrimaryKey();
```

The ejbLoad method must store the values that it retrieves and the state of the entity in instance variables so that the information is available to our custom methods. Our package entity has quite a few attributes, but for this example, we will capture only a couple. Declare instance variables on the PackageBeanBean class as shown below:

```
Integer Customer_ID;
Integer Status_ID;
String Description = "";
String PackageStatus = "";
```

After declaring the instance variables, the ejbLoad method can be written. The code for this method is listed below:

```
public void ejbLoad ()
throws java.rmi.RemoteException
{
    PackagePK myPK = null;
    Connection conn = null;
    Statement stmt  = null;
    ResultSet rs = null;

    // Get Primary Key
    myPK = (PackagePK)_entityContext.getPrimaryKey();

    try {
// get JDBC Connection class
        conn = getConnection();

        // Create a Statement instance
        // and send query
        stmt = conn.createStatement();
        stmt.execute("SELECT customer_id, status_id, description FROM
package WHERE package_id=" + myPK.Package_Key);

// get result set
        rs = stmt.getResultSet();

        // populate instance variables
        while (rs.next()) {
          Customer_ID = new Integer(rs.getInt("customer_id"));
          Status_ID = new Integer(rs.getInt("status_id"));
          Description = rs.getString("description");
        }

        // Get Status Description
```

```
        stmt.execute("SELECT description FROM order_status WHERE
status_id=" + Status_ID );
        // get result set
        rs = stmt.getResultSet();

        // populate instance variables
        while (rs.next()) {
           PackageStatus = rs.getString("description");
        }
      }
    catch (com.sybase.jaguar.util.JException je) {
        throw new java.rmi.RemoteException("", je);
    }
    catch (SQLException se) {
        throw new java.rmi.RemoteException("", se);
    }
    finally {
        try {
           if (rs    != null) rs.close();
           if (stmt != null) stmt.close();
           if (conn != null) this.releaseConnection(conn);
        }
        catch (SQLException se) {
           throw new java.rmi.RemoteException("", se);
        }
    }
}
```

The ejbLoad method is very similar to the ejbFindByPrimaryKey method. It gets a connection from the Jaguar database connection cache and runs SQL statements to get data for the entity (a Safari package) that is represented by the primary key value it holds. The data returned from the SQL statements in the result sets is processed and stored in the instance variables.

We will write two simple custom methods for our Entity Bean that allow a client to access the description of a package and the status that it is in. The two method signatures are listed below:

```
String getDescription()
String getStatusDesc()
```

To add a custom method that will be accessible to client applications, we must add them to the Remote interface. Highlight the Remote interface in PowerJ (com.safari.PackageBeanRemote) and use the popup menu or toolbar to insert a method for each publicly accessible method we want to create. PowerJ will automatically create methods with the same name and method signature in the Bean class. In the Bean class (com.safari.PackageBeanBean), implement each method as listed below:

```
public String getDescription() throws java.rmi.RemoteException
{
    return Description;
}

 public String getStatusDesc() throws java.rmi.RemoteException
{
    return PackageStatus;
}
```

Once we have completed this, we have finished our basic Package Entity Bean. Obviously we will not be able to update, create, or delete packages until we implement the ejbStore, ejbCreate, and ejbRemove methods. To deploy the Entity Bean, simply click on the JAR target and choose Deploy. PowerJ will handle compiling the classes, building the JAR file, and transferring the files to the Jaguar server. PowerJ will also correctly install the EJB component onto the Jaguar server and set its properties based on the type of Bean and the values chosen on the wizard so that it is ready to be used by client applications.

3.5   *What is a Session Bean?*

A Session Bean is an EJB component that does not model persistent data. Instead, a Session Bean represents lists of data, tasks, workflow, or business processes. Session Beans represent operations that are acted out on Entity Beans. For example, the Safari Shipping Company deals with packages and we have already written an Entity Bean that represents a single package. However, our Entity Bean does not, nor should it, include methods to perform business operations. The Entity Bean is responsible for setting and getting values and persisting state. Operations that are performed on the package, for example finding a package for a customer or changing its status as it is shipped to its destination, are handled in Session Beans.

Just because Session Beans do not deal with persistent data does not mean that they do not deal with databases. Session Beans can query databases and save data and information that is pertinent to a given task. Session Beans, however, should use Entity Beans to alter the state of a particular entity. For example, our FindPackage Session Bean, which we will create later in this chapter, can execute SQL statements to get a list of packages associated with a given customer. However, if the employee of Safari Shipping wishes to change the status of a package or indicate who signed for a given package, the Session Bean should use the Entity Bean methods to change the state instead of doing this work itself. Not only would the Session Bean be violating basic object-oriented rules by duplicating the work of the Entity Bean, but it could also cause the Entity Bean itself to be out of synch with its data until the container calls the ejbLoad method.

Client applications should interact with Session Beans instead of Entity Beans so that they are tied only to business tasks and not business data.

Session Beans do not deal with persistent data, so there is no concept of persistence. Any data that must be saved in a Session Bean must be handled by the developer by issuing SQL statements. A Session Bean can take advantage of database connection caches and the Jaguar Transaction Manager just like an Entity Bean.

Session Beans are handled differently than Entity Beans. Session Beans are probably closer to the EJB 0.4/CORBA Java components and PowerBuilder components that developers may be used to writing in Jaguar CTS 3.0x. Entity Beans are always "logically" stateful, representing the state of a particular entity. As noted previously, however, the handling of the actual Entity Bean instance varies between EJB container vendors. A Session Bean can be either stateful or stateless. Session Beans do not have finder methods because they are not associated with any particular entity. A client application gets a remote reference to a Session Bean using a create method. The create method on a Session Bean is radically different that the create method of an Entity Bean. On the Entity Bean, it is used to create a new persistent entity; however, on the Session Bean, the create method is used simply to get a remote reference to the Remote interface of the Session Bean so that the client can access methods and perform tasks.

A create method of the Home interface on a Session Bean must be declared to return a Remote reference to the Remote interface (EJBObject) of the Bean class. There must be a corresponding ejbCreate method on the Bean class that matches the signature of the one on the Home interface but the method is not required to do anything and returns a void (nothing). How the container handles the create method internally varies depending on whether or not the Session Bean class is stateless or stateful. However, the container always returns a remote reference that points to an instance of a Session Bean that is always dedicated to a single client as shown in figure 3.19. Session Beans are not used concurrently so they have only one method running at a time and there are no thread-safe issues. Like Entity Beans, loopbacks are not permitted in Session Beans by default, and according to the EJB specification are never allowed for a Session Bean.

A Session Bean is an EJB component that implements the javax.ejb.SessionBean interface. This interface has methods that are similar to those on the EntityBean interface. However, Session Beans do not represent persistent data so they do not have ejbLoad or ejbStore methods. In addition, the ejbCreate and ejbRemove methods do not serve the same purpose as they do in the Entity Bean. The methods of a Session Bean are even handled differently depending on whether the Session Bean is stateful or stateless.

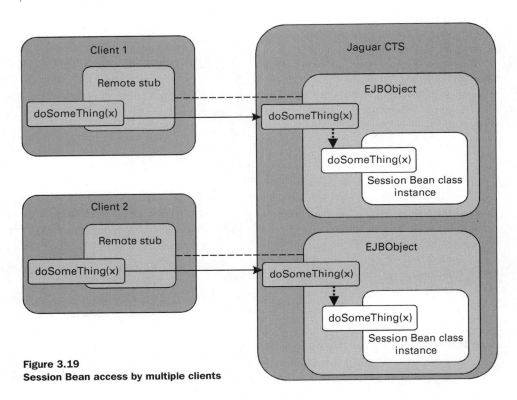

Figure 3.19
Session Bean access by multiple clients

3.5.1 *Stateful Session Beans*

Stateful Session Beans act on behalf of a single client and maintain state between method calls. Stateful Session Beans can accumulate data through method calls and then save information to the database based on business rules and the data on hand. When the client calls the create method, a new instance of the class is created or an available instance of the class is taken from the pool and bound to an EJBObject. The setSessionContext method is called to provide the SessionContext object. The ejbCreate method is also called and than the remote reference is returned to the client.

The Session Bean can now accept requests from the client. The Session Bean is considered active and dedicated to a client process until it is removed using the remove method, it has timed out (instance timeout property), or it has been passivated. Session Beans that maintain state can be passivated and activated, resulting in calls to the ejbActivate and ejbPassivate methods. If a Session Bean instance is passivated by the container, the client can still access it using the remote reference. When the client makes a request using the remote reference, the container will get an available instance of the Session Bean and activate it so that it can handle the client request automatically. This is all transparent to the client.

The remove method of the Session Bean is very different from the remove method of the Entity Bean. Because the Session Bean is not associated with an entity, the remove and corresponding ejbRemove methods do not need to DELETE any data. Instead, the ejbRemove method should clean up any resources that the Session Bean has opened. After the ejbRemove method finishes running, the instance of the Session Bean is disassociated with the EJBObject and the client session by the container and is either destroyed or placed in the pool.

The methods for a stateful Session Bean and their uses are listed in table 3.5.

Table 3.5   Methods for a Stateful Session Bean

Stateful Session Bean method	Description
setSessionContext	Called after instance is instantiated and before ejbCreate.
create	Called by client to get a remote reference to a stateful Session Bean; delegates the call to the ejbCreate method.
ejbCreate	Called by container when the create method is called on EJBHome object after the creation of the instance.
remove	Called by client to invalidate a remote reference to a stateful Session Bean; delegates the call to the ejbRemove method.
ejbRemove	Called by container when remove method is called on EJBHome/EJBObject object prior to the destruction of the instance.
ejbActivate	Called by container when instance is activated.
ejbPassivate	Called by container when instance is passivated.

3.5.2   Stateless Session Beans

The instance of a stateless Session Bean does not maintain state between method calls, and a single instance is able to service requests for many clients. The instance of a stateless Session Bean is made available to a single client when a method is invoked. When a method is executing, no other clients can access the Bean class instance. After the method is finished running, the instance of the Session Bean is made available to other client requests. This is similar to a Jaguar CORBA component that sets Auto Demarcation/Deactivation on.

The container manages the instances of a stateless Session Bean creating them as needed. When the container must create an instance of a stateless Session Bean because there are no available instances of the Session Bean class in the pool to handle a client request, the class is instantiated and the setSessionContext method is called to provide the SessionContext object. After that the ejbCreate method, which has no arguments, is invoked. The ejbCreate method is called only once in the life cycle of a stateless Session Bean.

Client calls to the create method on the Home interface are not delegated to ejbCreate later like they are for stateful Session Beans and Entity Beans. Instead, the container simply creates an EJBObject and returns an object reference to the client. The instance of the Session Bean is not associated with the EJBObject until a method is invoked. When a method is invoked, the container takes an available instance out of the pool and associates it with the EJBObject. After the method is completed, the instance is disassociated with the EJBObject and placed back in the pool. Stateless Session Beans are not activated or passivated, so the ejbActivate and ejbPassivate methods are never called because there is no data to maintain.

Calling remove on a stateless Session Bean does not cause the ejbRemove method to be called on the Bean class. Instead, it just invalidates the stub and releases the EJBObject. The ejbRemove method is called by the container when it is about to remove the instance from memory, usually to conserve resources.

The methods for a stateless Session Bean and their uses are listed in table 3.6.

Table 3.6　Methods for a Stateless Session Bean

Stateless Session Bean method	Description
setSessionContext	Called after instance is instantiated and before ejbCreate.
create	Called by client to get a remote reference to a stateless Session Bean.
ejbCreate	Called only once by container when instance is initially created. It is not called when create is called on the EJBHome object.
remove	Called by client to invalidate a remote reference to a stateless Session Bean.
ejbRemove	Called only once by container when instance is about to be destroyed. It is not called when remove is called on the EJBHome/EJBObject object.
ejbActivate	Not called.
ejbPassivate	Not called.

3.6　*How do I build a Session Bean in PowerJ?*

Our Jungle Safari Shipping Company will need a Session Bean to model the workflow involved in dealing with packages. We will build a stateless Session Bean in PowerJ 3.5 that is used to find packages. To create an Enterprise Java Bean, create a new target. When the New dialog opens, select the EJB 1.0 Component and click the OK button. On the next dialog, select the Session Bean (see figure 3.10). After choosing the Session Bean, the EJB Wizard will ask whether the Bean should be stateful or stateless, as shown in figure 3.20.

After deciding to build a stateless Session Bean, the wizard will ask us to supply the target name and location just like the Entity Bean. We will also need to supply

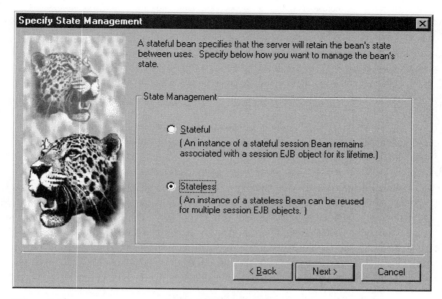

Figure 3.20 Choosing between stateful and stateless

the name of the Java package and the Java Bean name. Our Session Bean will be named FindPackageBean and will be placed in the same Java Package as our Entity Bean, com.safari, as shown in figure 3.21. The remaining wizard prompts will ask for the name of the Remote interface, the transaction support (Required is fine), and the Jaguar server and package (Safari) to deploy the component to.

Building a Session Bean is easier than writing an Entity Bean because we don't have to worry about implementing lots of ejbXXX methods or creating a primary key class. The Session Bean will need to perform database queries, so it will need to access the Jaguar database connection cache. This can be handled by adding protected user functions, getConnection and releaseConnection, which are the same as the ones used in the Entity Bean example.

Once these functions are added, the Remote interface methods need to be defined. On the Remote interface (com.safari.FindPackageBeanRemote) add a method with the following signature:

```
public TabularResults.ResultSet getPackages()
throws java.rmi.RemoteException
```

PowerJ will automatically add a method with the same signature to the Bean class (com.safari.FindPackageBeanBean). This method will be used to look up all the packages in the company and return a result set. The code sample is shown below:

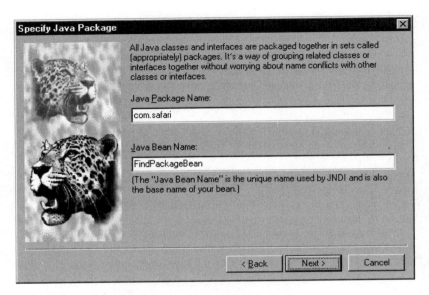

Figure 3.21 Specifying the Java package and Bean name

```
public TabularResults.ResultSet getPackages()
throws java.rmi.RemoteException
{
Connection conn = null;
    Statement stmt  = null;
    ResultSet rs= null;
    TabularResults.ResultSet CORBA_rs = null;

    try {
// get JDBC Connection class
      conn = getConnection();

      // Create a Statement instance
      // and send query
      stmt = conn.createStatement();
      stmt.execute("SELECT package_id, bill_of_laiding, description
FROM package");

      // get result set
      rs = stmt.getResultSet();

      // convert result set
      CORBA_rs = com.sybase.CORBA.jdbc11.IDL.getResultSet(rs);

    }
    catch (com.sybase.jaguar.util.JException je) {
       throw new java.rmi.RemoteException("", je);
    }
```

```
        catch (SQLException se) {
          throw new java.rmi.RemoteException("", se);
        }
        finally {
          try {
            if (rs   != null) rs.close();
            if (stmt != null) stmt.close();
            if (conn != null) this.releaseConnection(conn);
          }
          catch (SQLException se) {
            throw new java.rmi.RemoteException("", se);
          }
        }
        return CORBA_rs;
}
```

The getPackages method is very similar to the methods we wrote on the Entity Bean. It uses the Jaguar connection cache to run SQL statements. A client application can use this list of packages to get a package ID for a particular package and use it to get a remote reference to an Entity Bean.

Once the method is finished, we can deploy the Bean to Jaguar CTS. To deploy the Session Bean, click on the JAR target and choose Deploy. PowerJ will handle compiling the classes, building the JAR file, and transferring the files to the Jaguar server. PowerJ will also correctly install the EJB component onto the Jaguar server and set its properties based on the type of Bean and the values chosen on the wizard so that it is ready to be used by client applications.

3.7   *What are EJB transactions?*

Anyone who has written a database application should be familiar with the concept of a transaction. Transactions are logical units of work consisting of one or more SQL statements that succeed or fail as a group. When dealing with transactions we are talking about changes to a database using Data Manipulation Language (DML) SQL statements (INSERT, UPDATE, DELETE). A transaction must be clearly marked as to where it begins and where it ends so that there is no question as to which SQL statements should be committed or rolled back when the transaction is ended. A successful completion of a transaction is committed and all the changes to the data are permanently recorded in the database. When an error occurs during a transaction, a roll back is issued and any changes that were made to the data during the transaction are removed by restoring the database to its original state before the transaction started.

In most applications the objects define the transaction boundaries and explicitly manage the commit or roll back of the transaction. The EJB specification outlines a new way to handle a transaction using declarative transactions that are controlled by the EJB container. Declarative transactions are transactions managed by the EJB container based on component attributes, which can be changed at runtime. If you are familiar with Jaguar CTS, than you will already understand the idea behind declarative transactions. Jaguar CTS already handled declarative transactions for all of the component types that it supports. These capabilities have been enhanced to comply with the EJB specification.

In order for declarative transactions to work, a Transaction Manager is needed. A Transaction Manager is an intermediary that sits in between the component and the database and handles the transaction context on behalf of a component. The Transaction Manager is responsible for correctly applying the changes to the database made in a transaction based on whether the component votes to commit or roll back the transaction. A Transaction Manager allows several components to take part in existing transactions or start new ones when a method is called, based on how the EJB properties are defined.

Jaguar components can take part in implicit (called container-managed transactions in the EJB specification) or explicit (called Bean-managed transactions in the EJB specification) transactions. An implicit transaction is a transaction for which boundaries and outcome are managed by the Jaguar Transaction Manager. An explicit transaction is managed by the component itself. When implicit transaction management is used, the component no longer can commit or roll back a transaction because it does not know if it is at the end of the transaction or not. The EJB container keeps track of this for the component, based on the transactional attributes of the component and the way it has been called. Instead of directly managing the outcome of the transaction by issuing a commit or rollback, a component instead votes on whether a transaction it is involved in should succeed or fail. A unanimous vote to succeed by all participants in the transaction will tell the container to commit the transaction when it ends. Any vote to roll back, however, will result in the container rolling back the transaction when it ends.

TIP   To take advantage of the Jaguar Transaction Manager, components must use database connections from the Jaguar connection cache.

The EJB container, in this case the Jaguar Transaction Manager, allows transactions to span multiple components and method calls in the same Jaguar kernel without any additional work by the developer using the transactional attributes. Every component that is deployed on the Jaguar server has a transaction property that determines whether or not the component supports Jaguar transactions and how inter-component calls are handled. The transactional property is set when the component is deployed to Jaguar CTS, based on the values chosen during development.

Table 3.7 lists the EJB transactional attributes and how inter-component calls are handled. In the description, the caller of the component can either be a client application or another EJB component.

Table 3.7   EJB Transactions

EJB 1.0 Transaction Attributes	EJB 1.1 Transaction Attributes	Description
TX_NOT_SUPPORTED	NotSupported	The component does not take part in the transaction of the caller. The component does not execute within a transaction.
TX_SUPPORTS	Supports	The component takes part in the transaction of the calling client/component. The component does not take part in a transaction if the caller does not have a transaction.
TX_REQUIRED	Required	The component always takes part in a transaction. When the caller has no transaction, the container starts a new transaction for the component. If a caller has a transaction, the component executes within the same transaction as the caller.
TX_REQUIRES_NEW	RequiresNew	The component always takes part in a new transaction that is managed by the container. Whenever the component is called, it starts a new transaction. If the caller has a transaction, it is a separate transaction from the components.
TX_MANDATORY	Mandatory	The component must take part in the caller's transaction. If the caller does not have a transaction, calls to this component fail with a TransactionRequiredException.
TX_BEAN_MANAGED	*	The component explicitly manages its own transaction. If a caller is involved in a transaction, the component operates in a separate transaction.
-	Never	The component must never be invoked by a caller with a transaction. If the caller has a transaction, calls to this component fail with a RemoteException; otherwise, the component will execute without a transaction.

*In EJB 1.1, Entity Beans cannot manage their own transactions. Session Beans with a transaction type of "Bean", which is specified in the deployment descriptor, can manage their own transactions and do not set a transaction attribute.

NOTE   Beans that do not have their transactional property set to TX_BEAN_MANAGED cannot access the UserTransaction object. A Bean that manages its own transactions with the UserTransaction object defined in the JTA must be set to TX_BEAN_MANAGED.

Voting in EJB is handled implicitly. After a method is completed the default vote is to commit a transaction. If an exception is thrown by the method, then the method may end up voting to roll back the transaction. Exception handling and voting is handled differently in EJB 1.0 and EJB 1.1. In EJB 1.0, any exception thrown during a container-managed transaction will cause a transaction to be rolled back. A component can take part in a transaction that is not container-managed when a client application or EJB component that is explicitly managing a transaction invokes a method on an EJB component with a TX_SUPPORTS, TX_REQUIRED, or TX_MANDATORY transaction attribute. In EJB 1.1, transactions are rolled back when a system exception (any Exception that extends java.rmi.RemoteException or java.lang.RuntimeException) is thrown by a method, but not when an application exception is thrown. To be on the safe side, a method in an EJB component should always vote to roll back transactions explicitly using the EJBContext, object rather than rely on throwing exceptions when a problem occurs.

The EntityContext and SessionContext interfaces both extend the EJBContext. The EJBContext provides two methods that are related to transactional control: the setRollbackOnly method and the getRollbackOnly method. The getRollbackOnly method is used to determine if the current transaction has already been marked for rollback. This method can be used to avoid processing that cannot be committed when a transaction is marked to be rolled back already. The setRollbackOnly method can be used by a component to vote to roll back the transaction that it is involved in.

The client application, or EJB component, that initiates the start of a transaction is called the root of the transaction as shown in figure 3.22. All other components join the transaction of the root component based on their transactional attributes. When the root method is finished executing, the EJB container handles the commit or rollback of a pending transaction by counting the votes of all the components and methods in the transaction.

To illustrate the transactional attributes and how they are used in an inter-component call, let's look at some examples using figure 3.22. If the root component has a transactional attribute of TX_REQUIRED, the container starts a container-managed transaction when a client application calls the method doX. If Bean A is marked as TX_SUPPORTS, then the method doY will execute in the same transaction as the method doX on the root component. If Bean B is marked as TX_REQUIRES_NEW, then the method doZ will *not* execute in the same transaction as the method doX on the root component. Instead, the container will start a new transaction and Bean B will become the root component of the new transaction. Assume Bean C has a transactional attribute of TX_REQUIRED. When Bean B calls the doMore method on Bean C, it will execute within the transaction started in the doZ method. Based on the transactional attributes and calling pattern of the

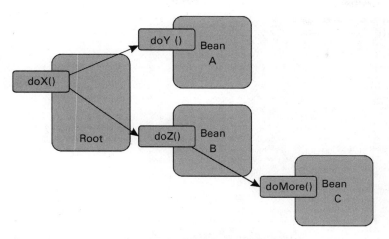

Figure 3.22   A look at a transaction that spans multiple components

components, the EJB container is managing two separate transactions. If Bean B votes for a rollback, all the data changes made in both Bean B and Bean C are rolled back. However, the changes made in the original root component with method doX and Bean A are not affected by this and can save their changes.

The transactional attributes can be set during the development of the EJB Bean and altered after deployment using the Jaguar Manager. To view or change the transactional attribute of an EJB component, highlight the component name and click on File | Component Properties. Then select the Transactions tab of the Component Properties dialog as shown in figure 3.23.

Each method can also have its own transactional support specified, unless it is TX_BEAN_MANAGED. If this is so, then the methods cannot have a different transactional attribute from the component. To access the transactional attributes of a method, select the component in the Jaguar Manager. Expand the Interfaces folder under the component. The methods are all listed under the Remote interface. Highlight the method and choose File | Method Properties.... A dialog similar to the one in figure 3.23 will open. Make any changes required and click OK to save.

In addition to the transactional attributes, the transaction isolation levels for a component and a method of an EJB component can also be set. The isolation level of a component or method determines how it will retrieve data from a database as shown in figure 3.24.

NOTE   The EJB 1.1 specification does not require transaction isolation levels to be set. This property will not be supported in future releases of Jaguar CTS.

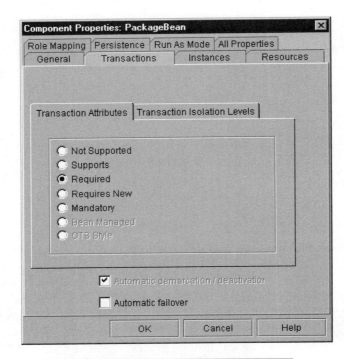

Figure 3.23
The Component
PropertiesTransactions tab

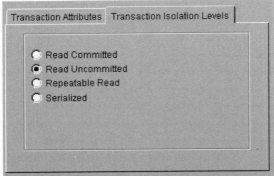

Figure 3.24
Transaction isolation levels

3.8 *How does a client access an EJB?*

An EJB client must get a remote reference to the Remote interface (EJBObject) of an EJB component before it can invoke methods on a Bean. In order to get a remote reference to an EJB component, the client must have a remote reference to the Home interface (EJBHome) of the EJB component, which allows it to get a remote reference to the Remote interface. The EJB specification specifies that the

Java Naming and Directory Interface (JNDI) be used to look up and get Home interfaces. Four steps are required by a client before it can call methods on an EJB component. These are:

1   Get a JNDI context.

2   Perform a lookup using the EJB name and get a reference to the Home interface.

3   Cast the object returned by the lookup to the Bean's Home interface.

4   Use the create or find methods on the Home interface to get a reference to the Remote interface.

These steps are illustrated in figure 3.25. JNDI allows a client to find and access an EJB Home interface. In order to find the Home interface, the client needs to know the location of the JNDI server and the name that the EJB it is interested in using is stored under. The JNDI Context object must be initialized so that the vendor implementation of their Naming Service is used. An EJB container is responsible for implementing a Naming Service for EJB components and providing a JNDI driver for it.

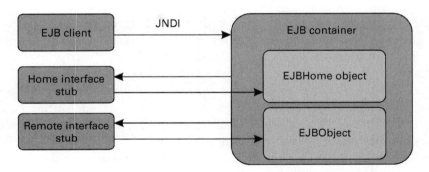

Figure 3.25   Getting a remote reference to an EJB component

WARNING   The EJB component model uses different stubs than a CORBA component, and they are not compatible. An EJB component needs both home and remote stubs, whereas the CORBA component needs only a single stub to the object.

A client can use the remove method of the EJBObject to invalidate the remote reference to the Bean. What happens to the Bean depends on the type. Calling remove on a Session Bean will invalidate the remote reference on the client. Calling remove on an Entity Bean actually deletes the entity data from the database as well as invalidating the remote reference.

3.9 How does a PowerJ client access an EJB component on Jaguar CTS?

A PowerJ or any other Java client can use JNDI to access an EJB component deployed to the Jaguar server. In order to perform the lookup, the client application should use the Bean Home Name as shown in figure 3.26. The Bean Home Name is found on the General tab of the Component Properties dialog of the EJB component and is stored in the Jaguar property com.sybase.jaguar.component.bind.naming.

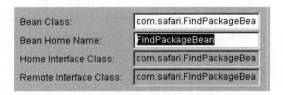

Figure 3.26
The Bean Home Name

JNDI provides an interface to work with many different naming services. The service provider class that implements the JNDI interface for a particular naming service needs to be specified in the INITIAL_CONTEXT_FACTORY property of the InitialContext object. In order to access an EJB on Jaguar CTS using JNDI, the Context object INITIAL_CONTEXT_FACTORY property must be set to com.sybase.ejb.InitialContextFactory. This value will vary for each EJB server vendor. The PROVIDER_URL property is used to specify the protocol, server location, and port number where the naming service is located.

After setting up the properties for the JNDI Context object, the client can get a reference to the object as follows:

```
    javax.naming.Context jndi_cxt = new javax.naming.InitialContext
(props);
```

Once the client has a reference to the JNDI Context object, it can be used to perform a lookup. The object that is returned by the lookup method should be cast to the Bean's Home interface as shown in the code sample below:

```
FindPackageBeanHome PkgeHome = null;
PkgeHome=(FindPackageBeanHome)jndi_cxt.lookup("FindPackageBean");
```

The Java code to use JNDI to access an EJB on Jaguar CTS is listed below:

```
java.util.Properties props = new java.util.Properties();
// Initialize JNDI for Jaguar
```

```
props.put(javax.naming.Context.INITIAL_CONTEXT_FACTORY, "com.sybase.ejb.Ini-
   tialContextFactory");
props.put(javax.naming.Context.PROVIDER_URL, "iiop://localhost:9000");
try {
     // Get JNDI Context
     javax.naming.Context jndi_cxt = new javax.naming.InitialContext (props);

     // Lookup Home interface and cast it
     com.safari.FindPackageBeanHome PkgeHome = (com.safari.FindPackageBean-
Home)jndi_cxt.lookup("FindPackageBean");

     // Create EJBObject and get remote reference
     com.safari.FindPackageBeanRemote PkgeRemote = PkgeHome.create();

     // Call methods using PkgeRemote
}
catch (javax.naming.NamingException ne) {
     // Handle error
}
catch (javax.ejb.CreateException ce) {
     // Handle error
}
catch (java.rmi.RemoteException re) {
     // Handle error
}
```

In order to use EJB components in PowerJ, generate the EJB 1.0 stubs in the Jaguar Manager. Because PowerJ does not use the system CLASSPATH, the location for the stubs must be specified in the PowerJ IDE. Place %JAGAUR%\html\classes in the Global Classpath of PowerJ, which is located on the Global Classpath tab of the PowerJ Properties dialog shown in figure 3.27. The PowerJ Properties dialog can be accessed under the Tools | Options... menu option.

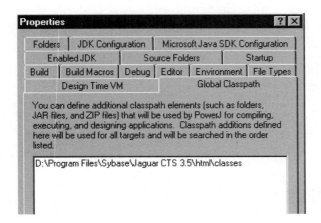

**Figure 3.27
PowerJ Properties—Global Classpath**

3.10 *How can I access an EJB component from PowerBuilder or a CORBA client?*

CORBA clients can access EJB components on Jaguar CTS using the SessionManager interface to get a Home interface. The EJB components do not require any additional changes or need CORBA stubs, instead the client application uses the EJB stubs through a CORBA ORB rather than JNDI.

The code to initialize the ORB and get the Manager and Session objects is the same. The first difference between using the CORBA component and an EJB is in the lookup of the session object, the Bean Home Name is specified instead of the Package/Component name.

```
obj = session.lookup("FindPackageBean");
```

The object that is returned by the call to lookup needs to be narrowed to the Bean's Home interface using the Home interface Helper class.

```
FindPackageBeanHome EJBPackageHome = FindPackageBeanHomeHelper.narrow(obj);
```

Once the remote reference is narrowed to the proper interface, the Home interface can be used to get a remote reference to the Remote interface. Once this is successfully obtained, using create or findXXX methods, the client can call methods.

```
PkgeRemote = EJBPackageHome.create();
```

In Java the code looks like this:

```
java.util.Properties props = new java.util.Properties();
props.put("org.omg.CORBA.ORBClass", "com.sybase.CORBA.ORB");

org.omg.CORBA.ORB orb = org.omg.CORBA.ORB.init((String[])null, props);
org.omg.CORBA.Object obj = orb.string_to_object
("iiop://localhost:9000");

SessionManager.Manager manager = SessionManager.ManagerHelper.
narrow(obj);
SessionManager.Session session = manager.createSession("","");

obj = session.lookup("FindPackageBean");
com.safari.FindPackageBeanHome EJBPackageHome = com.safari.FindPackageBeanHome-
    Helper.narrow(obj);
try {
    PkgeRemote = EJBPackageHome.create();
    // Call methods using PkgeRemote
}
catch (javax.ejb.CreateException ce) {
    // Handle Error
}
catch (java.rmi.RemoteException re) {
    // Handle Error
}
```

A PowerBuilder client can also access EJB components using the same technique. Before the PowerBuilder client can attempt to access EJB components, the Jaguar Proxy Wizard needs to be used to generate stubs for the SessionManager objects and the EJB components that will be accessed as shown in figure 3.28.

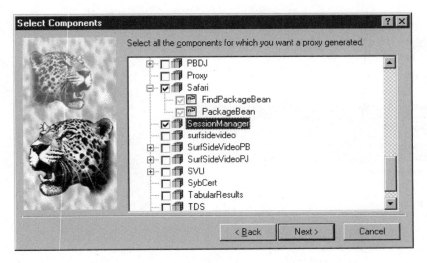

Figure 3.28   Generating proxies for EJB components in PowerBuilder

Once this is done, the code for PowerBuilder to access an EJB looks like this:

```
JaguarORB          myORB
CORBAObject        myCORBAObj
Manager            myManager
Session            mySession
FindPackageBeanHome myHome
FindPackageBeanRemote myRemote
string             myORBoptions

SetPointer(HourGlass!)
myORBoptions=""
myORB = CREATE JaguarORB
// initialize ORB
myORB.init(myORBoptions)

myResult = &
myORB.string_to_object("iiop://localhost:9000", myCORBAObj)
IF myResult= 0 THEN
    // narrow to Manager
    myCORBAObj._narrow(myManager, "SessionManager/Manager");
    // create Session
    mySession = myManager.createSession("","")
    // lookup Home interface for Bean
```

```
    myCORBAObj = mySession.lookup("FindPackageBean")
    // narrow to Home interface
    myCORBAObj._narrow(myHome, &
"com/safari/FindPackageBeanHome")

    // get remote interface using create
    myRemote = myHome.create()

    // Call methods on EJB using myRemote
ELSE
    mle_status.Text = "Error getting Manager Object"
END IF
```

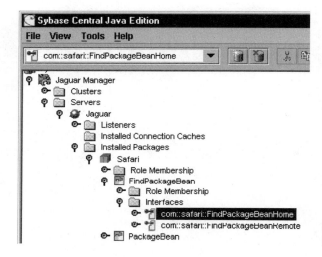

Figure 3.29
EJB interfaces

TIP When narrowing the Home interface, make sure that the whole interface name is used. Otherwise, PowerBuilder will not be able to handle this.

For example, use com/safari/FindPackageBeanHome instead of safari/FindPackageBeanHome, or FindPackageBeanHome. The whole interface name can be found in the Jaguar Manager under the Interface folder for the component as shown in figure 3.29.

Servicing the jungle

4.1   *What is a service component?*

Service components are designed to run in the background under the control of the Jaguar CTS server. They perform background and batch processing that is not invoked by a client application. Instead, service components are started by the Jaguar CTS server when it starts up. Service components implement three standard methods, `start()`, `run()`, and `stop()`,which affect its life cycle. The `start()` method is invoked when the Jaguar server is started, and is invoked again only after the server is physically restarted. Refreshing the service component or the Jaguar server from inside Jaguar Manager does not cause the start method to be executed again. Immediately upon return from the start method, the server invokes the run method. The run method is where the bulk of the processing occurs. Once the run method has finished running, the service component is finished and will not perform any more processing unless the Jaguar server is physically restarted. Developers routinely implement an infinite loop inside the run method to keep the background process going continuously while the server is running. The thread is often put to sleep for an arbitrary period of time after each loop iteration. The `stop()` method is invoked when the server is refreshed, shutdown, or the service component itself is refreshed.

4.2   *What does the service component interface look like?*

Service components are really regular components that are specialized in the sense that they have implemented an interface composed of three methods, which are invoked by the Jaguar server instead of a client application or another component. The three methods are subroutines (return `void` in Java or `(None)` in Power-Builder) and must be have the following method signatures:

```
void start()
void run()
void stop()
```

When developing a service component using Java, pay particular attention to the fact that the component must implement the *methods* as opposed to the *Java interface* CtsService::GenericService. Confusion often arises over the terminology that a service component must implement the CtsService::GenericService interface. Creating a Jaguar component that implements an IDL interface means defining the methods of the interface, not specifically stating that you're implementing the interface as you would normally do using Java. The problem with implementing the CtsService::GenericService interface is that it requires the class to implement the base CORBA remote object interface. This is due to the fact that

CtsService::GenericService extends org.omg.CORBA.Object. Starting with Jaguar 3.5, it is possible to implement the CtsServices::GenericServiceOperations interface if you are using Java. This new interface is a recent addition to CORBA, and requires the class implement the necessary operations.

TIP   Any component that implements the three methods listed above can be installed as a Jaguar service on a Jaguar server through the Jaguar Manager.

Components that implement the required methods for executing as a service are not limited or restricted to the service methods. In other words, a component can implement the service methods described here as well as any number of other methods.

4.3   What are the `start()` method's responsibilities?

The `start()` method is used to initialize the service properly. Technically, there are no mandatory initialization steps required, but most services maintain some small amount of stateful data that needs to be set up properly. The Jaguar server will automatically invoke this method once on every installed service when the server is starting. The method will be invoked again only after the Jaguar server is physically restarted. It is generally accepted protocol for a service to make a log entry announcing itself as being properly initialized and ready to go to work. Common initialization in services include creating an instance variable for access to the Jaguar log.

If you need to make intercomponent calls from inside the `start()` method, you may encounter an error situation. This is because Jaguar may not have started the name service yet, making it impossible to look up the requested name context. To get around this problem, open up the Jaguar server's properties. Find the following property and set it equal to `start` instead of the default value of `run`.

```
com.sybase.jaguar.server.bindrefresh=start
```

This property tells Jaguar CTS to bind itself with the Naming Service during startup rather than after it is running.

4.4   What are the `run()` method's responsibilities?

The `run()` method is responsible for performing the actual work of the service. Jaguar automatically invokes this method after the completion of the `start()` method. Jaguar never invokes the `run()` method more than once, leaving it up to the developer to implement some type of infinite loop if the service is to remain running for the life of the Jaguar server. If the service's intent is to perform an operation exactly once, do not implement any form of a loop inside the method, allowing it to return immediately.

Research conducted by the authors indicated that in refreshing the Jaguar server or the service component from Jaguar Manager, Jaguar executes the stop method but the thread of the run method continues without interruption. In researching this, we used a service component with a local variable responsible for tracking the iteration count. The component logged iteration 38 to srv.log, the service component was refreshed from inside Jaguar Manager, and the stop method was executed. After the arbitrary sleep period specified in the loop, the run method logged iteration 39 to srv.log.

It is imperative that the run() method periodically step aside, suspending itself for a fixed amount of time. This suspension ensures that the service thread doesn't hoard server resources, lowering overall server performance. Later in this chapter we will look at how to put a thread to sleep.

If the run() method doesn't contain any code, then the service will stop.

4.5   What are the `stop()` method's responsibilities?

The stop() method is called automatically by Jaguar when the server is being shut down, refreshed, or the service component is refreshed. Also, it is possible to programmatically call the stop method from inside the start or run methods. This method should be used to perform any cleanup required by the service. In rare situations, it may even be necessary to store the service's state. The overall goal of the stop() method is to stop the execution of the run() method in services performing continuous background processing. For example, an instance variable could be set. This variable is checked first inside every iteration of the run() method loop to determine if the loop should be exited.

WARNING   There have been documented bugs where the stop method is not invoked even when the Jaguar server is shut down properly through Jaguar Manager.

4.6   How should I define a service component's properties?

First and foremost, Sybase strongly recommends *against* transactional services in the Jaguar CTS online books. Simply stated, transactions don't belong inside a service. Period. Jaguar would attempt to deactivate a service component after a transaction, defeating the intended purpose of service. This does not mean that a service cannot access a database, it instead means that the service component should not form any dependencies on Jaguar's transactional capabilities. In the event that your service requires Jaguar's transactional capabilities, implement a component (preferably stateless) that performs the transactional work. The service component can then create an instance of the stateless component and invoke a method on that component.

Clients typically should not need to talk to a service component directly. In the event logic needs to be accessed by both the service and clients, move that logic into a separate component—preferably a stateless component with concurrency enabled. Now you can access the logic from the service through an intercomponent call and from the client without having to maintain multiple sets of source code.

4.7 How do I configure a Jaguar service?

PowerBuilder developers should never have to go through any additional steps from inside Jaguar Manager to configure a single threaded service to execute inside Jaguar when deployed from the IDE. However, PowerJ and other development environments require additional steps after the deployment of the component to set it up as a service. We will walk through the necessary steps for setting up the service here.

The *Jaguar CTS Programmer's Guide* in the online books provides a great recipe for adding your service component to the Jaguar server's list of services.

1 Start the Jaguar Manager.

2 Expand the Servers folder

3 Select the server to which you wish to add the service.

4 Display the property sheet for the server, choosing Server Properties from the File menu.

5 Navigate to the All Properties tab page.

6 Locate the `com.sybase.jaguar.server.services` property in the list by highlighting it and clicking the Modify button.

7 Edit the value of the field by adding the name of your service component(s) to the list. Use the form Package/Component. In the event there are already services installed on the server, separate the service names with a comma.

8 Click OK to close the Modify Properties window.

9 Click OK to close the Server Properties window.

10 Refresh or restart the Jaguar server to run the service.

4.8 How can I dictate the number of threads Jaguar should run on my service?

It is possible for Jaguar to spawn multiple service threads inside a single component instance or multiple service component instances, each running on a single thread. The actual setup and deployment of the component into this type of environment is dependent upon a number of things.

The importance of the instance properties of any service component cannot be stressed enough. You may wish to earmark this question and refer back to it when you are designing and deploying your services. In the next couple of paragraphs, we will cover the different combinations and the various results in depth.

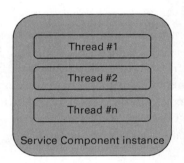

Figure 4.1   A single instance of service component running multiple threads

When creating a service component, the *Jaguar CTS Programmer's Guide* in the online books indicate that the Sharing option on the Instances tab of the Component Properties dialog should be selected. When sharing is on, Jaguar will create one and only one instance of the component in memory. Also, if the concurrency property is set to false and bind thread is set to true, the component can safely store data in instance variables initialized inside of the start() method. If, however, concurrency is set to true and bind thread is set to false, we are indicating that we have a thread-safe component (in other words, written in PowerJ). This combination of settings results in a single instance running multiple threads inside it, as seen in figure 4.1.

Alternatively, it is possible to turn off sharing on the service component and increase the number of requested threads. Actually, when sharing is turned off, we aren't requesting a larger number of threads. In fact, we are requesting a larger number of instances, each running in its own thread. The combination required to achieve this result is to set sharing to false, concurrency to true, and bind thread to false. This combination of settings results in multiple instances with each running a single thread, as depicted in figure 4.2.

The latter approach of spawning multiple instances can be useful in cases where you have a queue that needs to processed, and you have a multiprocessor machine. If the sharing property is set to false, the concurrency property is set to true, and bind thread set to false, each instance of the component will access the queue (preferably implemented as a shared component with concurrency set to false to ensure the next entry in the queue isn't pulled off by two different service components) and grab the next item to be processed.

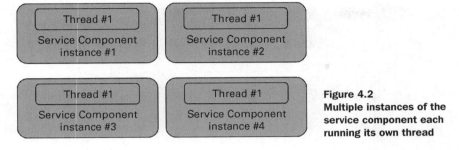

Figure 4.2
Multiple instances of the service component each running its own thread

For example, consider this real world example of where multiple instances would provide value to overall application performance. The Jungle Safari Shipping Company needs to print several documents for each package entered into its system at its shipping hubs. As each package is entered, the report requests are added to the end of a FIFO queue (a shared component with concurrency set to false, or a database table). The company's Jaguar servers are running multiple instances of the reporting service. Each instance of the service would process a report, in parallel. In figure 4.2, we could simultaneously be processing and printing four different reports taken from the queue.

At this point, it should be clear that there is a monumental difference between service components based on how their instance properties are set. Despite the differences described above, the number of threads or instances Jaguar should spawn at startup is specified in square brackets after the name, where *n* is an integer representing the number of threads.

When naming your servicing in the `com.sybase.jaguar.server.service` property of the server, include a set of square brackets after the component's name. Set the value in between the square brackets with any positive integer. This number will tell Jaguar the number of requested threads or instances, again depending upon your service component's instance settings. In the example shown in figure 4.3, the service component someService inside of the package BackgroundTasks will be run using ten threads (it has both sharing and concurrency set to true).

When the Jaguar server encounters the square brackets on the service name, it invokes the `run()` method from the different threads until it reaches the requested number of threads. Alternatively, it creates the requested number of instances and invokes the `run()` method on each instance.

Regardless of the setting of the service component's Shared property, Jaguar will invoke the `start()` method once, and each thread will terminate upon conclusion of the `run()` method.

When implementing a service that runs in multiple threads, and synchronized access to shared data is not necessary, maximum performance is achieved when the

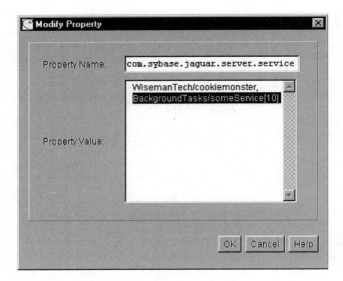

Figure 4.3
The number of threads or
instances Jaguar should spawn
are indicated

Concurrency property is set to true and the Bind Thread property is set to false. This is important to remember. The concepts of concurrency and bind thread were discussed in detail in chapter 2. Refer to that chapter for more detailed coverage on these properties.

4.9 Why are services better implemented by Java, instead of PowerBuilder?

The Java language inherently provides better support for executing a service class in a multithreaded environment. This is because Java is a multithreaded language, and PowerBuilder is not.

The PowerBuilder VM does not allow multiple requests to be processed on a single instance of a component class at one time.

PowerBuilder supports asynchronous parallel processing on a client through the invocation of the `SharedObjectx()` family of methods. However, this isn't multithreaded in the true sense of the word. The technical requirements of developing a multithreaded application are very complex and beyond what most traditional PowerBuilder developers may have ever encountered. The following is not intended to produce an argument about PowerBuilder's multithreaded capabilities, but to point out some facts regarding PowerBuilder. PowerBuilder doesn't natively provide the ability to suspend or resume a thread. PowerBuilder doesn't provide any context-switching mechanism for a thread (such as the ability to raise or lower the priority of the thread to cause a context switch). PowerBuilder does not natively expose any thread synchronization objects to coordinate access to shared thread data between threads (there are no mutexes, critical sections, or semaphores). Lastly, PowerBuilder DataStores on Microsoft Windows internally use a form of TLS. For a more detailed description of how PowerBuilder uses TLS, review the discussion in chapter 2 of the Bind Thread component property.

PowerBuilder's multithreaded limitations become a disability when developing components that are to be deployed as a Jaguar service. Because a Java service component can easily take advantage of Jaguar's multithreaded environment, it becomes clear that a typical Java service component will out perform a typical PowerBuilder component. Depending upon the activities of the service, this performance advantage could be substantial.

Because a PowerBuilder component inherently uses a form of TLS inside of the PowerBuilder virtual machine on Windows NT, *all* PowerBuilder components, regardless if they are a service or not, need to seriously contemplate the settings on the Sharing, Concurrency, and Bind Thread properties. These combinations were also discussed in detail in chapter 2.

WARNING   There is a documented bug with the PowerBuilder wizards. They do not deploy shared or service components correctly. The wizards, as well as the Project painter, do not provide an interface to disable the Concurrency option. You must use Jaguar Manager after deploying one of these types of components to manually disable the Concurrency option.

4.10 *How do I control the execution frequency of a service component?*

The service component is responsible for determining its own life. As we stated earlier in this chapter, Jaguar never invokes the run() method more than once, leaving it up to the developer to implement an infinite loop if the service is to remain running for the life of the Jaguar server. Putting the thread into a sleep state at the end of the loop (before the next iteration) is strongly recommended in order to keep overall server performance high, and eliminate situations where the thread may takeover the CPU.

In Java, use the java.lang.Thread.sleep() method to put a thread to sleep. This method takes a single argument; the number of milliseconds to suspend the thread. For other component types, Jaguar includes a C library libjdispatch.dll that provides the JagSleep() method. This method takes a single argument; the number of seconds to suspend the thread. It can be used to safely suspend execution of the thread calling the routine, and it can also prevent the thread from taking over the server's CPU.

WARNING	Under no circumstances should a PowerBuilder component use the `Yield()` function inside of the service in place of calling `JagSleep()`! The `Yield()` method was not designed to be thread-safe, and in fact, there would be no break in the service execution because the component would merely yield to itself.

For PowerBuilder developers, the external function declaration that can be used to put their component to sleep is as follows:

```
subroutine JagSleep(long seconds) &
    library "libjdispatch.dll"
```

WARNING	Never call the system's sleep routine or any other routine that suspends execution of the current process. Doing so will result in a suspension of the entire Jaguar server process. The two methods disclosed above are designed to suspend only the current thread, allowing other threads inside Jaguar to continue their execution.

4.11 *How can I communicate with a service component from a client connection?*

Actually, the preferred solution is one that never requires a client to communicate directly with a service component. Instead, consider moving the common business logic out to a separate stateless component. The service can then make an intercomponent call to this stateless component from inside of the `run()` method and the client can access the component as it does any other stateless component, as displayed in figure 4.4. If the client needs to communicate information to the service—for instance, how long to sleep in between executions—set up a shared component to store the data.

Figure 4.4 shows a stateless component with two methods, one that actually performs the business and another that is merely a wrapper method to set the timer delay. This wrapper method fully encapsulates the client from the shared object—clients don't even know it exists, providing even greater flexibility down the road if a different architecture needs to be implemented, such as moving the timer delay into a database. When the service component wakes up, it makes an intercomponent call to the stateless component's `doMyWork()` method. After the method returns, the service makes a call to the shared component's `getSleepDuration()` method. The return value from this method indicates the number of seconds the service should go to sleep.

Because the service will start automatically when Jaguar starts, initially the client won't be able to connect and indicate the timer delay through the `setTimer-Interval()`. To accommodate this, the shared component should have logic incorporated that establishes a default sleep value. To do this, declare an instance (or class) constant and name it `DEFAULT_SLEEP` and set it to an arbitrary number of seconds. Also, define an instance variable and name it `requestedSleep`. In the `getSleepDuration()`, implement a simple IF...THEN statement:

```
If the requestedSleep is equal to 0, then
     return DEFAULT_SLEEP
else
     return requestedSleep
```

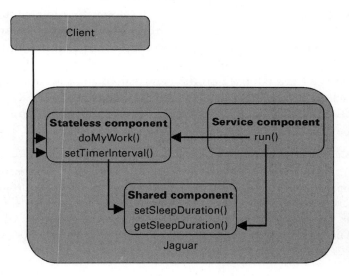

Figure 4.4
A strong service architecture allows clients to execute the logic as well

If the service component was developed in Java, and the component has concurrency set to true, there is another option for communicating with the service component. The CtsServices::ControlService interface documents an interface for controlling running services, including the ability to return a value back to the invoking client. The method is named `control()`, and it takes a single string as a parameter. Service components supporting the `control()` method would make decisions based upon the string value passed.

Because the method supports passing in only a single string, you may wish to design the function to accept a comma-delimited or a URL-formatted argument string. For example:

```
timerDelay=2000&Var1=value1&var2=value2&var3=value3.
```

In this way, the client can use the single control method to communicate multiple values to the service. The method could then update a static class variable (instance variable) that is used as the argument in the call to `java.lang.Thread.sleep()`, resulting in a change to the amount of time the thread slept.

Using the CtsServices::ControlService interface isn't an option if the service component was developed using PowerBuilder. This is due to PowerBuilder's lack of multithreading capability and the fact that PowerBuilder service components typically have concurrency set to false.

4.12 *How do I write a Java service component?*

Writing a Java service component will require the developer to implement a class which extends `java.lang.Object`. To do this, create a new workspace inside PowerJ. Add a new target to the workspace of type Java classes. In this example, the target will be called `jungleservice`. Add a Standard Class to the target by selecting New…, switching to the Class tab page on the New dialog, and selecting Standard Class. Name the package JaguarJungle and the class notificationservice. By default, the class extends `java.lang.Object` and is correct. Click the Finish button on the Class wizard after entering in these names.

WARNING The EJB specification dictates how a container (Jaguar) must manage an EJB component's life cycle and the EJB specification does not currently address service components. Also, EJB components can only execute inside of a single thread. For these reasons, EJB components, regardless of type, should not be used as Jaguar services, although it may appear to be possible.

All Jaguar services must implement the three documented service methods:

```
public void start() throws java.rmi.RemoteException;
public void run() throws java.rmi.RemoteException;
public void stop() throws java.rmi.RemoteException;
```

Define these three methods inside of the JaguarJungle.notificationservice class. Remember to add the import `com.sybase.jaguar.server.*` statement in order to access the Jaguar server log file. Next, go into the implementation of the `run()` method and write the service logic. For example, the following code will execute inside Jaguar every five seconds for a total of five times before terminating.

```
public void run() throws java.rmi.RemoteException
  {
    // _runCnt is a class variable defined as:
    // private static int _runCnt = 0;
```

```
while (_runCnt < 5)
  {
  //Increment our run count
  _runCnt ++;
  try
    {
    //remember to import
    //com.Sybase.jaguar.server.*;
    Jaguar.writeLog( true,
       "JaguarJungle: Notification service ran!" );

    // do whatever this service

    //does on each iteration
    // sleep now for 5000 milliseconds
    Thread.sleep(5000);
    } catch (InterruptedException ie) {
     System.err.println( ie.toString() + " " +
        ie.getMessage() );
    } catch (Exception e ) {
     System.err.println( e.toString() + " " +
        e.getMessage() );
    }
  }
}
```

After building the Java class file, it will need to be manually moved into a directory accessible to Jaguar prior to defining the new component inside of Jaguar Manager. Java class files should be stored inside %JAGUAR%/html/classes directory. In this specific example, the directory would be %JAGUAR%/html/classes/JaguarJungle/.

After moving the `.class` file, start Jaguar Manager and create a new package named JaguarJungle, if it doesn't already exist. Highlight the package and choose Install Component… from the File menu. Choose the Import from Java File option and click the Next button. Using the Browse button, locate the `.class` file under %JAGUAR/html/classes/JaguarJungle. Enter a component name that is different from the class name specified in Component class name, as pictured in figure 4.5. For our example, we will call the component `notifier`.

WARNING When entering the name for the component, be sure to use a different name from that specified in the Component class name field. If these names are the same, the skeleton files will overwrite one another and not compile successfully!

After clicking the Finish button, the wizard generates all the necessary IDL for the new component. The Component Properties dialog will automatically display for review.

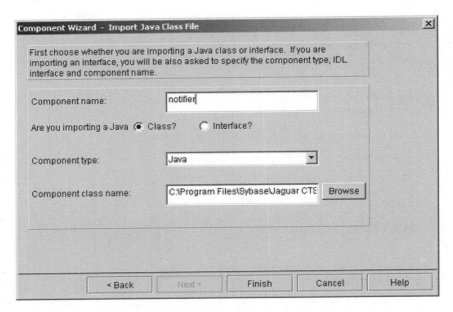

Figure 4.5 **The component name and class names must vary**

After successfully installing the component inside Jaguar Manager, add the service to the server's `com.sybase.jaguar.server.service`, as described earlier in this chapter. The name of the service in our example would be JaguarJungle/notifier. Make sure the new package is listed under the Installed Packages folder. If not, install the package in the server before continuing.

Before restarting the server, it is necessary to generate and compile skeleton files for this component. Skeleton files are the server-side equivalent of client stub files, defining the methods exposed by the component. Skeletons are necessary for Jaguar to access and invoke the service methods. In the event this step is skipped, the Jaguar server log file actually enters a reminder in the log file "Did you remember to generate skeletons?"

To generate skeletons, highlight the JaguarJungle package and choose Generate Stub/Skeleton… from the File menu. Choose the Generate Skeletons checkbox and click the Generate button. The system-generated skeleton files will need to be compiled. To compile the skeletons, access the DOS command line and navigate to the %JAGUAR%/java/classes/JaguarJungle/ directory. Compile the skeletons using the following command:

```
javac *.java
```

After restarting the server, the service would produce the following entries in the Jaguar srv.log file, highlighted in bold:

```
May 17 18:00:47 2000: Started: JaguarJungle/notifier
May 17 18:00:47 2000: Running: services...
May 17 18:00:47 2000: Running: CosNaming/NamingContext
May 17 18:00:47 2000: Running: Jaguar/GarbageCollector
May 17 18:00:47 2000: Running: CtsServlet/ServletService
May 17 18:00:47 2000: Running: JaguarJungle/notifier
May 17 18:00:48 2000: JaguarJungle:Notification service ran!
May 17 18:00:48 2000: Stopped: CosNaming/NamingContext
May 17 18:00:53 2000: JaguarJungle:Notification service ran!
May 17 18:00:58 2000: JaguarJungle:Notification service ran!
May 17 18:01:03 2000: JaguarJungle:Notification service ran!
May 17 18:01:08 2000: JaguarJungle:Notification service ran!
May 17 18:01:13 2000: Stopped: JaguarJungle/notifier
```

Notice that the interval between executions is five seconds, as requested. Be aware, however, that a Jaguar server with a high workload may not produce perfect results as witnessed here.

4.13 How do I write a PowerBuilder service component?

PowerBuilder service components are created through the standard Jaguar Component wizard. This wizard automates the generation of Jaguar service components written in PowerBuilder, significantly lowering the required effort to deploy a Jaguar service compared to the previous Java service component example. To access the wizard, choose File...New from the menu, go to the Start Wizards tab page, and select Jaguar Component. Step 5 of the wizard prompts for the type of component. Selecting Service here will instruct PowerBuilder to automatically generate a component with the three required methods of a service: start(), stop(), and run(). Leave the default transaction support option of Not Supported.

WARNING The PowerBuilder wizard responsible for generating the Jaguar service component automatically inserts a block of comments describing the purpose of each method. The comments for the stop method are misleading, stating that Jaguar never invokes the stop method. Whenever an administrator uses Jaguar Manager to refresh or restart the Jaguar server, or the service component is refreshed, the stop method is executed.

Open up the generated nonvisual object and write the service logic. Remember to declare a local external function that will put the component's thread to sleep for a fixed duration. Use the subroutine declaration documented earlier in this chapter for the `JagSleep()` method. After you've completed writing the service, deploy it to Jaguar and restart the server in order for the service to be recognized and started.

Our PowerBuilder example will use the same logic as that found in the EJB service earlier. The following code is for the service `run()` method. We obtain a handle to the server log through the `GetContextService()` method. We use an instance variable to keep track of the number of times the logic has executed, and after the fifth time the service will terminate. The service will execute inside Jaguar every five seconds for a total of five times before terminating.

```
ErrorLogging lel_jag

THIS.GetContextService( "ErrorLogging", lel_jag )

//ii_runCnt is an instance variable
DO WHILE ( ii_runCnt < 5 )

  ii_runCnt ++

  lel_jag.Log( "JaguarJungle:" + &
     "NotificationService ran!" )

  //Do whatever this service does
  //on each iteration

  //sleep for 5 seconds
  JagSleep( 5 )

LOOP
```

4.14 *How do I add custom properties to a component?*

A final option for communicating initialization parameters into a service is through the properties of a component. In fact, this technique isn't strictly limited to service components, as all components can take advantage of this concept. In situations where the client doesn't need to control the values (but administrators desire some form of control over the way the service behaves), or any component, components support user-defined properties.

Administrators can go in through Jaguar Manager, define new properties and update existing properties through the All Properties tab page of the Component's Properties dialog. In chapter 6, we will be discussing the Jaguar::Repository interfaces and the ability to read the properties of a component. To add a customer property, click on the Add button. Preferably, the name of the property would be your company's web site URL listed backwards, plus the name of the property. For example, `com.aegisconsulting.myproperty`, as seen in figure 4.6, is assigned the value of foobar.

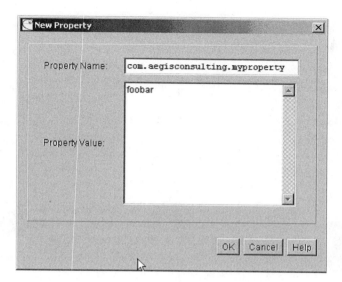

Figure 4.6
This illustration demonstrates how to add your own custom properties to a component

4.15 How do I implement a shared component in Java?

Components in general, and especially service components, may need to take advantage of a shared component to store common data. Earlier in this chapter, we discussed the architecture of allowing a client and a service to communicate and execute common business logic, and we talked about the architecture in figure 4.4.

Creating shared components in Java is possible, although the use of an EJB component is ill-advised. Although it may seem possible to configure an EJB to behave as a shared component, EJB components were not intended to work in that way. Session Beans by definition are distinct for each client. Entity Beans accomplish the goals of a shared component in practice.

Writing a shared component in Java is similar to writing a service component in Java. Developers have no mandatory interface requirements. That is to say that the component is free to implement whatever functions are necessary to achieve the business goals, and developers do not have to implement the service methods. After generating the .class file, deployment of the shared component is identical to that of a service component. When the Component Properties dialog automatically displays for review after running the Import Java Class File wizard, be sure to mark the component as shared by turning Sharing on. Also, as a shared component, it is not necessary to update the server's com.sybase.jaguar.server.service property, and the server does not need to be restarted in order to access the component.

Factory objects 5

5.1 What is the difference between interface and implementation?

This chapter addresses designing a solid interface and using a factory to instantiate remote components. But first, let's step back and make sure that everyone is using the same definitions. An *interface* is defined as the collection of an object's public method signatures. An *implementation* is the actual code behind the public method signatures that provides the functionality. An interface does not define component properties. CORBA and COM do not permit direct access to an object's properties. In reality, many development environments provide the necessary logic to access public properties through well-defined accessor methods, even though it appears you are accessing the property directly. *Accessor methods* are the infamous getXXX() and setXXX() methods that act as wrappers around a property. If a property is read-only, then there is no setXXX() method defined.

Defining the interface of a Jaguar component is fundamental to using the component. Without a well-defined interface, there wouldn't be any way to interact with a component. Although it isn't necessary for a developer to fully understand IDL, it sure does help from time to time. The IDL is automatically generated through the use of a development environment such as PowerBuilder or PowerJ. These environments have been tightly integrated with Jaguar.

NOTE IDL is defined by the Object Management Group as a standard language for defining component interfaces. Chapter 3, "OMG IDL Syntax and Semantics," in the CORBA V2.2 specification, defines IDL. Printable versions of this document can be downloaded from the following URL:
http://www.omg.org/corba/index.html
Although Jaguar defines IDL for EJB components, it is important to point out that an EJB component does not use IDL to define its interface. Instead, it uses Java interfaces.

A critical point to stress here is the difference between the public interface exposed by a component and the implementation of the component. A client should *never* have to know how a component provides or implements certain functionality—this is the basis of the idea of encapsulation. This was one of the fundamental reasons why the client caching design covered in chapter 2 was regarded as a poor design for maintaining stateful data on a stateless component. Instead, client objects should depend solely on the published interface of a given class, and not rely on the class implementation. The tip below is a good heuristic (rule of thumb) for developers to follow.

> **TIP** Clients should remain ignorant about the concrete classes that implement a component type, and instead commit themselves only to the abstract class defining the interface.

The lesson here is so important that an entire set of design patterns have been documented to help developers understand how to properly abstract the process of component creation. These patterns are collectively known as *Creational Patterns*, and are fully documented in many of the design patterns books, such as *Design Patterns* by Gamma et. al.

5.2 How do I code to an interface instead of an implementation?

If Safari's team had collectively decided on using a homogenous development environment for each of the broadcast components, it would have been very straightforward to create a single abstract class, say `n_cst_broadcaster`, as a PowerBuilder example. It would have stubbed a public `of_broadcast()` method and a large number of precoded, protected infrastructure methods. Each broadcaster would inherit from this abstract class and override the `of_broadcast()` method appropriately, implementing the broadcaster-specific code and forming a heavy reliance on the underlying infrastructure. Needless to say, a similar approach could have been taken in Java using PowerJ as well.

The heuristic we defined refers to hiding the concrete classes from the client. A picture is worth a thousand words, or in our case, the code is worth a thousand words. The following snippet of pseudocode shows how *not* to code. This Power-Builder example breaks our heuristic and ends up declaring each type of broadcaster:

```
n_cst_broadcaster_email              lnv_email
n_cst_broadcaster_fax                lnv_fax
n_cst_broadcaster_print              lnv_print
n_cst_broadcaster_pager              lnv_pager

CHOOSE CASE <how am I going to broadcast today>
    CASE EMAIL
        icn_jag.CreateInstance( lnv_email, &
            "Broadcasters/n_cst_broadcaster_email)
            lnv_email.of_broadcast( my message text )
    CASE FAX
            icn_jag.CreateInstance( lnv_fax, &
                "Broadcasters/n_cst_broadcaster_fax)
                lnv_fax.of_broadcast( my message text )

END CHOOSE
```

Notice how the client defines five variables, one for each broadcaster. This is a classic example of a client written to an implementation and not to an interface. This is largely due to the fact that the client is extremely knowledgeable about the concrete classes, and as a matter of fact, dependent upon the concrete classes, and it has no reason to be. To add another broadcast medium would require additional code and a complete recompilation and redistribution of the program.

Now consider the next snippet of PowerBuilder pseudocode where the client is indeed ignorant about the type of component with which it is interfacing:

```
n_cst_broadcaster      lnv_broadcaster

icn_jag.CreateInstance( lnv_broadcaster, &
    "Broadcasters/" + ls_className )

lnv_broadcaster.of_broadcast( my message text )
```

In this refined example, the object declares a single variable and invokes the `of_broadcast()` method. The client has committed only to the interface described by the abstract class, and did not define any concrete classes. Note that `is_className` contains the concrete classname, but it is merely a string. In fact, this string was read from the database table that is populated by each customer when they choose how they want to be notified about the delivery of their package(s). Consider the following facts as you keep in mind that Safari is using both PowerJ and PowerBuilder for developing their broadcast components:

Fact: It isn't possible to inherit from an object written in a different language.

Fact: It isn't possible to write a base-class that works across heterogeneous development environments like PowerBuilder and PowerJ.

Fact: It isn't possible to dynamically invoke a method on a Jaguar component.

Have you ever looked at the exported source code of a proxy object for PowerBuilder or a Java stub for PowerJ? These files consist of nothing more than a description of the public interface of a given component. Let's take a look at the system-generated PowerBuilder proxy object listed below, followed by a Java stub. Both examples are from the JaguarJungle/junglestore shared object, a shared object that implements the shared object described in chapter 4.

```
$PBExportHeader$junglestore.srx
$PBExportComments$Proxy imported from Jaguar
global type JungleStore from CORBAObject
end type
global JungleStore JungleStore

forward prototypes
  public:
    function Long getsleepduration () alias for "getsleepduration"
```

```
    function Integer setsleepduration (Long alv_seconds) alias for "setsleep-
  duration"
end prototypes

package JaguarJungle;

/**
 ** Generated by Jaguar CTS 3.5 - Tue May 09 13:27:39 CDT 2000
 **
 ** from JaguarJungle::JungleStore (file ..\JungleStore.idl
 **
 ** Please do not modify this file.
 **/

public interface JungleStoreOperations
{
    public int getsleepduration()
        throws CTS.PBUserException;

    public short setsleepduration
        (int alv_seconds)
        throws CTS.PBUserException;
}
```

In the case of PowerBuilder, only a single proxy object is generated. For Java, five system-generated files are actually created, but in the interest of space, only one is listed here. Notice both contain nothing more than the public interface of the object—in this case a pair of accessor methods.

When you declare a proxy variable or stub in a script, the development environment (PowerBuilder or PowerJ) is going to merely look at your script and ensure that you are calling methods that are going to exist on the Jaguar component. Notice that no properties (instance variables) have been exposed.

When you invoke the PowerBuilder Connection object's `CreateInstance()` method, you provide a reference variable that is used throughout the script to invoke methods on the remote object, and you provide a string. This string represents the package/component you wish to create. PowerBuilder does not have the capability to statically bind the string inside your script with the reference variable provided. PowerBuilder can *only* support late binding (runtime).

Similarly in PowerJ, after associating a stub with an application, developers have the ability to narrow down from the abstract to a more specific interface through the use of a string. Figure 5.1 shows the Interface Creation tab page (available by looking at the properties of a stub dropped on a form). Pay particular attention to the first radio button. This option permits a developer to specify a string variable that will contain the name of the component to which it is to narrow. The component must support the requested interface you are narrowing to, otherwise an exception will be thrown.

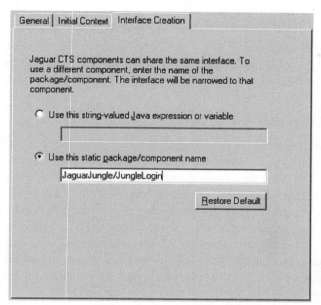

Figure 5.1
Shown here is the PowerJ interface
for dynamically specifying the
interface to narrow to

Think about this: It is possible to compile your application into an executable, even if Jaguar CTS is not up and running, regardless of the development environment. This is because the compiler does not bind your string to the proxy/stub reference variable until runtime. Even when the binding occurs at runtime, the binding is to the public interface exposed by the Jaguar component, not the name of the package/component listed in the string.

In most situations, you will be required to have the proxy/stub present in your project. Most business applications are not conducive to reusing a particular interface, but when you encounter these situations, we encourage you to design a strong public interface and write the client to the interface, not the implementation.

As a final note, be advised the CORBA IDL doesn't support method overloading, events, or NULL argument values. Sybase has implemented proprietary extensions in Jaguar to support these scenarios. If you use the EAServer ORB, function overloading will work successfully with Java and PowerBuilder clients. However, MASP and ActiveX clients do not support method overloading, and when these applications call a component that employs method overloading, developers will have to make a hard-coded decision on which method to invoke and call that function using the mangled name.

5.3   *How do I specify an IDL interface?*

Initially, Safari has identified that their broadcast notification service will include e-mail, fax, and pager. They've decided to keep the public interface small. In fact, it will only have a single method exposed at this time. Here is a language-neutral definition of this interface.

```
int broadcastMessage( String msg )
```

Now that the public interface has been formally defined, the respective development teams set out to write their components. Recall that the team has decided to use PowerBuilder to develop the fax component, while PowerJ will be used for the email and paging components. The web client is going to dynamically provide a list of available broadcasters to the customer. In chapter 6, we will demonstrate code that can be used to validate certain interfaces are implemented by a component.

When creating the respective Broadcaster components, each team will ensure that they implement the agreed-upon interface. In PowerBuilder, one of the developers should create an ancestor class that implements the broadcaster interface. PowerBuilder doesn't support any other mechanism beyond the use of inheritance and developer discipline to ensure the concrete classes implement the method. In PowerJ (Java), this process can and should be more formalized, and the compiler can ensure that the developer did indeed provide an implementation of the `broadcastMessage()` method through the use of a Java interface. One of the developers should formally define this broadcaster interface, and each developer should add this interface to his or her respective EJB component's `Implements` property, as pictured in figure 5.2.

Adding the `broadcaster` interface to the Attributes of the Bean tells the Java compiler to ensure that all the required methods of the interface have been included in the Bean. However, there is no corresponding IDL generated and deployed to Jaguar. In fact, the JaguarJungle/Broadcaster interface must still be manually added to each component regardless of the development environment.

When a component is deployed from PowerBuilder or PowerJ, an arbitrary interface name is automatically specified. The interface name used is the name of the package and the name of the component, but it could be anything that makes sense. Through Jaguar Manager, it is possible to change or extend the interfaces supported by a particular component. Access the All Properties tab page on the component's properties dialog and modify the `com.sybase.jaguar.component.interfaces` property, as picture in figure 5.3. Each interface is separated with a comma ",". We've added a new interface called JaguarJungle::Broadcaster to the component, as depicted in figure 5.3. Each broadcaster component developed and deployed by the Safari developers should add this interface through Jaguar Manager.

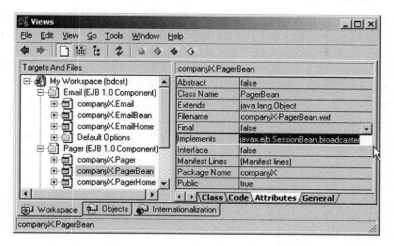

Figure 5.2   The Java broadcaster interface is being added to the Implements clause

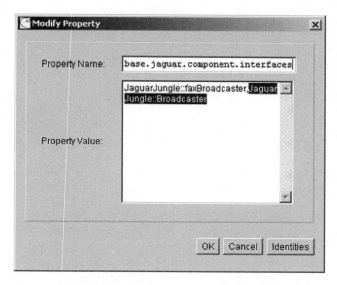

Figure 5.3   The new addition of the JaguarJungle::Broadcaster interface

5.4   What are the JaguarORB and CORBAObjects in PowerBuilder?

The JaguarORB object is jointly responsible with the CORBAObject for allowing a PowerBuilder client application to behave in the same fashion as a CORBA compliant client application, much like a C++ application in fact. These two objects combine to expose a greater capability than that of the Connection object. Although it is possible to combine the use of the Connection and JaguarORB/CORBAObject objects, usually one or the other is used exclusively. In the event you do use a combination of these approaches, make certain that any transactional processing occurs start-to-finish on a single approach. Point being, transactions will not span multiple client connections because each connection will be assigned its own Jaguar session ID.

At this point it is worthwhile to emphasize that an overwhelming majority of PowerBuilder clients do *not* need to utilize either the JaguarORB or CORBAObject objects. In fact, the majority of applications will work just fine using the more traditional Connection object to interact with remote Jaguar components from a Power-Builder client. In those rare events where you need the extra power and flexibility offered by JaguarORB and CORBAObject, the rest of this section is for you!

The first method you'll need to familiarize yourself with on JaguarORB is init(). The init() method can be invoked many times; however, it creates a new internal instance of the object on only the first invocation and uses this instance for the 2nd through *n*th calls. The init() method takes a single parameter; a string containing the initialization parameters. Conceptually, this method is identical to the SQLCA.DBParm property in that it can contain single or multiple properties. In the event you are going to supply multiple initialization parameters, separate each parameter using a comma.

For most of the properties, it is possible to set up a Jaguar environment variable in the System Properties of the machine. In the event both an environment variable is specified and an initialization parameter is set, the value of the initialization parameter takes precedence.

Chapter 7 provides detailed coverage of the various parameters that can be set. We will postpone any discussion on ORB initialization until then.

NOTE   We will be using the JaguarORB in PowerBuilder, and like other system nonvisual objects, we should inherit from JaguarORB and create n_jagorb in order to access the error! event and provide a foundation to build upon. For all the examples in this chapter that reference JaguarORB, we will be using n_jagorb to represent the extended concrete class.

WARNING   Before you begin any work with JaguarORB, it is very important to generate the proxy objects for the CosNaming and SessionManager packages and add them to your library list. Without these components, your code will not compile!

In the following script, we are going to declare two variables, one of type `n_jagorb` and another of type CORBAObject. CORBAObject is the PowerBuilder equivalent of an org.omg.CORBA.Object instance. The CORBAObject doesn't expose any events, and the `constructor!` and `destructor!` events documented in the PowerBuilder 7.01 help file is a mistake.

NOTE   Developers should never have to manually instantiate a CORBAObject. CORBAObjects are instantiated on the Jaguar server as a result of a method invocation and the local CORBAObject is set as the reference variable to the remote object. Pay particular attention to the proxy source code discussed earlier in this chapter. Recall that PowerBuilder proxies are descendants of CORBAObject.

After instantiating the JaguarORB, we will initialize it using the `init()` method, establishing our initial set of ORB parameters. For this example, we are going to initialize ORBNameServiceURL and ORBLogFile. Notice we don't have to instantiate the CORBAObject, in other words, we don't need to invoke CREATE.

```
n_jagorb        lnv_orb
CORBAObject     lco_nameservice
String          ls_parms

//Create the JaguarORB object
lnv_orb     = CREATE n_jagorb

//Prepare the initialization string
ls_parms    = "ORBNameServiceURL='iiop://localhost:9000'," + &
              "ORBLogFile='orblog.txt'"

//Initialize JaguarORB
lnv_orb.init( ls_parms )
```

Once the ORB is properly initialized, we are ready to resolve the Jaguar name service and bind that service with the declared CORBAObject. Resolving the Jaguar name service occurs when the `resolve_initial_references()` method of the ORB is invoked. The first parameter is typically "NameService" and the second parameter provides a reference to a CORBAObject. In the future, values in addition to "NameService" may be supported, but at present this is the only one. After this method has returned, our CORBAObject is now a reference variable for the remote Jaguar name service.

```
lnv_orb.resolve_initial_references("NameService", lco_nameservice)
```

At this point, it is important to stress that if the parameters provided for initialization were wrong or for some other reason a connection with Jaguar couldn't be established, `resolve_initial_references()` is not going to provide a legitimate reference variable in the CORBAObject. Because we don't want to encounter a NULL object reference at runtime, it is *very* important to check the return code of `resolve_initial_references()` to ensure that our CORBAObject is legitimate. Let's revise our code to include some exception handling.

```
n_jagorb        lnv_orb
CORBAObject     lco_nameservice
String          ls_parms
Integer         li_rtn

//Create the JaguarORB object
lnv_orb     = CREATE n_jagorb

//Prepare the initialization string
ls_parms    = "ORBNameServiceURL='iiop://localhost:9000'," + &
              "ORBLogFile='orblog.txt'"

//Initialize JaguarORB
lnv_orb.init( ls_parms )

li_rtn      = lnv_orb.resolve_initial_references( "NameService", &
              lco_nameservice)

IF li_rtn <> 0 THEN
   MessageBox("Alert!", "Unable to connect to Jaguar's name service!")
   DESTROY lnv_orb
   HALT
END IF
```

Before we can do any real work with JaguarORB and CORBAObject, we need to get our hands on an instance of CosNaming::NamingContext. When referencing this context, it is important to remember to preface with "omg.org/" to specify we want the OMG naming context implementation. We will declare a variable of type NamingContext (we received this proxy when we generated the proxies for CosNaming and SessionManager earlier) and, remembering to specify the OMG's naming context, the result looks like this:

```
NamingContext  lnc_context

li_rtn      = lco_nameservice._narrow( lnc_context, &
              "omg.org/CosNaming/NamingContext")

IF li_rtn < 0 THEN
   MessageBox("Alert!","Unable to establish a Jaguar naming context!")
   DESTROY lnv_orb
   HALT
END IF
```

WARNING   The PowerBuilder 7.01 online help states the `_narrow` method returns a 1 on success and a −1 on failure; however, the function routinely returns a 0, which can be interpreted as success.

Once we have a handle to a naming context, we are able to go after the ORB factory.

5.5   *What is an ORB Factory?*

An ORB, or object request broker, is responsible for channeling the communication between client and server objects. Clients think they have instantiated a local object that implements the business methods, but in reality the local object is merely the client-side ORB. During this instantiation, the ORB physically locates a remote object capable of fulfilling the request. When a client invokes a method on the object, the ORB intercepts the call, and is responsible for handling all the network traffic required to forward the request to the remote object, including the responsibility of passing it any provided parameters. The ORB patiently waits for the remote object to return a result, and this result is then handed over to the client who made the request.

A factory is responsible for ultimately providing the client with the ability to create the instance of a particular concrete class. The unique feature of a factory is that it is able to provide these class instances without requiring the client to have knowledge of the concrete class. More specifically, the client is *not* required to have formally declared a variable of the type of the concrete class. The client merely has to know what interface it is interested in. To reiterate the theme of this chapter, we should always try to design a closely related family of components around a stable, published interface.

A single Jaguar component can support a number of different interfaces, up to sixteen. The factories' unique ability to provide a generic CORBAObject allows the client to cast the object to any proxy or stub, assuming the returned CORBAObject supports the interface documented by the proxy or stub. Working with the CORBAObject, we can eliminate most if not all of the need for a client to have any knowledge about the concrete classes that ultimately provide the implementation of a particular interface. A loose analogy here is synonymous with the concepts behind PowerBuilder's CREATE USING feature. The string we use to instantiate the concrete class could come from *anywhere*.

Factories are based on the creational design pattern known as the Abstract Factory, or Kit. In our case, we are working with concrete factories since our factories are capable of serving up an instance of only a single class at any point in time.

Every Jaguar component must support at least one interface. In PowerBuilder, whenever you deploy your component to Jaguar, a module with the same name as your package and an interface with the same name as your component is created (or updated). It is purely a coincidence that these names are the same. In PowerJ, you are presented with a finer control of these setting through the EJB wizards.

In our case, we are working with concrete factories, not abstract factories. This means that each concrete class will require its own unique factory in order to be instantiated on the client. It is possible to provide only a single proxy (or nonvisual object) that represents the abstract class interface of many concrete classes. In other words, there is no physical requirement that if five Jaguar components implement the same interface that five physical proxies exist on the client. One proxy could be used to gain access to all five of the physical components through five factories where each factory corresponds to a single concrete class.

Because our factories are tied to a single concrete class at any point in time, clients will routinely have a number of factory instances, and development experience and design will dictate the scope of those instances—either global, instance, local, or in a rare situation, shared. Remember, the benefit of a factory is to allow a client to switch configurations or business rules by simply changing out or using the business rule's reference variable on another concrete factory that implements the business rule's interface.

5.6 *How do I use an ORB factory inside PowerBuilder client?*

PowerBuilder provides two distinct mechanisms for accessing an ORB factory. The first, and most prevalent method, is to use the Connection object to establish a connection with a Jaguar server and invoke the `CreateInstance()` method of the Connection object, specifying the package and component names. This method was discussed in detail in the prelude to this book, *Jaguar Development with PowerBuilder 7*. In this section, we will focus on the more obscure method, utilizing JaguarORB and CORBAObject to achieve the same results offered to us by the Connection object. To stress a point made earlier, usually the Connection object exposes more than enough features so that PowerBuilder developers do not have to resort to the more complicated, albeit more powerful, method described here.

With our newfound knowledge about a concrete factory, let's discuss how we are able to instantiate one. To instantiate a factory, we will need to use the `resolve()` method on the NamingContext instance our CORBAObject created for us in the last step. The `resolve()` operation takes a textual name and looks for a matching name context inside of the Jaguar name server's namespace. When a match is found, the corresponding bound object is retrieved and an instance of that object is created on the server. The name provided must be an exact match to that of the bound name, otherwise the method will fail. Name contexts, namespaces, and binding will be discussed in much greater detail in chapter 7.

The `resolve()` method is responsible only for locating the bound object, not determining the type of the object. This responsibility rests with the client, and it is referred to as *narrowing*. Narrowing is accomplished on the client by casting the generic CORBAObject returned to that of the specialized concrete class (proxy or stub) that documents a specific interface. For instance, to create a concrete factory for Safari Shipping's Fax Broadcaster object, we must first resolve the name context. Using the returned name context, we retrieve an instance of a concrete factory object that is capable of providing the client with a handle to a remote component instance. The `create()` method on the concrete factory is invoked, passing the appropriate user ID and password. The factory goes to work, creating an instance of the target on the server and returning a generic CORBAObject to the client. The client must take this CORBAObject and narrow (or cast) it to a specific reference variable.

NOTE   The Fax Broadcaster is a standard PowerBuilder stateless component that implements the JaguarJungle/Broadcaster interface described earlier in this chapter. The remaining code examples in this chapter assume the Fax proxy has been added to the library list.

```
NameComponent   lncmp_comp[]
Factory         lnf_factory
CORBAObject     lco_fax
Fax             lnv_fax
lncmp_comp[ 1 ].id   = "JaguarJungle/fax"
lncmp_comp[ 1 ].kind = ""

lco_fax = lnc_context.resolve( lncmp_comp )
lco_fax._narrow( lnf_factory, "SessionManager/Factory" )
lnv_fax = lnf_factory.create( "jagadmin", "" )
```

The NameComponent used in this script represents the structure of the naming context. The NameComponent is implemented as an unbounded array. Each position in the array is used to map to a corresponding level of the namespace. Again, chapter 7 will delve deeper into these Jaguar naming services.

The *kind* attribute of a NameComponent is also an IDL string, and it is used to provide descriptive power for names while remaining syntax-independent. Examples include "c_source", "object_code", "executable", "postscript", and " ".

Okay, let's take a quick review as we return to our code example. First, we initialized our ORB through JaguarORB, created an instance of the NamingContext component, and used that component to resolve the n_demo class, resulting in a factory capable of producing the specifically requested concrete class, or in this case, the n_demo component. Here's what our cumulative code looks like:

```
n_jagorb        lnv_orb
CORBAObject     lco_nameservice, &
                lco_fax
NamingContext   lnc_context
NameComponent   lncmp_comp[]
Factory         lnf_factory
String          ls_parms
Integer         li_rtn
Fax             lnv_fax
String          ls_msg

//Create the JaguarORB object
lnv_orb        = CREATE n_jagorb

//Prepare the initialization string
ls_parms        = "ORBNameServiceURL='iiop://localhost:9000'," + &
                "ORBLogFile='orblog.txt'"

//Initialize JaguarORB
lnv_orb.init( ls_parms )

li_rtn          = lnv_orb.resolve_initial_references( "NameService", &
                lco_nameservice)

IF li_rtn <> 0 THEN
   MessageBox("Alert!","Unable to connect to Jaguar's name service!")
   DESTROY lnv_orb
   HALT
END IF

//Documentation claims 1 on success, but we received a 0
li_rtn          = lco_nameservice._narrow( lnc_context, &
                "omg.org/CosNaming/NamingContext")

IF li_rtn < 0 THEN
   MessageBox("Alert!","Unable to establish a Jaguar naming context!")
   DESTROY lnv_orb
   HALT
END IF

//Name of the Package/Component we want to create
lncmp_comp[ 1 ].id   = "JaguarJungle/fax"
lncmp_comp[ 1 ].kind = ""

//Find the name context and get a factory capable of producing it
lco_fax = lnc_context.resolve( lncmp_comp )

//Cast the CORBAObject to a Factory object
```

```
li_rtn = lco_fax._narrow(lnf_factory, "SessionManager/Factory")

IF li_rtn < 0 THEN
  MessageBox("Alert!","Unable to establish the requested Factory!")
  DESTROY lnv_orb
  HALT
END IF

//Ask the factory to create an instance of the object for us
lco_fax = lnf_factory.create( "jagadmin", "" )

//Cast the CORBAObject to our interface reference variable
li_rtn = lco_fax._narrow( lnv_fax, "JaguarJungle/fax" )

IF li_rtn < 0 THEN
  MessageBox("Alert!","Unable to create component instance!")
  DESTROY lnv_orb
  HALT
END IF

//Broadcast the message!
ls_msg = "Package 1234 delivered on 03Jun00 at 11:17AM!"
lnv_fax.broadcastMessage( ls_msg )
```

To stress an earlier point, it is neither necessary for the client to CREATE a CORBAObject, nor is it necessary for the client to CREATE the Fax object before it is narrowed.

At this point, we are ready to add the final modification to our code. We need to determine if the remote object we are creating supports a particular interface; in our case that interface is JaguarJungle/Broadcaster. This test may be necessary because Jaguar components can support up to sixteen interfaces, and the interface you are going after is different from the name context of the component.

To check for interface support on a CORBAObject, we invoke the _is_a() method, specifying the name of the interface as an IDL string. We can then use the Boolean response of the method to determine if we can safely narrow the object and invoke the well-known methods of the interface. Let's revise our code to perform this check. To emphasize, the pending code modification would be placed between the following two lines of code from earlier:

```
//Ask the factory to create an instance of the object for us
lco_fax    = lnf_factory.create( "jagadmin", "" )

//Cast the CORBAObject to our interface reference variable
li_rtn     = lco_fax._narrow( lnv_fax, "JaguarJungle/fax" )
```

Now, let's look at that modification:

```
//Declare the following variable at the top of the script
//Boolean    lb_validInterface

//Ask the factory to create an instance of the object for us
lco_fax    = lnf_factory.create( "jagadmin", "" )
```

```
lb_validInterface = &
    lco_demo._is_a("JaguarJungle/Broadcaster")

IF lb_validInterface THEN
    //Cast the CORBAObject to our
    //interface reference variable
    li_rtn       = lnv_corba._narrow( lnv_fax, &
        "JaguarJungle/fax" )

    ...  //remaining code
ELSE
    //Handle the error!
    //Doesn't support the interface!!
END IF
```

The _is_a() method on CORBAObject looks at the properties of the object it found to determine if the object supports the requested interface. If the object does indeed implement that interface, the method returns true. Based on this result, it is possible to confidently narrow the object to the desired interface and then invoke any of the well-documented methods of the interface.

To review some of the lessons, we have learned a number of techniques using JaguarORB and CORBAObject that would allow the PowerBuilder client to determine dynamically at runtime if a particular component supports a particular interface—in our case, the JaguarJungle/Broadcaster interface. Developers can write any number of broadcasters, making the appropriate entry in the database to announce the presence of a new broadcaster. When customers visit the Safari Shipping web site, they can be presented with a list of available notification broadcasters to pick from. When the package is delivered, they will receive the delivery information from Safari Shipping via their selected medium.

5.7 What is the PowerJ InitialContext object?

PowerJ provides an elegant drag-and-drop development interface for writing components or applications. Components and applications will use the InitialContext object from the Jaguar page of the component palette. Placing the Jaguar.Initial-Context object onto the view allows you to establish a connection with a Jaguar server and invoke components remotely.

After placing the object, go into the Views window and select the Objects tab page at the bottom of the right hand pane (under the treeview). Expanding the treeview reveals a jctx_1 object. Highlight this object and click on the Properties tab page under the left hand pane of the Views window. This is where you configure the component or application to communicate with Jaguar. Let's go over what each tab page exposes to the developer.

General	Contains the programmatic name of the InitialContext object used throughout the source code
Jaguar CTS Server	Indicates where the Jaguar CTS Server is physically located. Specifically, this points to one or more name servers to be used to look up components. The default location is `localhost`. Alternatively, developers are able to programmatically specify the location by using string-valued Java expressions or variable.
Authenticated session	When developing a client application, developers will request an authenticated session. When developing components, developers will request the internal Jaguar CTS session.
Naming and SSL	The use of EJB requires the use of the `javax` naming services. Typically, this option will be checked. One of the downfalls of EJB's debut in Jaguar CTS is that developers are no longer afforded the luxury of ignoring the type of component they are going to interact with. PowerBuilder components will require a CORBA initial context factory, while EJB components will require an EJB initial context factory. More details of this issue will be covered in chapter 7 when we talk about naming services.
ORB properties	Initialization properties for the ORB. These will be covered in depth in chapter 7.
ORB arguments	The equivalent of command line arguments passed to the ORB. These are similar to the ORB properties defined above, and a more detailed discussion will take place in chapter 7.

5.8 How do I import Jaguar stubs into PowerJ?

PowerJ provides a slick wizard that automatically generates stubs and adds Jaguar components to the component palette. This wizard is accessible from the Components menu by selecting the Add Jaguar Component... menu item. Stepping through the wizard allows you to specify the location of the Jaguar server, as well as selectively pick what components to import and where on the component palette to place them. After importing your Jaguar components, use drag-and-drop to place the component's interface onto the form.

After placing a Jaguar interface stub onto the visual form, go into the Views window and select the Objects tab page at the bottom of the right hand pane (under the treeview). Expanding the treeview reveals the name of the component just placed on the form. Highlight this object and click on the Properties tab page under the left hand pane of the Views window. This is where you associated the component with the InitialContext object setup earlier.

At this point, drag-and-drop the component into your script. The PowerJ reference card will appear, presenting a list of valid methods for the component.

5.9 *How do I use the CORBA ORB factory inside of a PowerJ client?*

In PowerJ, the `org.omg.CORBA.*` package exposes the ORB factory. Before you are able to access anything on Jaguar, the ORB must be properly initialized. In addition, the stubs of the corresponding Jaguar components should have been compiled and added to the `CLASSPATH`.

NOTE PowerJ developers will depend on the `org.omg.CORBA.*` and `com.sybase.CORBA.*` packages to configure the ORB properties. The ORB properties will be discussed in more detail inside chapter 7.

The techniques described here can be accomplished in a more automated fashion by using the drag-and-drop features of PowerJ and the InitialContext object, as described in section 5.7. With that out of the way, let's walk through the hand-coded approach in Java of accessing an ORB.

```
//assumes the following import is present
//import com.sybase.jaguar.system.*;

org.omg.CORBA.ORB orb = null;
org.omg.CORBA.Object nameSvce = null;
org.omg.CosNaming.NamingContext nc = null;
org.omg.CosNaming.NameComponent comp_nc[];
Factory compFactory = null;

Repository JagRep = null;
Property jagProp[];

try {
  // setup properties to initialize ORB
  Properties props = new Properties();
  props.put("org.omg.CORBA.ORBClass", "com.sybase.CORBA.ORB");
  props.put("org.omg.CORBA.NameServiceURL",
    "iiop://localhost:9000");

  // initialize ORB and get ORB object
  orb = ORB.init((String[]) null, props);

  // obtain initial Naming Service object reference
  nameSvce = orb.resolve_initial_references("NameService");

  // narrow (cast) Object to the NamingContext type
  nc = NamingContextHelper.narrow(nameSvce);

  // Create the name component for the Jaguar component
  comp_nc = {new NameComponent("Jaguar/Repository", "")};
  org.omg.CORBA.Object objectRef = nc.resolve(comp_nc);
  compFactory = FactoryHelper.narrow(objectRef);
```

```
JagRep =
  RepositoryHelper.narrow(
     compFactory.create("jagadmin", ""));

jagProp = JagRep.lookup( "Component", "SVU/SVULogin");
} catch (Exception e) {
  log("CORBA exception:" + e.getMessage());
}
```

First, we set up the ORB properties in the `props` variable, naming the ORBClass to use and the complete URL to the Name Server(s). Multiple name servers would be listed here, delimited by a semicolon. These properties are then passed to the `ORB.init()` method, where the ORB is initialized. After successfully initializing the ORB, we need to get a handle to our naming services. Remember, these naming services are responsible for translating our Package/Component string into a list of servers capable of fulfilling requests for the corresponding physical object. The name service object (`nameSvce`) is treated like any other object and must first be narrowed down to a naming context before use.

Once we have established our naming context (`nc`), we use that context to resolve a request for the Jaguar/Repository component by invoking `nc.resolve(comp_nc)`. Resolving the name obtains a list of servers capable of fulfilling requests for that object's class. We take the return CORBA object and once again must narrow it first. This narrowing creates a factory capable of producing the requested component, in this case Jaguar/Repository.

We call the component factory's `create()` method, instructing Jaguar to make a physical instance available for requests. At this point, the instance Jaguar has created is now bound to the client's session. Next, we invoke our method on the component, `lookup()` in this example, and store the results in the `JagProp` variable.

If we wanted to create an instance of a different component, we would substitute the Package/Component name of Jaguar/Repository with something else, and then work with the `xxxxxHelper.narrow()` methods from that component's stubs.

Peering into the Jaguar interface repository

6

6.1 What is the interface repository?

Jaguar CTS ships with a number of proprietary Sybase components. The components serve a very important task—they are Jaguar's interface to the rest of the world. Many of Sybase's tools, including PowerBuilder and PowerJ, rely on these components inside their various Jaguar wizards.

Each of the public interfaces exposed by these components are documented inside the *Interface Repository* (IR). The IR can be viewed inside the web browser through the following URL:

http://localhost:8080

By default, this address can be accessed only from a browser running on the same machine as the Jaguar server, unless the administrator opened up port 8080 to the world by changing the address from localhost to the machine's IP address or to the machine's name.

NOTE   For those familiar with CORBA, an IR is used with DII stubs. Sybase does not provide a formal CORBA InterfaceRepository. The home page displayed at http://localhost:8080 labels the collection of Jaguar HTML documents as Interface Repository Documentation, and the header of each page therein provides a link named Interface Repository. For continuity, this chapter will use interface repository and IR to refer to the collection of HTML documents.

The myriad of documents found inside the IR can actually be updated to include the components and interfaces developed by your organization. To accomplish this, open Jaguar Manager and use the Generate HTML option found on the right mouse button menu for any server, component, or IDL entry inside Jaguar Manager.

Throughout the rest of this chapter, we will be looking at the various components found inside of the IR and demonstrate how you can take advantage of the services exposed by them.

6.2 What is the Jaguar repository?

The *Jaguar repository* stores all of the information about the Jaguar server, including but not limited to all data regarding packages, components, and database connection caches. More specifically, the Jaguar repository contains the IDL files, property files, and required libraries to create an instance of the component, such as DLLs, JARs, or PBDs. To stress the importance of the repository, if someone were to delete the Jaguar repository, they would render the entire Jaguar installation useless. Yes, the repository is that important.

Jaguar uses a hierarchical set of folders inside of the repository to contain everything needed for accessing and implementing every installed package. This repository by default is located at %JAGUAR%/Repository, where %JAGUAR% represents the full installation path of the Jaguar server.

TIP   Jaguar's reliance on the repository cannot be stressed enough. If you are looking to provide a quick backup of a Jaguar server, copy the entire %JAGUAR%/Repository directory, including all subdirectories, the afconfig.dat file and all `java/classes`. This technique has proven useful for synchronizing Jaguar servers in disparate, nonnetworked locations for end-user acceptance testing. In fact, this technique can be streamlined further to capture only a single package. However, care must be taken to ensure that all the required files for the component or package are captured and copied. Later in this chapter, we will discuss the Jaguar::Repository `files()` method, which reports all the files used by Jaguar for a specific package.

6.3   *What is the general structure of the Jaguar repository?*

As a caveat to answering this question, let me emphasize here that this book *strongly* recommends that you utilize the Jaguar Manager for your day-to-day interactions with the repository. The purpose of this section is to provide a better understanding of the purpose and importance of the repository design. Many people will tell you that it is the design of the repository that makes the Jaguar application server stand out from the crowd.

WARNING   Sybase reserves the right to change the structure of the repository with new releases of Jaguar CTS. Any code that is used to access the Jaguar repository should rely on the Jaguar::Repository component instead of directly accessing files.

To generalize, the repository is home for three types of files. Each of these file types plays a critical role in the implementation of the application server. These file types are:

- Property files (.PROPS)
- Interface definition language files (.IDL)
- Implementation files (such as .PBD or .DLL or .CLASS)

Property files contain the properties displayed in the All Properties tab page found on almost every type of entity inside the Jaguar Manager. *IDL files* contain the CORBA representation of the public interface exposed by each module inside the repository. The *implementation files* are those files, which contain the actual implementation of the interfaces documented by the IDL. An example is the Power-Builder library deployed as a .PBD file, or a Java class file inside a .JAR file.

Now that we have a basic understanding of the three general types of files we will encounter inside of the repository, let's take a look at the underlying folder structure. If you are at a computer, pull up Windows Explorer (assuming you are under Windows NT) and follow along!

%JAGUAR%/Repository

This is the top level of the repository. You will see eight folders, each with a fairly self-explanatory name. Let's step through these folders in alphabetical order.

%JAGUAR%/Repository/Cluster

The Cluster subdirectory contains .PROPS files for the clusters set up on the Jaguar Server. This properties file contains the underlying details of the cluster. Clusters are covered in detail in chapter 1.

%JAGUAR%/Repository/Component

The Component subdirectory contains a folder for each package on the Jaguar server. Each of these packages will be listed inside Jaguar Manager under the Packages branch, and only a subset of these packages will actually be listed under the Servers/Jaguar/Installed Packages branch.

The name of each component inside a package must be unique to that package. In other words, it is possible for a component named "widget" to be deployed inside of multiple packages. These components may or may not be the same "widget" component. Conceptually speaking, a developer could make the rationalization that a database table is to a package as a column is to a component.

Regardless of the development language of the component, there will be a number of .PROPS files for each component installed inside that package. In the event that one or more of the components was developed using a language other than Java, there will be another level of subdirectories with names corresponding to the related component. These directories represent the lowest level of the repository, and contain the actual implementation files generated by the development environment, such as PowerBuilder.

%JAGUAR%/Repository/ConnCache

When working with connection caches inside Jaguar Manager, the cornerstone All Properties tab page is conspicuously missing. Jaguar stores core Connection Cache properties, among other things, inside a file named `afconfig.dat`. This file is encrypted, so there isn't much to view and there certainly isn't anything to manually manipulate. Connection Caches can have properties in addition to those encrypted in the afconfig.dat file, and this folder is the holder for the `.PROPS` file that contains these properties. The `.PROPS` file must be named `<connection cache name>.PROPS`. For example, we discussed the com.sybase.jaguar.conncache.check property in chapter 1. To implement this property, create a text file by hand and save it in this folder.

%JAGUAR%/Repository/IDL

Every Jaguar package is documented using IDL files. The top level contains an IDL file for each package. These package IDL files are typically mirrored by separate folders with the same name as the package. Each of these folders contains IDL files corresponding to the components associated with the package. It is important to understand that the purpose of any IDL file is to document modules and interfaces, as opposed to the more commonly manipulated packages and components.

%JAGUAR%/Repository/Listener

The Listener subdirectory contains a `.PROPS` file for each installed listener on the Jaguar server. To oversimplify, a listener is responsible for associating a protocol with a particular TCP/IP socket. A socket is a combination of a host name or IP address and a port number. The `.PROPS` file contains a listener name, TCP/IP host address, TCP/IP Port, and a specific network protocol such as IIOP, HTTP. For more details on TCP/IP, see chapter 8.

%JAGUAR%/Repository/Package

The Package subdirectory contains a `.PROPS` file for each package on the Jaguar server. These property files contain the properties listed on the All Properties tab page of the package inside Jaguar Manager. To access the All Properties tab page, expand the Packages branch of the primary Jaguar Manager treeview, click the right mouse button on a package and select Package Properties... .

To see Jaguar Manager in action, while looking at the All Properties tab page, click the Add button. A dialog appears prompting for a *property name* and a *property value*. Typically, the property name consists of the company's Internet address listed backwards followed by the name of the property, such as `com.wisemantechnologies.myproperty`. The value is always stored as a string, making it the developer's responsibility to cast it to the appropriate data type in the code. After adding a new property and a value here and clicking the OK button, opening up the .PROPS file inside of WordPad reveals the additional property/value pair.

%JAGUAR%/Repository/Security

The Security subdirectory contains the .PROPS files, as well as other files, responsible for Jaguar's security system. Excluding the .PROPS files, each file is binary encrypted and contains the underlying details of the security profiles. Security profiles are responsible for establishing the relationship between a Jaguar listener and a certification. Also, the certificate database is stored in this directory.

%JAGUAR%/Repository/Server

The Server subdirectory typically contains a .PROPS file for each logical server on the Jaguar Server. This properties file contains the underlying details of the Jaguar Server. See chapter 1 for details on logical servers.

In practice, when a developer is actively developing a Jaguar service, every once in awhile the service may misbehave, causing Jaguar to hang at startup or even worse, abruptly crash. To remove the rogue service from the startup list, developers can open up the server's properties file and delete the name of the service component from the list. If it truly was their service causing the startup problems, Jaguar should start up normally once it removed from the .PROPS file. Afterwards developers are free to attempt to fix their code and try the whole thing over again. The property name listing the server's services is `com.sybase.jaguar.server.services`.

If the server participates in any role with a Jaguar Cluster, other files (additional `.PROPS` and `.CYCLE` extensions) responsible for synchronizing a Jaguar cluster may be present inside this directory.

%JAGUAR%/Repository/Servlet

The Servlet subdirectory contains the .PROPS files for any installed servlets. Chapter 10 demonstrates how to create and install a basic servlet.

6.4　How do I use the Jaguar::Repository interface?

The Jaguar::Repository interface contains very powerful methods to create, modify, and delete entities inside the Jaguar Repository. Sybase uses the term *Entity* to refer to the various objects stored inside the Jaguar Repository. The following list represents some of the more common well-known Jaguar entity types:

- Component
- ConnCache (DBMS Connection Cache)
- Interface
- Listener
- Method
- Module
- Package
- Role
- Security
- Server
- Servlet

Using the Jaguar::Repository component, it is possible to inspect the properties of all of these entity types. However, different entities permit different levels of manipulation, depending upon the version of Jaguar installed. For example, in Jaguar CTS 3.0.x, it is not possible create or manipulate the properties of a Connection Cache.

6.4.1 Generating the "Jaguar" package proxies

A Jaguar component proxy represents an available Jaguar server component. Another commonly accepted name for a proxy is *stub*, and these two terms can be used interchangeably. Creating the necessary proxies to access the component is the first step when calling methods on any component, and this holds true for components included with Jaguar as part of the initial IR. To reiterate, these proxies are generated using identical methods to those used to generate the proxies for any user-defined object.

PowerBuilder developers will use the Proxy Project, while PowerJ developers will select the Add Jaguar Component... from the Components menu. Regardless of the environment, including the following, the Jaguar package covers all the examples in this chapter unless otherwise noted.

If your development environment is PowerJ, the component tab page you specify to store the Jaguar package stubs should contain the following:

- com.sybase.jaguar.system.Management
- com.sybase.jaguar.system.Monitoring
- com.sybase.jaguar.system.Repository

If your development environment is PowerBuilder, the following proxies and structures should be present in your library search path before attempting to use any of the examples presented in the rest of this section. The list of objects include:

- fileviewer proxy
- genericservice proxy
- jvmdebugger proxy
- management proxy
- monitoring proxy
- repository proxy
- writer proxy
- data structure
- list structure
- logfileid structure
- monitordata structure
- monitorkeys structure
- properties structure
- property structure
- view structure

6.5   *How can I read the properties on an entity?*

Using the Jaguar::Repository `lookup()` method, developers can read in the entire set of properties for a single entity. Unfortunately, the Jaguar 3.x API does not contain a method for looking up a single property, nor does it provide the ability to look up multiple properties on multiple entities in a single method call.

The Jaguar interface repository documents the `lookup()` method as follows:

```
Jaguar::Properties lookup(in string entityType,
    in string entityName )
    raises Jaguar::LookupError
```

The first argument, `entityType`, can be any of the well-known entity types listed above. Check with the IR for a complete list of available well-known entities. The second argument, `entityName`, is the name of the entity you want to look up. For example, if you wanted to inspect the properties of the Jaguar::Repository component, the entity type would be Component and the entity name would be Jaguar/ Repository.

TIP   The entity name provided in the lookup function must be of the type provided in the entity type argument. Otherwise, Jaguar CTS will not find it.

The `lookup()` method returns the `properties` data type. In PowerJ the properties data type is a sequence, which is a single-dimension Java array of the Jaguar::Property data type. Inspecting the `properties` structure in PowerBuilder reveals that the only property inside of the structure is an unbounded array named `item` of data type `property`. The `property` data type is another structure, and it contains two properties, `name` and `value`. The `name` property contains the name of the entity property, for example, com.sybase.jaguar.component.type. The `value` property contains the corresponding value of the entity property. These name/value pairs can be read, manipulated, and even optionally put back into the entity inside of the Jaguar Repository, depending on the type of entity and the version of Jaguar.

In chapter 3, we demonstrated an EJB component that connected to a database by specifying the name of the Jaguar connection cache. In general, hard-coding values such as database names is not recommended. Let's rewrite that code to take advantage of the `lookup()` method.

```
try
{
    //remember to import the following:
    //import org.omg.CORBA.*;
    //import Jaguar.*;

    static ORB orb;
    java.util.Properties props = new
        java.util.Properties();

    props.put("org.omg.CORBA.ORBClass",
        "com.sybase.CORBA.ORB");

    orb = ORB.init((java.lang.String[])null, props);

    /* Get parameters from the repository */
    Jaguar.Repository repository =
        Jaguar.RepositoryHelper.narrow(
          _orb.string_to_object("Jaguar/Repository"));

    Jaguar.Property[] compProps =
        repository.lookup("Component",
        "yourPackage/yourComponent");

for (int i = 0; i < compProps.length; i++)
    {
        if (compProps[i].name.equals("yourProp.dbname"))
        {
            _dbName = compProps[i].value;
        }
```

```
    }
} catch (java.lang.Throwable _ignoreexception) {
    /* handle exceptions */
}

//... use the _dbName to setup JDBC and continue
```

Notice that the preceding code example uses the `string_to_object()` method. Components making intercomponent calls can obtain object component references for other components located on the *same* server through this method. The IOR string is specified as Package/Component. This coding technique is server-side only, and will not work when executed on a client. Because of Jaguar's load balancing and high availability techniques (unless accessing a component included with Jaguar out of the box, such as Jaguar/Repository), a better approach is to go through the name server. We'll discuss naming services in chapter 7.

TIP   When accessing the Jaguar/Respository component from a Jaguar component, it is recommended that the `string_to_object()` method using the Package/Component name always be used to get the object reference so that the repository that is being accessed is on the same server as the Jaguar component.

Here is a small code segment in PowerBuilder that demonstrates reading some Jaguar component properties from inside a Jaguar component using the repository component:

```
CONSTANT STRING DIET_LEVEL = &
    "com.wisemantechnologies.cookiemonster.dietlevel"

//Jaguar Related Declarations
TransactionServer    ltrx_jag
repository           ljag_repository
ErrorLogging         lel_jag
Properties           props

//Working variables
Long    ll_Max, &
        ll_Cnt

String ls_dietLevel

THIS.GetContextService( "TransactionServer", ltrx_jag )

IF isValid( ltrx_jag ) THEN

    THIS.GetContextService( "ErrorLogging",  lel_jag )
    ltrx_jag.CreateInstance( ljag_repository, &
        "Jaguar/Repository" )
```

```
//Lookup the properties for cookie monster
props  = ljag_repository.lookup( "Component", &
            "WisemanTech/CookieMonster" )

//How many properties are we looking at here?
ll_Max    = UpperBound( props.Item )

//Find the property which indicates the diet level
FOR ll_Cnt = 1 TO ll_Max

  IF Lower( props.Item[ ll_Cnt ].Name ) = &
      DIET_LEVEL THEN
        ls_dietLevel = props.Item[ ll_Cnt ].Value
        lel_jag.Log("Diet level: " + ls_dietLevel)
    END IF
  NEXT
END IF
```

If you are going to be reading a lot of the properties of a component throughout your code, and the values of the properties do not change very often, it is recommended that you cache the values of the properties on the client. Inside of Java, you could use a hash table for each entity, storing the name and values for future reference. PowerBuilder developers can implement a similar approach by creating a single class with a cache to store the values. The cache would be a DataStore, and the external data object would contain the following three attributes:

- Entity
- Name
- Value

Create a single method inside of the class to look up a specific property on a specific entity. For example, your lookup function could use the following function signature and contain the following high-level logic:

```
int of_getProp(string entity, ref string value)

Filter the DataStore for the requested entity

Get the matching row count

If there are no matching rows, then
    Read in the properties for the requested entity
End if

Do a Find() on the DataStore for the requested Name (property)

If we find a row that matches then
    Store the value in the string reference argument.
    return success
Else
    Set the string reference argument to NULL
    Return failure
End if
```

In the event you are using a DataStore, use the `Filter()` method as a quick mechanism to sort out rows that are unimportant in the property query; for example, a filter on the entity you are looking up. Alternatively, use the `Find()` method to locate the property—this is much faster than writing a slow FOR...NEXT loop and inspecting every property for a match. Remember, every entity property is treated as a string, and it is the developer's responsibility to cast the value to the appropriate data type.

6.6 How can I use the keyword context service to read properties?

The keyword context service is a PowerBuilder-specific feature, and can be used as an alternative to using the Jaguar::Repository's `lookup()` method to read the properties of the current component. Here is a sample PowerBuilder script which demonstrates the use of the keyword context service. This example returns the first value of the requested property, if it is found.

```
contextKeyword      lkw
String              ls_values[], &
                    ls_property, &
                    ls_propValue
integer             li_rc, i

getContextService("keyword", lkw)

ls_property = "com.sybase.jaguar.component.type"

li_rc = lkw.getContextKeywords(ls_property, ls_values)

CHOOSE CASE li_rc
    CASE IS > 0
        ls_propValue = ls_values[1]
    CASE ELSE
        ls_propValue = ""
        THIS.of_LogError("Error in accessing the property")
END CHOOSE

RETURN ls_propValue
```

> **TIP** The contextKeyword object cannot be used to access Jaguar properties on anything but the current component that runs the code. It also cannot be used to modify Jaguar properties

6.7   *How can I create or modify the properties on an entity?*

As a caveat to this section, not every entity supports creation and/or modification of properties. This is further complicated by differences between versions. For instance, in version 3.0.x, it is not possible to programmatically create and define a connection cache. The code fragments required to manipulate properties are fairly straightforward. If the code compiles successfully but doesn't produce the desired results at runtime, chances are you are trying to manipulate an entity that isn't allowed to be manipulated. Refer to the IR and the online books for a complete list of modifiable entities for your version of Jaguar.

The first rule to learn when modifying the properties of an entity is very important. Earlier in this section, it was disclosed that the `lookup()` method can read only the entire set of properties for a given entity and that it is not possible to read in a single property value. The behavior of the `lookup()` method sets the tone for the `define()` method, documented below. The `define()` method must update *all* the properties for the entity, and it is not capable of updating a single property. To reiterate, when updating an entity's properties, it is the caller's responsibility to `lookup()` all the current properties, add or remove any properties as required, and pass the entire updated property set back through the `define()` method.

The Jaguar interface repository documents the `define()` method as follows:

```
void define(in string entityType,
    in string entityName,
    in Jaguar::Properties props)
    raises Jaguar::UpdateError
```

The first two arguments are identical to those covered for the `lookup()` method. The only difference is that instead of returning the `properties` data type, one is passed in as the third argument.

NOTE   Jaguar defines the method's third argument as a single variable of type properties. When generating proxies for the Jaguar repository in Power-Builder, the third argument of the `define()` method may come across mapped as Property[] versus Properties. If this occurs, the situation can be corrected by exporting the proxy out to a text file. Open up the proxy in your favorite text editor, such as Notepad. Replace "Property props[]" with "Properties props" and import the proxy back into your library. Once completed, the `define()` method works as documented in the IDL.

Back to our example: If we wanted to change the DIET_LEVEL property from the code example above for the lookup method, we could add a define call at the end:

```
CONSTANT STRING DIET_LEVEL = &
    "com.wisemantechnologies.cookiemonster.dietlevel"

//Jaguar Related Declarations
TransactionServer        ltrx_jag
repository               ljag_repository
ErrorLogging            lel_jag
Properties              props
//Working variables
Long                    ll_Max, &
                        ll_Cnt
String                  ls_dietLevel = "1234"

THIS.GetContextService( "TransactionServer", ltrx_jag )

IF isValid( ltrx_jag ) THEN

    THIS.GetContextService( "ErrorLogging",  lel_jag )
    ltrx_jag.CreateInstance( ljag_repository, &
        "Jaguar/Repository" )

    //Lookup the properties for cookie monster
    props    = ljag_repository.lookup( "Component", &
                   "WisemanTech/CookieMonster" )

    //How many properties are we looking at here?
    ll_Max   = UpperBound( props.Item )

    //Find the property which indicates the diet level
    FOR ll_Cnt = 1 TO ll_Max

      IF Lower(props.Item[ll_Cnt].Name) = DIET_LEVEL THEN
        props.Item[ ll_Cnt ].Value = ls_dietLevel
        lel_jag.Log("Increased diet level: + ls_dietLevel)
      END IF

    NEXT

    //Add a new property here!
    ll_Max ++

    props.Item[ ll_Max ].Name      = &
    "com.wisemantechnologies.message"

    props.Item[ ll_Max ].Value     = &
    "How about them Buckeyes?!?"

    ljag_repository.define( "Component", &
       "WisemanTech/CookieMonster", &
       props )
END IF
```

6.8 *How can I look up all the entities installed on Jaguar?*

Thus far in this chapter, we have focused exclusively on viewing and manipulating the properties of an entity, typically a component. This capability of looking at and manipulating properties only scratches the surface of what the Jaguar::Repository interface is capable of achieving.

The Jaguar Manager application uses the Jaguar::Repository interface, among others. If you think about it, if the Jaguar Manager is able to do something, chances are (with a few exceptions), you are able to accomplish the same thing in your custom application or component.

If we wanted to look up all the entities of a particular type, such as packages, we can use the Jaguar::Repository component's `items()` method.

The Jaguar interface repository documents the `items()` method as follows:

```
Jaguar::View items(in string entityType,
     in string entityName)
          raises Jaguar::LookupError
```

The entityType argument can be any well-known entity. The entityType argument acts as a filter to limit the information returned when the entityName argument equals the empty string (""). In this situation, the method returns only the top-level items of the specified type. For example, to return a list of all Packages:

```
View lv_packages

//Get a View of all of the packages on the Jaguar Server
lv_packages = ijag_repository.items( "Packages", "" )
```

When an entityName is specified, the `items()` method returns the details for the named entity of the specified entityType, if a match is found in the repository.

The returned data type is a `View`. A `View` is conceptually identical to that of a two-dimensional unbounded array—unbounded in both directions. To say it another way, a `View` is a table that can contain an unlimited number of rows and an unlimited number of columns, and the `View` table is defined on a method-by-method basis.

The `items()` method `View` contains four columns, shown below in table 6.1.

Table 6.1   The method `View`

Column 1	Column 2	Column 3	Column 4
entity type	simple name	Entity name	description

Upon detailed inspection, the `View` structure contains a single unbounded array named "item" of data type List. A `List` contains an unbounded array named "item" of data type String. In this way, the rows are represented by the top level item[]

array, and the columns are represented by the nested item[ ]. Therefore, all values in this table are of data type String. Building on the earlier sample where we read in all the packages on the Jaguar server, the following code reads the entity name of the first package returned in the view.

```
View      lv_packages
String    ls_entityName

//Get a View of all of the packages on the Jaguar Server
lv_packages = ijag_repository.items( "Packages", "" )

//Read the entity name of the 1st package
ls_entityName = lv_packages.Item[ 1 ].Item[ 3] )
```

An analogous metaphor for the View/List relationship is one of a table's Rows/Columns. The View item[ ] could have been called row[ ] and the List item[ ] could have been called column[ ].

In this next example, we will be building a treeview containing every package and component currently installed on your Jaguar Server, identical to the treeview pictured in figure 6.1 from the Jaguar Component Wizard in PowerBuilder 7.

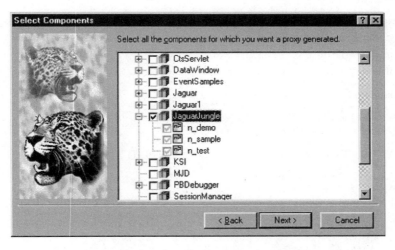

Figure 6.1   This treeview lists installed packages/components on Jaguar

Using everything we have learned about the items() method, we can now implement our own version of the select components treeview shown in figure 6.1 in one of our own applications. The following code assumes you have a Window with a treeview named tv_components, and that you have already established a connection to Jaguar inside of a Connection instance variable called icn_jag.

```
View lv_packages, &
     lv_components

Long ll_componentMax, &
     ll_componentCnt, &
     ll_packageMax, &
     ll_packageCnt, &
     ll_parentHandle, &
     ll_serverHandle

TreeViewItemltvi_parent, &
ltvi_child

IF isValid( ijag_repository ) THEN

   //Insert the Jaguar Server as the root of the TreeView
   ll_serverHandle= tv_components.InsertItemLast( 0, &
      "Jaguar (" + icn_jag.Location + ")", 1 )

   //Get a View of all of the
   //packages on the Jaguar Server
   lv_packages = ijag_repository.items( "Packages", "" )

   //How many packages are there?
   ll_packageMax = UpperBound( lv_packages.Item )

   //Setup the constant Parent TreeViewItem settings
   //that are common to each Package
   ltvi_parent.Children   = TRUE
   ltvi_parent.Level      = 1
   ltvi_parent.PictureIndex   = 2
   ltvi_parent.SelectedPictureIndex   = 2

   FOR ll_packageCnt = 1 TO ll_packageMax
      //Grab the name of the current package
      ltvi_parent.Label = &
           lv_packages.Item[ ll_packageCnt ].Item[ 3]

      //Add the current package
      //to the TreeView under the Server
      ll_parentHandle = &
        tv_components.InsertItemLast( ll_serverHandle,&
                                      ltvi_parent )

      //Get a View of all of
      //the components for the current package
      lv_components = &
          ijag_repository.items( "Component", &
             lv_packages.Item[ ll_packageCnt ].Item[ 3] )

      //How many components are there?
      ll_componentMax = UpperBound( lv_components.Item )

      FOR ll_componentCnt = 1 TO ll_componentMax
        //Add the current component
        //to the TreeView under the Package
```

```
         tv_components.InsertItemLast( ll_parentHandle, &
            lv_components.Item[ll_componentCnt].Item[ 3],3)
      NEXT
   NEXT
ELSE

   MessageBox("Connection", &
      "Invalid Jaguar Connection Object!")

END IF
```

6.9   *How can I look up the interfaces a component implements?*

A single Jaguar component is capable of implementing sixteen interfaces. This means that a single component provides all the well-known functions of each interface supported. To view the interfaces supported by a single component, we will use the Jaguar::Repository `interfaces()` method. Programmatically, a developer connects to a remote instance of a component that supports, for example, five interfaces. The client code will typically narrow (or cast) the generic class to that of a specific interface. From that point forward in the code, only the methods of the narrowed interface are supported. (For more details on narrowing to a specific interface, review chapter 5.) This approach is different from the CORBAObject's `_is_a()` method in that it returns a list of interfaces, whereas the CORBAObject's method returns a Boolean to indicate if a particular interface is supported.

The Jaguar interface repository documents the `interfaces()` method as follows:

```
Jaguar::List interfaces(in string component)
      raises Jaguar::LookupError
```

The component argument should be in the form of package/component. For example, the following code returns the IDL interfaces implemented by the Jaguar::Repository component we have been working with in this chapter.

```
List   llist_intf

//Get all the IDL interfaces supported by Jaguar/Repository
llist_intf = ijag_repository.interfaces("Jaguar/Repository")

MessageBox("Interface", llist_intf.item[ 1 ] )
```

Earlier, we talked about the List structure, and indicated that it contained an unbounded array named item[] of data type String. To determine the number of interfaces returned from the `interfaces()` method, pass the List's item[] array to PowerBuilder's `UpperBound()` function. The Jaguar::Repository component supports the IDL:Jaguar/Repository:1.0 interface.

PowerBuilder developers using the JaguarORB and CORBAObject approach (as opposed to the more common Connection object) can exploit the `is_a()` method of the CORBAObject to determine if the object supports a particular interface before attempting to narrow the object. Java can use an equivalent method using the ORB class in the `org.omg.CORBA` package. Alternatively, both PowerBuilder and Java components can use the `interfaces()` method and look for the matching interface.

6.10 What are the Jaguar management components?

The Jaguar management components loosely describe the Jaguar::Management and Jaguar::Monitoring components. Collectively, these two components provide the developer with a rich interface for providing integrated Jaguar management capabilities inside an application.

6.11 How can I use Jaguar environment variables?

In chapter 1, we took a closer look at the serverstart.bat file used to run the Jaguar server. In the beginning of the batch file, we witnessed the establishment of %JAGUAR% to point to the root path of Jaguar. It is possible to define your own custom environment variables inside of this batch file. One nice benefit of defining your own Jaguar environment variable is that the value is easily accessible for any component, as well as any client connection. Uses are limited only by your imagination. In the following example, I've added the "foobar" environment variable to serverstart.bat and set it up in tribute to Kernighan and Ritchie's "Hello World" program.

```
@echo off
cls
SETLOCAL
set JAGUAR=D:\Program Files\Sybase\Jaguar CTS 3.0
cd %JAGUAR%\bin
set foobar=Hello World!
```

6.12 How do I access Jaguar environment variables?

Now that we have been formally introduced to Jaguar environment variables, we need to look at the programmatic requirements to read these environment variables. The Jaguar API is very limited with regard to environment variables, providing only the `getEnv()` method to access a predefined environment variable from the server's runtime environment.

The Jaguar interface repository documents the `getEnv()` method as follows:

```
string getenv(in string var)
```

At this time, there is no documented API for soliciting a collection of all the environment variables from Jaguar—the developer must know the name of the variable they are interested in. If the environment variable is undefined, the method returns an empty string—so always check the return value.

We recommend, however, that you consider using component properties instead of this technique. Component properties can be administered from Jaguar Manager running across a network, and they can be updated dynamically by refreshing the package/component.

Administering Jaguar environment variables requires the entire server to be restarted to take effect. One nice benefit of defining your own Jaguar environment variable is that the value is easily accessible for any component, as well as client connection. Uses are limited only by your imagination.

6.13 How can a component determine the name of the server it is running in?

A component has two options to find out the name of its Jaguar server. The first method uses the `getServer()` method, while the second uses the `getEnv()` method. Clients should rely on the Jaguar naming server's ability to provide location transparency (not knowing where a component actually lives), so this method is suggested for statistical or auditing purposes only.

The Jaguar interface repository documents the `getServer()` method as follows:

```
string getServer()
```

If you were going to use the `getEnv()` method, look up the %SERVERNAME% environment variable. Recall that this variable is established inside the server-start.bat file.

6.14 What server properties can be monitored remotely?

Jaguar Servers expose a monitoring API that allows administrators to view overall application server load and performance. This API is located inside of the Jaguar::Monitoring component. It is important to always refer to the IR for the most recent and up-to-date constants that can be monitored, because constants are routinely added as new versions are released.

When implementing a remote Jaguar Server monitor in PowerBuilder, it is necessary to declare these constants manually. In PowerJ, import the `com.sybase.jaguar.system.*` package to gain direct access to these constants.

NOTE A PowerBuilder example of the Jaguar::Monitoring component is available for download from the book's web site. A Java example is included with the interface repository documentation directly below the definition of the `monitor()` method.

The Jaguar::Monitoring interface defines a large number of constants organized into the following groups. Each monitoring group is documented in greater detail in the tables that follow, including a reference to the decimal equivalent for Power-Builder developers. The following logical monitoring groups are defined.

- Components
- Connection caches
- Network-HTTP
- Network-HTTPS
- Network-IIOP
- Network-IIOPS
- Network-TDS
- Network-TDSS
- Requests
- Sessions

Each of the above monitoring constants yields a snapshot value. In other words, the value returned when querying any of these constants is representative of the value at that instance in time and the value is most likely going to change when queried again. For each snapshot value there are corresponding cumulative values for last maximum and peak. A cumulative counter represents a value that will only increment—never decrement. In addition to these numerical counters, it is also possible to look at the amount of process time required.

6.14.1 *Component statistics*

Component statistics provide details on the number of active components (components currently in use), the number of pooled components (components not currently active but instantiated), and the number of invoked components. These are listed in table 6.2.

Table 6.2   Component statistics

MONITOR_COMPONENT_ACTIVE	8
MONITOR_COMPONENT_COMPLETE	16

MONITOR_COMPONENT_INVOKE	4
MONITOR_COMPONENT_POOLED	12
MONITOR_COMPONENT_ROLLBACK	20

6.14.2 *Connection cache statistics*

Connection cache statistics are useful for tracking the servers that are interacting with remote databases. If the number of *forced* connection caches is high, this is a good indication that the system may need to increase the number of available connections or that load balancing may need to be implemented or expanded. These are listed in table 6.3.

Table 6.3   Connection cache statistics

MONITOR_CONNCACHE_ACTIVE	24
MONITOR_CONNCACHE_CLOSED	28
MONITOR_CONNCACHE_FORCED	32
MONITOR_CONNCACHE_INVOKE	36
MONITOR_CONNCACHE_NOWAIT	40
MONITOR_CONNCACHE_OPENED	44
MONITOR_CONNCACHE_REOPENED	176
MONITOR_CONNCACHE_WAITED	48

6.14.3 *HTTP/HTTPS network statistics*

These statistics can monitor the amount of web (HTTP/HTTPS) traffic and the amount of time the Jaguar server is spending handling web requests. Jaguar also automatically records the number of hits on the server as well as the number of hits on a page. Depending on which section of the Jaguar documentation you read, it incorrectly states this data is stored in the log file %JAGUAR%\bin\httpstat.dat. In actuality, the file "httprequest.txt" inside of the %JAGUAR%\bin directory is used to track the HTTP statistics. In addition to this log file, the directory also contains the "httperror.txt" and "httpservlet.txt" files. These are listed in table 6.4.

Table 6.4   HTTP/HTTPS network statistics

MONITOR_NETWORK_HTTP_READ_BYTES	52
MONITOR_NETWORK_HTTP_TOTAL_BYTES	60
MONITOR_NETWORK_HTTP_WRITE_BYTES	56
MONITOR_NETWORK_HTTPS_READ_BYTES	64
MONITOR_NETWORK_HTTPS_TOTAL_BYTES	72
MONITOR_NETWORK_HTTPS_WRITE_BYTES	68

6.14.4 IIOP/IIOPS/TDS/TDSS Network Statistics

IIOP/IIOPS/TDS/TDSS statistics maintain detailed read/write values for each of these listener protocols. These are listed in table 6.5.

Table 6.5   IIOP/IIOPS/TDS/TDSS network statistics

MONITOR_NETWORK_IIOP_READ_BYTES	76
MONITOR_NETWORK_IIOP_TOTAL_BYTES	84
MONITOR_NETWORK_IIOP_WRITE_BYTES	80
MONITOR_NETWORK_IIOPS_READ_BYTES	88
MONITOR_NETWORK_IIOPS_TOTAL_BYTES	96
MONITOR_NETWORK_IIOPS_WRITE_BYTES	92
MONITOR_NETWORK_TDS_READ_BYTES	100
MONITOR_NETWORK_TDS_TOTAL_BYTES	108
MONITOR_NETWORK_TDS_WRITE_BYTES	102
MONITOR_NETWORK_TDSS_READ_BYTES	112
MONITOR_NETWORK_TDSS_TOTAL_BYTES	120
MONITOR_NETWORK_TDSS_WRITE_BYTES	116

6.14.5 Request statistics

These request statistics keep track of the number of protocol specific requests Jaguar is responding to. These are listed in table 6.6.

Table 6.6   Request statistics

MONITOR_REQUEST_HTTP	128
MONITOR_REQUEST_HTTPS	132
MONITOR_REQUEST_IIOP	136
MONITOR_REQUEST_IIOPS	140
MONITOR_REQUEST_TDS	144
MONITOR_REQUEST_TDSS	148

6.14.6 Session statistics

Session statistics keep track of the number of protocol specific sessions Jaguar is managing. These are listed in table 6.7.

Table 6.7   Session statistics

MONITOR_SESSION_HTTP	152
MONITOR_SESSION_HTTPS	156
MONITOR_SESSION_IIOP	160
MONITOR_SESSION_IIOPS	164
MONITOR_SESSION_TDS	168
MONITOR_SESSION_TDSS	172

6.14.7 Cumulative statistics

Each of the above monitor constants can be combined with any of the constants below. The combination of these constants (adding them together) results in the last maximum, peak maximum, or process time for the specific area. Consider this example:

MONITOR_SESSION_IIOP returns the number of current IIOP sessions.

MONITOR_SESSION_IIOP + MONITOR_LAST_MAXIMUM returns the number of maximum IIOP sessions since Jaguar was started. These are listed in table 6.8.

Table 6.8 Cumulative statistics

MONITOR_LAST_MAXIMUM	1
MONITOR_PEAK_MAXIMUM	2
MONITOR_PROCESS_TIME	124

6.15 *How should I initialize my component, .ini files, or component properties?*

Storing values, such as the parameters for getting connected to the database or who the last user was to log in successfully, has traditionally been the job of an initialization (.ini) file. With the advent of Windows 9*x* and NT, many developers began to rely more on the Windows Registry, per Microsoft's suggestion to store this type of information. While these techniques are clearly the best choice when dealing with the client, they may not be the best choice when dealing with a Jaguar component.

The first thing to consider is that an .ini file is not an integrated part of the Jaguar repository, at least not by default. Even if you place the .ini file in a directory in repository, Jaguar will view the file as foreign and totally ignore it. Problems begin to manifest themselves when the environment is or is going to be set up to provide high availability/load balancing and someone runs the Synchronize option inside of Jaguar Manager (for more details on synchronization and clustering, review chapter 1). As a review, when running the synchronization, Jaguar includes only property files, IDL files, class files (for Java components), shared objects or DLLs (for C/C++ components), and PBDs (for PB components) when setting up the target server. Notice that this list does not include .ini files, registry entries, bitmaps, and so on.

After running a synchronization, extra steps may be necessary to propagate the remaining dependencies, such as registry entries, to each server. Even with this limitation, .ini files do have the advantage of allowing similar settings/info to be changed/accessed by any number of components without having to go through the steps of adding or modifying the values on a component-by-component basis.

It is possible to define a comma-delimited list of dependent files inside the `com.sybase.jaguar.component.files` property. The files listed here will be included when a cluster synchronization is fired off, and eliminate the necessity of manually copying over other dependent files. Using the `lookup()` and `define()` methods described earlier in the chapter, it is possible to programmatically read and set this property. This technique proves especially useful for .ini files.

TIP   Place any .ini files used by your components in the %JAGUAR%\bin directory so Jaguar can easily find them.

As an alternative to utilizing an .ini file to store initialization values, developers can define their own component properties using Jaguar Manager and then read these values in programmatically. To add your own user-defined properties to a component, open up Jaguar Manager and drill down through the treeview to your package or component, shown in figure 6.2.

Figure 6.2   Accessing Package Properties

Go to the All Properties tab page and click Add to add a new property. The dialog displayed in figure 6.3 requires a property name and a property value. The property name is typically your company's URL backwards, minus the www prefix, plus the name of the property. Remember, programmatically all property values are treated as strings!

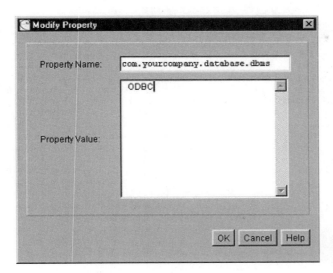

Figure 6.3
Adding a property

For example, Sybase properties begin with com.sybase.property_name. Your properties should be defined as com.yourcompany.<SectionName>.<KeyName> where <SectionName> and <KeyName> are conceptually equivalent to their cousins inside the .ini file. Consider this example .ini file turned into a component property and displayed in figure 6.4.

Table 6.9   Sample .ini file

[Database]
DBMS=ODBC
DBParm=ConnectString='DSN=MyDSN;UID=dba;PWD=sql'

Table 6.10   Sample Component Property Names

com.yourcompany.database.dbms
com.yourcompany.database.dbparm

There is a downside to this approach when the component is being developed with PowerBuilder, but it can be compensated for. PowerBuilder's project painter doesn't provide an interface to manage user-defined component properties, so developers will have to resort to using Jaguar Manager. PowerJ exposes the Environment Properties on the Deploy tab page of an EJB 1.0 component.

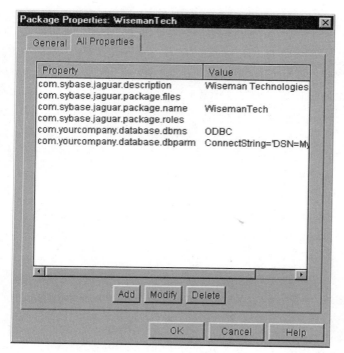

Figure 6.4
Two new Properties for "your company"

6.16 How do I use CtsSecurity::AuthService for my own authentication service?

Jaguar exposes the CtsSecurity::AuthService interface for developing proprietary user authentication routines. Developing a proprietary authentication routine may more adequately suit the security policies of your environment; for example, connecting to a database connection cache to validate the credentials of a potential user.

When developing an authentication component using Java, pay particular attention that the component must implement the *methods* as opposed to the *Java interface* CtsSecurity::AuthService. An in-depth conversation regarding the rationale behind this is found in chapter 4, where Jaguar services are discussed.

Sybase includes a very detailed Java component that fully demonstrates a user-configurable authentication service. This example can be found at the following path: %JAGUAR%/html/classes/Sample/AuthServiceDemo. Included is an HTML file that fully documents how to compile, install, and test the authentication service.

Because Java is already well documented, we will only demonstrate a Power-Builder component here. This component will be capable of servicing authentication requests. In PowerBuilder, it will be necessary to import the proxies for the

CtsSecurity package. Create a proxy project and select the entire CtsSecurity package to get all the necessary objects.

After you have the proxies added to your library list, create a new standard Jaguar component using the Jaguar component wizard from the Object tab page of the New dialog. In our example, we will name the nonvisual n_authdemo and the Jaguar component, SecurityDemo. We'll place this component inside a package called JungleSecurity. Be sure to indicate a transaction support option of Not Supported and check the Auto Demarcation/Deactivation check box.

The CtsSecurity::AuthService interface is only a single method. The Jaguar interface repository documents the checkSession() method as follows:

```
long checkSession(in CtsSecurity::SessionInfo sessinfo)
```

The return value must be either AUTH_SUCCEED (0) or AUTH_FAIL (1), as defined in the CtsSecurity package. We recommend you declare two local constants at the top of the checkSession() method to eliminate any ambiguity regarding the interpretation of a literal value.

The checkSession() method will be invoked by Jaguar for every new client session after Jaguar has verified authentication and before it continues processing the client request of that session. Additionally, Jaguar will invoke the method once the session expires, as dictated in the server property com.sybase.jaguar.server.authtimeout.

The only argument to the method is a SessionInfo object. This object exposes a number of useful methods routinely used in providing an authentication service. Methods on this object provide the ability to inspect the host name, listener, supplied user ID (name) and password, as well as the peer IP address from which the connection is originating.

The following PowerBuilder code represents the shell of a basic authentication service. In this example, we write out to the server log the user ID and password, and always authenticate the session. Obviously, in the real world this algorithm would need to be taken many steps further, probably including a database connection or something similar to validate the user's credentials.

```
CONSTANT LONG AUTH_SUCCEED = 0
CONSTANT LONG AUTH_FAIL = 1

ErrorLogging lel_jag

GetContextService( "ErrorLogging", lel_jag )

lel_jag.Log("JungleSecurity: Start checkSession")

lel_jag.Log("JungleSecurity: User ID: " + &
    sessinfo.getName() )

lel_jag.Log("JungleSecurity: Password: " + &
```

```
sessinfo.getPassword() )
RETURN AUTH_SUCCEED
```

After saving your authentication component and successfully deploying it to Jaguar, use Jaguar Manager to set the new authentication service to your component. This is done by editing the server property `com.sybase.jaguar.server.authservice`. The value of this property should contain the package/component that implements the CtsSecurity::AuthService interface.

WARNING   Using build 35038 of Jaguar CTS 3.5 and PowerBuilder 7.02, we were unable to successfully deploy the component and continually received IDL definition errors from the PowerBuilder project painter.

When testing server-wide authentication services (and Jaguar services in general), it is possible that a component may not work properly and need to be debugged further. Symptoms could range from simply not being allowed to log into Jaguar, or in extreme cases, Jaguar crashing. Recall that the %JAGUAR%\Repository\Server directory contains the .PROPS files that drive the server. Close Jaguar and run WordPad (or your favorite editor), and open up the %JAGUAR%\Repository\Server\Jaguar.PROPS file. Locate the authservice property and reset it by removing your package/component's name. When you restart Jaguar, you should be able to log back into Jaguar (assuming you were able to successfully log in prior to the installation of your proprietary authentication service). This technique works well for removing rogue Jaguar services as well.

6.17   *What is a PowerBuilder cookie?*

PowerBuilder cookies are used inside the Jaguar repository when components are being developed and deployed from within a PowerBuilder Jaguar Project, and are not applicable for components developed in other environments. When the PowerBuilder project painter is used to deploy a package to Jaguar, Jaguar maintains copies of all the previous versions of each component inside of that package. The term that Jaguar uses is a "cookie" and they are represented inside of the component as 'C*xx*' where *xx* is a sequential number incremented each time the package is deployed from the PowerBuilder project painter. For example, C23 becomes C24.

There were only two locations we could find where Jaguar was able to consistently locate a dependency file, such as an .ini file. The first location was inside of the %JAGUAR%\bin directory. The second was any directory specified in the system's PATH environment variable. It appears that Jaguar will look through only the search path specified in the serverstart.bat file used to start/stop Jaguar. Here is how PATH is defined inside that batch when Jaguar is installed. Notice the addition of %PATH% at the end, concatenating the system path to the end of the list.

```
set PATH=.;%JDK_LATEST%\bin;%JAGUAR%\dll;%PATH%;
```

Knowing about the PowerBuilder cookie is important when you are referencing files. It has always been recommended that developers avoid hard-coding paths in front of a file name, and with the component path changing each time the package is deployed, it is unrealistic to store a hard-coded file path, including the path to an .ini file, inside of the actual component. If you did this, each time you deployed the component to Jaguar you would have to remember to change the hard-coded path.

NOTE Jaguar stores all the files necessary for the component inside the repository. The directory structure to locate the source files is

%JAGUAR%\Repository\Component\<PackageName>\
<ComponentName>\Cxx\

<PackageName> is the name of your package.
<ComponentName> is the name of your component.
Cxx is the PowerBuilder cookie number.

The cookie number is automatically incremented each time the package is deployed from PowerBuilder and cannot be dictated from the present PowerBuilder interface. However, by using the Jaguar Manager, it is possible to reset this cookie number by editing the component properties. Look for the com.sybase.jaguar.component.pb.cookie property and set it to the number you wish to use. *Do not include the letter C!* When Jaguar is refreshed, it will look in the *Cnn* directory, where *nn* is the number you provided.

TIP Jaguar does not delete old PowerBuilder cookies, resulting in a bloated repository. For example, one repository swelled to 2.5 GB! To regain that wasted hard drive space and automatically purge outdated cookies, you may wish to review and download the Jaguar CookieMonster available at Sybase Developers Network (SDN) under Third Party Resources.

Jaguar naming services

7

This chapter covers:

- Jaguar naming services
- ORB initialization parameters

7.1   *What are the Jaguar naming services?*

Jaguar naming services are a critical cog in the implementation of a load-balanced, highly available distributed architecture—especially if that architecture needs to support growth in the future with minimal effort and minimal client redeployment.

Jaguar naming services help implement what many people refer to as *location transparency,* or the idea that the client has no knowledge about the physical location of the object it is interacting with. This location transparency is accomplished by associating a logical name with a physical object. In the case of Jaguar, this logical name relates to the combination of a package and component.

When a Jaguar name server initializes, the logical names provided for the registered package/component combinations are stored conceptually in a virtual table in memory. The primary key of this table is the logical name. As such, it is not possible for two different package/component pairs to both use the same logical name. The establishment of the relationship between the logical name and the package/component is known as *binding,* as displayed in figure 7.1.

Binding

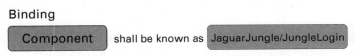

Figure 7.1   Associating a name with a component is known as *binding*

After each component is bound to a name, the combination of the bound name and its referenced physical object is referred to as the *name context,* as depicted in figure 7.2.

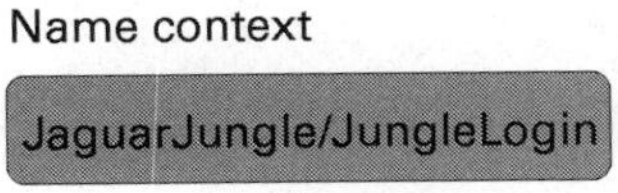

Name context

JaguarJungle/JungleLogin

Figure 7.2
The component name and location are known as the *name context*

Actually, binding is not restricted solely to package/component combinations. It is possible to bind a logical name with an existing named context, resulting in a hierarchy that is similar to the file system on your computer. The entire collection of name contexts constitute the *namespace,* displayed in figure 7.3.

In figure 7.4 we can see a more complex example of a namespace. In this example, we see three packages deployed to four different servers, each a member of the same Jaguar cluster. The first line of text under each server represents the name assigned to the server that one might see in the Windows NT Network Neighborhood. The second line of text represents the initial name context for the server. In

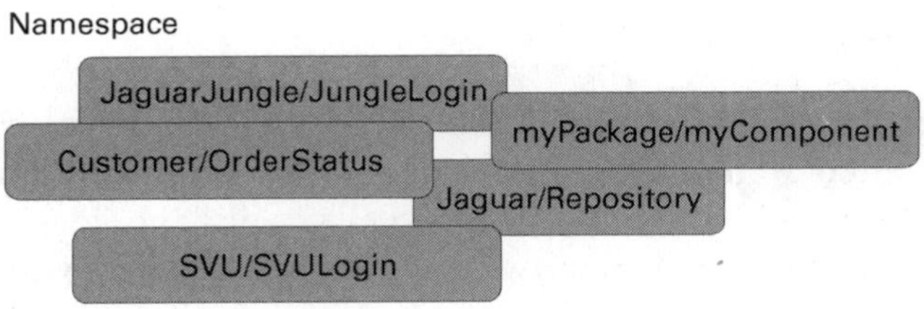

Namespace

JaguarJungle/JungleLogin

Customer/OrderStatus

myPackage/myComponent

Jaguar/Repository

SVU/SVULogin

Figure 7.3 A partial namespace

this cluster, the Jaguar name server (ServerD) would start first. To keep things simple, assume that there are no packages deployed to ServerD. After the name server is up and running, servers A, B, C, and E are started. Each of these servers will register its respective lists of available package/components. The name server uses this registration process to store the bindings for each server. An application wishing to reference Package1/ComponentX in the east coast operations would use the following URL:

iiop://serverD:9000/northamerica/us/east/Package1/ComponentX

The client has no knowledge if ServerA or ServerE is used to fulfill the request. Notice that the URL specifies the name server's host name. This is the power of location transparency. Also consider that the URL is nothing more than a text string, which means that each user in the system could be associated with their operational region. We could build the URL dynamically, based on values retrieved from the database.

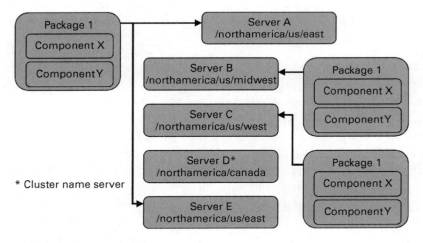

* Cluster name server

Figure 7.4 A Jaguar namespace

Remember when encyclopedias were sold in printed books instead of a CD-ROM? The master index for each encyclopedia cross-referenced entries throughout the entire collection. When a client wants to reference a remote Jaguar component where the location of the component is unknown, it looks to the namespace. The namespace is conceptually identical to the cross-referenced index of our encyclopedia. Our Jaguar namespace points to any number of Jaguar servers that can provide an instance of the requested component; and the order in which servers capable of fulfilling the request is arranged according to the load balancing properties of the cluster. Clients take this list of server URLs and resolve the component name with the referenced object, resulting in the instantiation of the component for the client on the first server in the list. For more details on load balancing, review section 1.18 in chapter 1.

When the client of a distributed application wants to create an instance of a component on a Jaguar server somewhere, the client must establish an initial connection to at least one Jaguar name server. It is worth noting that every Jaguar server can act as its own name server, but when participating in a cluster this may not be the case. For more details on setting up a Jaguar cluster, review section 1.8 in chapter 1.

When participating in a large cluster, it is possible to configure the Jaguar server to rely on another server to act as a name server on its behalf, or to configure the Jaguar server to rely on an external naming service, such as an LDAP server, operating in conjunction with Jaguar's naming service. A Jaguar server can be established as a name server inside of Jaguar Manager through the server's properties. Figure 7.5 shows the *Naming Service* tab page. To mark the server as a name server, check the Enable as a Name Serv checkbox.

Remember, a namespace can be physically represented as a hierarchy, and that a naming context is defined as the combination of the bound name and its referenced object at the lowest level. Jaguar administrators can arbitrarily define the initial context for each Jaguar server.

The initial context is responsible for creating this hierarchy, or level metaphor we've been describing (<Level1>/<Level2>/<Level3>/etc.). The initial context is established whenever a value is entered in the InitialContext field, displayed in figure 7.5. There is no need to specify a forward slash at the end of the entry. The number of levels implemented is arbitrary and depends on the geography or organizational unit administrators are trying to represent, as well as the number of servers involved.

For instance, if we had six Jaguar servers strategically located across North America, we could use the name service to provide logical names based on the region the server was intended to service. Each Jaguar server has one and only

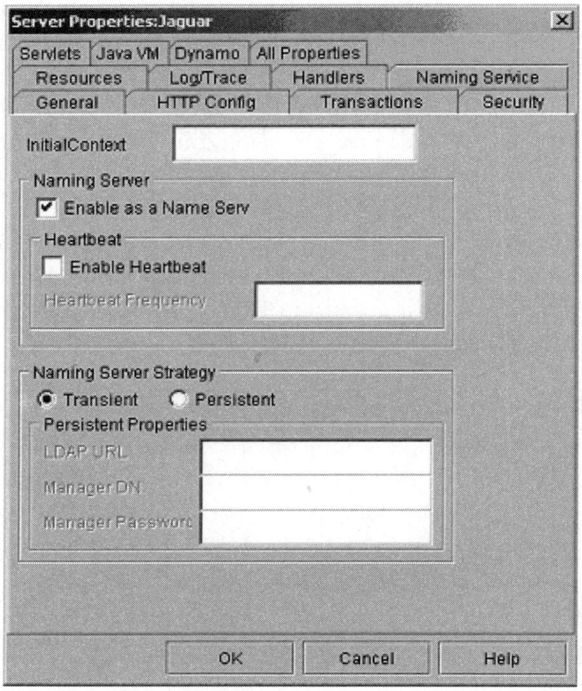

Figure 7.5
Jaguar Server Naming
Service Properties page

one initial context, and each server is by default bound to the servicing name servers of the cluster. The administrator could set up the initial contexts in our example as follows:

SafariShipping/northamerica/eastcoast

SafariShipping/northamerica/midwest**

SafariShipping/northamerica/southwest*

SafariShipping/northamerica/west

SafariShipping/northamerica/mexico

SafariShipping/northamerica/canada

* = Cluster Name Server with an IP address *(intentionally fake)* 265.127.1.3

** = Cluster Name Server with an IP address *(intentionally fake)* 265.127.1.4

When each of the above servers are started, after the name servers, the servers report in with the name servers, and the name servers assemble the namespaces. For instance, if the eastcoast server implemented PackageA/ComponentA, the name server would create the following binding:

SafariShipping/northamerica/eastcoast/PackageA/ComponentA

An application wishing to create an instance of PackageA/ComponentA would take each level and map it into the NameComponent array, and then fire off the query to the name server for that component. Here is a PowerBuilder code example which demonstrates this concept. The variable `inc_context` refers to a Naming-Context. Review chapter 5 for details on how to establish the naming context:

```
NameComponent   lncmp_comp[]
Factory         lnf_factory
CORBAObject     lco_demo
ComponentA      lnv_comp

lncmp_comp[ 1 ].id   = "safarishipping"
lncmp_comp[ 1 ].kind = ""
lncmp_comp[ 2 ].id   = "northamerica"
lncmp_comp[ 2 ].kind = ""
lncmp_comp[ 3 ].id   = "eastcoast"
lncmp_comp[ 3 ].kind = ""
lncmp_comp[ 4 ].id   = "PackageA/ComponentA"
lncmp_comp[ 4 ].kind = ""

//Ask the naming context to resolve our component
lco_demo = inc_context.resolve( lncmp_comp )

//Narrow the CORBAObject to a corresponding factory
lco_demo._narrow( lnv_factory, "SessionManager/Factory" )

//Ask the factory to create the object for us
lco_demo = lnf_factory.create( "jagadmin", "" )

//Narrow the CORBAObject to the component
lco_demo._narrow( lnv_comp, "PackageA/ComponentA" )

//invoke your methods
lnv_comp.of_doSomething()
```

Figure 7.6 shows a graphical representation of the logical steps that occur as a result of this code. When the name server receives a query from a client (step 1), the name server first locates the name context in the server's namespace for the given ID, displayed in figure 7.6. In our example, the name context refers to levels 1 through 3. The last level is always used to denote the bound object (package/component). Once the name server resolves the object reference, it returns a factory which knows where and how to create an instance of the requested object (step 2). This is only a factory, not an actual instance of the requested object. The client narrows the returned CORBAObject to a named reference variable of type `Factory`, which is part of the SessionManager package that comes with Jaguar CTS. The client then invokes the `create()` method on the factory (step 3) which results in the creation of an actual instance of the named object on the target server. The factory's `create()`

method returns a CORBAObject back to the client (step 4), where the client must further _narrow() it to the a declared reference variable. At this point, the client invokes the methods of the component. Pay particular attention to the fact that the client only knew about the name servers of the cluster, and did not use hard coded component location information.

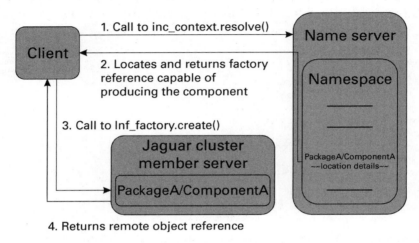

Figure 7.6   The steps a client goes through to create a component instance

In the event administrators chose to leave the initial context blank on all the servers, then we would have only needed the first position of the array, since package and component are always tied together and represent the desired object.

In PowerBuilder, developers can use either the Connection object or the JaguarORB object to establish Jaguar name server connectivity. PowerBuilder clients may not need to use the CORBA naming service explicitly and can instead opt to simply use the built-in name resolution that happens automatically through the CreateInstance() and Lookup() methods of the Connection object. In fact, the Connection object uses CORBA naming service, but hides a large amount of the implementation details of CosNaming from the developer. If a decision is made to use the CORBA naming service explicitly instead, it is important to remember to include the proxies for the naming service interface found in the CosNaming and SessionManager packages from Jaguar. Many people have asked what the "Cos" stands for—Common Object Services, and CORBA supports a number of common services in addition to the naming service we are talking about here. In PowerJ, developers use either the InitialContext object or the combination of org.omg.CORBA.* and SessionManager.* packages to connect to a Jaguar server.

The first object, InitialContext, is appropriately named; the object is responsible for providing a handle to the initial naming context of the specified naming servers for creating instances of the server-side components.

NOTE   In order to present the details on the naming services in a consistent flow, the code examples through the rest of this section will be primarily in Power-Builder.

Developers should try to leverage the combination of the CORBA naming services and the power of the creational design patterns exposed by the ORB. From a PowerBuilder developer's perspective, use of the JaguarORB and CORBAObject results in a drastically different approach to remote component instantiation when compared to the more familiar Connection object, but the client would be CORBA compliant.

NOTE   We should emphasize that the examples in the online help file for JaguarORB and CORBAObject has some inaccuracies. The online books included with PowerBuilder are an improvement.

7.2   How do I initialize my ORB to use naming services?

Before you are able to access anything on Jaguar, the ORB must be properly initialized. PowerBuilder exposes two options, the `options` property of the Connection object and the `init()` method of the JaguarORB object, and in PowerJ, the org.omg.CORBA.* package exposes the ORB object which contains the equivalent `init()` method. This section focuses on initializing the ORB. To review the role and use of a Factory object, please review chapter 5.

In PowerBuilder, the `init()` and the `options` property both use a single string containing the initialization parameters. In the event you are going to supply multiple initialization parameters, separate each parameter using a comma.

In PowerJ, use a java.utils.Properties object and invoke the `put()` method for each name/value pair you wish to use to initialize the ORB.

For most of the properties, it is possible to set up a Jaguar environment variable in the System Properties of the machine. In the event both an environment variable is specified and an initialization parameter is set, the value of the initialization parameter takes precedence.

Let's cover some of the supported initialization parameters. PowerJ developers will depend on the `org.omg.CORBA` and `com.sybase.CORBA` packages to configure the ORB properties. Table 7.1 represents a list of the more common initialization parameter names for the different environments.

Table 7.1   Common initialization parameters for PowerBuilder and PowerJ

PowerBuilder	PowerJ
ORBNameServiceURL	com.sybase.CORBA.NameServiceURL
ORBHttp	com.sybase.CORBA.http
ORBRetryCount	com.sybase.CORBA.RetryCount
ORBRetryDelay	com.sybase.CORBA.RetryDelay
ORBProxyHost	com.sybase.CORBA.ProxyHost
ORBProxyPort	com.sybase.CORBA.ProxyPort
SocketReuseLimit	com.sybase.CORBA.socketReuseLimit
ORBClass	org.omg.CORBA.ORBClass

We will be discussing each one of the parameters listed, and some others, in greater detail. For convenience, we will be using the PowerBuilder parameter name as the heading.

7.2.1   *ORBNameServiceURL*

This parameter is by far the most important and the one that is always included in establishing ORB connectivity from Java and PowerBuilder clients using CORBA::CosNaming. This property is not necessary when using ActiveX clients, or when clients are using SessionManager::*. ORBNameServiceURL is responsible for establishing the IIOP URL for the Jaguar server providing the name service. The corresponding environment variable name, if set up, must be JAG_NAMESERVICEURL. The parameter specifies the URL to the name service using the following syntax:

iiop://hostname:port/initial-context

When specifying this property in PowerBuilder, be sure to enclose the entire string in single quotes. This is one of those little things that could result in your scratching your head for a couple of hours trying to figure out why you are getting an undocumented return value of –6 from resolve_initial_references() in the code, or so we discovered.

The initial context portion of the URL is optional. In the event you do specify an initial context, e.g. USA/Sybase/, all names that you resolve with the context are assumed to be relative to this location in the namespace hierarchy.

As with the Connection object's Location property, this parameter can expose multiple name servers (if you are using a Jaguar cluster), with each server separated by a semicolon.

The default value for this property is dependent upon the client. Java applets use a default of iiop://download-host:9000/ while other clients use iiop://local-host:9000/.

The following example demonstrates setting up the ORB from inside of Java:

```
java.util.Properties props = newjava.util.Properties();

props.put("org.omg.CORBA.ORBClass","com.sybase.CORBA.ORB");
props.put("com.sybase.CORBA.NameServiceURL","your-URL-here");

ORB orb = ORB.init((String[]) null, props );
```

The following example demonstrates setting up the ORB from an ActiveX client:

```
myURL        = "iiop://myserver:9000"
Set myORB    = Server.CreateObject("Jaguar.ORB")
myORB.init("-ORBlogFile=c:\myorb.log")

Set obj      = myORB.string_to_object( myURL )
myMgr        = obj.Narrow_("SessionManager/Manager")

Set obj      = myMgr.createSession("jagadmin","***")
mySession    = obj.Narrow_("SessionManager/Session")

Set myFactory = mySession.lookup("package/component")
Set myBusObj  = myFactory.Narrow_("SessionManager/Factory")
myFactory.Create()
```

7.2.2 *ORBHttp*

This parameter indicates if HTTP tunneling should be used when connecting to the server. Valid values include "true" (use tunneling first) and "false" (try plain IIOP and if the connection is refused, switch to HTTP tunneling). The default value is false and is appropriate in environments where some users connect through firewalls and some do not.

In the event your corporate firewall doesn't allow IIOP packets through, set this parameter to "true" to get around the problem. Setting the value to true merely eliminates the overhead of waiting for the IIOP connection to be refused before switching to tunneling.

7.2.3 *ORBLogIIOP*

This parameter determines if the ORB logs all IIOP protocol traffic. As with ORBHttp, valid values are "true" and "false" with the default of false. The corresponding environment variable name, if set up, must be JAG_LOGIIOP. The traffic logged by this paramenter is intended to be used as a debugging tool. In fact, the log is not proprietary to Sybase but instead is dictated by the CORBA specification found at http://www.omg.org. The specification provides more insight about the log and the information that is sent across in the IIOP packets.

If this parameter is set to true, you must specify the ORBLogFile parameter as well.

7.2.4 ORBLogFile

This parameter establishes the path and name of the file where all client execution status and error messages are logged. The corresponding environment variable name, if set up, must be JAG_LOGFILE. By default, no log file is established.

7.2.5 ORBCodeSet

This parameter determines the code set the client uses when communicating with Jaguar. This setting is by default "iso_1" and should rarely have to be changed. The corresponding environment variable name, if set up, must be JAG_CODESET.

7.2.6 ORBRetryCount

When the client initially attempts to connect to Jaguar and fails, this parameter determines the number of times to automatically retry. The default is to attempt to connect to Jaguar five times. The corresponding environment variable name, if set up, must be JAG_RETRYCOUNT.

7.2.7 ORBRetryDelay

In the event the client wasn't able to establish connectivity with Jaguar on the first attempt, this parameter determines the number of milliseconds to wait before trying again to establish a connection with Jaguar. The default is 2000 (2 seconds). The corresponding environment variable name, if set up, must be JAG_RETRYDELAY.

7.2.8 ORBProxyHost

This parameter establishes the machine name or the IP address of a Secure Sockets Layer (SSL) proxy. More specifically, this parameter along with ORBProxyPort, are used in situations where there is a proxy server or firewall doing network address translation. These parameters tell the ORB client to ignore the endpoints in the Profile[] from the IOR and to instead use the settings from these parameters.

7.2.9 ORBProxyPort

This parameter establishes the port number of the SSL proxy.

7.2.10 SocketReuseLimit

This parameter controls the number of times the client's connection may be reused to call methods from one server. The default value is 0, or no limit. The default setting is ideal for short-lived clients or single-threaded clients, but may have a negative impact on multithreaded client connections that typically invoke many methods from servers in a cluster.

When the default value is left for multithreaded clients, the load-balancing capabilities of the cluster may be compromised. This is because the end point list can get stale, where the clients become accustomed to using servers they have already established connections with rather than distributing the processing load across the cluster's servers. Sybase testing revealed that a setting of 10 to 30 is an adequate starting point in this situation. Typically, this setting is more prominently tweaked when Jaguar is operating in a web server environment. In a single-threaded client, the speed advantage of a cached socket is much faster than bouncing around from server to server on new sockets.

Without this option, we could possibly never load-balance back to a member server of a Jaguar cluster that failed because of cached sockets. A client ORB would only open new sockets on this server when its own cache is flushed.

7.2.11 *ORBClass*

The name of the package used to implement the ORB is typically com.sybase.CORBA. ORB. There is no default value for this property, so be sure to include it.

7.2.12 *com.sybase.CORBA.local*

Server-side components use this initialization parameter to indicate whether the ORB reference can be used to issue intercomponent calls in user-spawned threads. The default value is true, and means that all intercomponent calls are made in memory. It also requires that each call must be issued from the thread spawned by Jaguar. When false, components are able to make intercomponent calls from user-spawned threads. This property doesn't apply to PowerBuilder components because PowerBuilder components are not multithreaded, as discussed in chapter 4.

Now that we know what the various parameter initialization settings are, let's look at some scripts that demonstrate how to set up these parameters from the different development environments.

7.3 *How do I initialize the ORB in PowerBuilder?*

In chapter 5, we reviewed a number of detailed examples of using the JaguarORB. At that point in the book, we made a blanket statement about the initialization parameters, deferring to this chapter. Review chapter 5 for details on implementing the JaguarORB. For details on using the Connection object, see the predecessor to this book, *Jaguar Development with PowerBuilder 7*.

7.4   *How do I initialize the ORB in PowerJ?*

Java application developers will use the java.util.Properties object, setting the desired properties through the `put()` method. The properties are then passed to `org.omg.CORBA.ORB.init()`. To avoid hard-coded properties, developers could specify the properties as command-line arguments of the application. Properties specified through the command line will always take precedence over the corresponding properties specified through java.utils.Properties.

7.5   *How do I initialize the ORB in a Java applet?*

Applet developers have two choices for initializing the Jaguar ORB. ORB properties can be set up by constructing a Properties object and pass that to the `org.omg.CORBA.ORB.init()` method, or the properties can be set up as parameters in the HTML applet tag used to load the applet. Properties provided as name/value pairs inside of a param tag of the applet will always take precedence over the corresponding properties specified through java.utils.Properties. To ensure that hard-coded property values are used at runtime, pass the applet parameter as null.

What to do
when your Jaguar
is caught in the Web

This chapter covers

- Internet and web primer
- How to build web applications using Jaguar CTS
- An overview of PowerDynamo

8.1 *What is the World Wide Web?*

The Internet and the World Wide Web (or Web) have engulfed the information technology industry. In fact, it has started to dominate every aspect of our lives. We can buy, sell, and research just about anything on the Internet. Dot-com companies dominate commercials and most companies today at least advertise having a web site. Internet companies drive the stock market and boast gaudy P/E ratios and market caps while telecom companies and cable companies are trying to make Internet access faster and easier for everyone. In the software industry, the Internet has made getting trial versions of products easier to obtain, and most products and drivers have regular maintenance patches and upgrades available on the vendor's web site.

It is important to point out that the Internet and the Web are not the same, although the terms are becoming nearly synonymous in today's vocabulary. The popularity of the Internet has been spurred on by the ease of use provided by web technologies, particularly the web browser, which adds a graphical interface to the Internet environment.

The Internet is a global network of interconnected networks. This network provides access to servers, information, and services around the world. The Internet is based on the TCP/IP network communication protocol. All machines and servers need to have TCP/IP installed and configured in order to communicate on the Internet. Servers on the Internet can provide several different services to clients, some common ones include FTP, SMTP, Telnet, Gopher, and HTTP.

The World Wide Web, also known as the web, is not the Internet. The Web is a distributed computing architecture and is just one of many services (HTTP) that servers on the Internet provide. While the Web is often deployed on the Internet, it can also be implemented on a completely independent corporate network, known as an intranet.

DEFINITION   INTRANET   A network that is based on web technologies and is confined to an organization is called an intranet. An intranet is typically deployed over a corporate network and often provides access to the Internet. Internet access, however, is not a requirement. Because an intranet architecture is in a more controlled environment and is used to perform daily business tasks, the browser typically relies on plug-ins, Java applets, and database connectivity to provide a richer client-side application.

The web architecture relies on the client/server model of communication where a client application requests information and services from a server application. However, the Web is based on a thin client that can access information anywhere using a web browser application, unlike the larger, more specialized GUI client applications that interact directly with a database and are typically what is meant by the term "client/ server" in today's IT terminology.

8.2 How does the Web work?

The web architecture is defined by the technologies it needs, including the TCP/IP and HTTP communication protocols, web browsers, and a web server. In the web architecture the web browser requests an HTML page from a web server. The web server (or HTTP server) is designed to listen for a client's HTTP requests and to provide the documents they ask for. The web architecture is illustrated in figure 8.1.

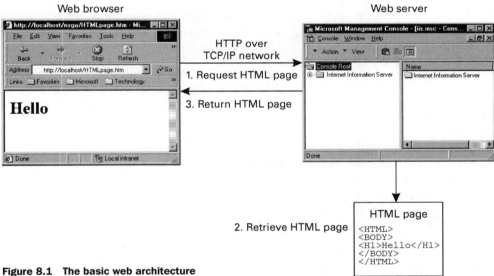

Figure 8.1   The basic web architecture

The web browser is a client application that can communicate with web servers over HTTP and request, receive, interpret, and display information from a web server. The capabilities of the Web have expanded greatly beyond the core web service of requesting and receiving HTML documents. Web browsers have been enhanced to handle more files types through either built-in capabilities or by installing plug-ins. Some examples of file types that most browsers can handle on their own are the JPG and GIF image formats while Adobe's Portable Document Format (PDF) files are widely supported through a plug-in, the Adobe Acrobat Reader. In addition to requesting and displaying files, the browser is now capable of executing code on the client-side by interpreting scripts embedded in the HTML documents that are usually written in JavaScript. The leading browsers also have a built-in Java virtual machine making them capable of running Java programs.

Before discussing the details of building a web application with Jaguar CTS, it is important to have an understanding of some of the underlying technologies.

8.3   *What is HTML?*

Most information on the Web is stored in documents using HTML (HyperText Markup Language). These HTML documents are platform independent hypertext files that contain textual information marked with tags. These tags are used to tell the browser to do something special besides display text. They can be used to define the way the data is presented. They can also embed information and additional resources within them. These additional resources include images, files, scripts, controls, and programs. They can also provide links to other documents that can be on the same web server or on any other accessible web server.Here is a sample of HTML:

```
<html>
<body>
<h1>Hello</H1>
</body>
</html>
```

The browser translates this so that the user sees the display as shown in the browser in figure 8.1.

The HTML is based on Standard Generalized Markup Language (SGML), which conforms to International Standard ISO 8879. The World Wide Web Consortium manages the HTML language. For more information about HTML, visit the World Wide Web Consortium site at the following address:

http://www.w3.org/MarkUp/

8.4   *What is a URL?*

When a browser makes a request on the Web, it does so using the Uniform Resource Locator (URL) standard. The URL identifies the communication protocol, the file or resource that is being requested, and where the file or resource is located, including the server and the path. The syntax for the URL is listed below:

protocol://host {:port}/path/file_name

The protocol describes the service that is to be used to access the resource (i.e. HTTP, File, FTP). The next part of the request tells us the IP address of the server and on what port the application we are interested in is listening on. A web server usually listens on port 80, which is the default for the HTTP service, so it is usually not required. The server location is usually expressed using a domain name rather than the IP address, but either can be used. The final part of the request tells us the path and name of the resource that is being requested. An example is:

http://www.aegisconsulting.com/index.htm

In the example above we are requesting an HTML page named index.htm from the root directory on the server that hosts the www.aegisconsulting.com domain. For more information about URLs, see RFC 2396 and the World Wide Web Consortium site, at the following address:

http://www.w3.org/Addressing/

8.5   What is HTTP?

The HyperText Transfer Protocol (HTTP) is an application-level communication protocol that runs over TCP/IP. HTTP allows multimedia content to be exchanged across a network to diverse platforms. HTTP is a stateless, object-oriented protocol that uses the client/server model of issuing requests and returning a response. For more information about HTTP, see RFC 2616 and the World Wide Web Consortium site, at the following address:

http://www.w3.org/Protocols/

An HTTP transaction or session is made up of four basic steps.

1   Connect to the web server
2   Request a file/resource
3   Receive a file/resource or an error
4   Disconnect from the web server

The stateless character of HTTP arises from the fact that the client is disconnected from the server after a request has been resolved. Let's review this in the context of retrieving an HTML page with an image from a web server. When the client browser requests an HTML page, it connects to the web server and issues the request. The web server handles the request, locates the document, and sends the requested HTML page to the client application and then disconnects. The browser translates the HTML and presents the information to the user. During the translation, the browser notes that an image is required based on the <IMG> tags. When an HTML page requires additional resources, in this case an image, it must issue another request to the web server. The additional resource could also be any other content type, for example a Java applet. To finish loading the HTML page, the browser must reconnect to the web server and request the image. After the image is received the browser is disconnected. This process is repeated for all the images and resources contained by the HTML document as illustrated in figure 8.2. This makes the web architecture inherently slow. A newer version of the HTTP protocol, HTTP 1.1, allows several requests to be made in the same connection before disconnecting, helping to speed up the retrieval of HTML documents. However, it is still not connection-based because the browser is disconnected from the web server after the page and all the files it requires are downloaded.

The steps in an HTTP 1.1 transaction that downloaded an HTML page and an image are shown in figure 8.2 and listed below:

1 Connect to the web server
2 Request an HTML page
3 Receive the HTML page
4 Request the image file
5 Receive the image file
6 Disconnect from the web server

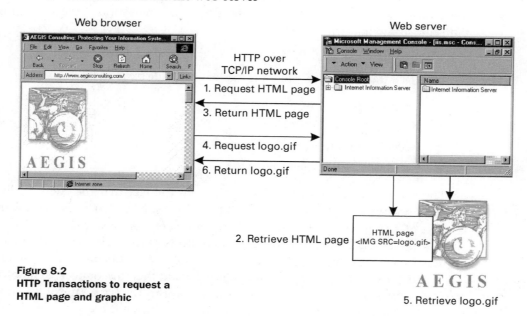

Figure 8.2
HTTP Transactions to request a
HTML page and graphic

8.6 What is TCP/IP?

TCP/IP (Transmission Control Protocol/Internet Protocol) provides a set of network communication protocols that performs the tasks of both the transport and network layer of the Open Systems Interconnection (OSI) Reference Model. The OSI Reference Model, developed by the ISO (International Organization for Standardization), is used to divide the services provided by network protocols into seven layers. TCP/IP is one of the most popular networking stacks and is the standard protocol on the Internet. This is due to the wide support of hardware platforms including Windows, UNIX, DOS, and NetWare, and also the broad support of network protocols and physical architectures including Ethernet, Token Ring, Frame Relay, and ATM.

8.7 What is IP?

The Internet Protocol (IP) provides network-to-network communications, which is known as routing. To facilitate routing, IP is responsible for providing an internetwork addressing scheme and routing data to the correct network and machine. IP does not rely on the physical addresses of each node. Instead, it uses a logical addressing scheme that allows the physical network to change without having to propagate these changes to the upper layers of the network stack. The logical address is translated into a physical address using the Address Resolution Protocol (ARP).

The IP address is a 32-bit number that is often represented in dotted decimal notation. A typical IP address in the dotted notation would be represented as follows:

161.125.23.116

Each portion of the IP address in the dotted notation represents the decimal value of a byte (8 bits) of information. The decimal number 161 is represented as 10100001 in binary. The entire IP address 161.125.23.116 can be represented by the following binary number, 10100001 01111101 00010111 01110100. These octets, as each portion of the IP address are sometimes known, can range in value from 0 to 255.

Identifying a machine (or node) on an internetwork requires two pieces of information–the network the machine is attached to (the network ID) and the address of the machine (the host ID) on that network. The IP address actually represents both of these. The first part of the address is called the network ID or net ID, and it defines a unique network address. The second part is the host ID, which defines a unique machine on the network identified by the net ID.

So which part of the IP address is the net ID and which part is the host ID? That depends on the IP address in question. IP addresses are divided into classes and depending on the class an address belongs to, a different number of bits is allocated for each ID. The classification of IP addresses allows network administrators to design a network infrastructure that can have lots of networks (each with few hosts), or have a few networks (each with several hosts). There are five classifications of IP addresses, of which only the first three (A, B, and C) are put to use on the Internet. The remaining two are reserved for special functions. The IP address classifications are listed in table 8.1. Only machines on the same network can communicate without a router. Two machines are on the same network when they have the same net ID. If the net IDs are different, the two machines will not be able to communicate even if they are connected through the same hub.

Table 8.1   IP address classifications

Classification	First octet range	No. octets for Net ID	No. octets for host ID	Subnet mask
A	1–126	1	3	255.0.0.0
Reserved	127	-	-	-
B	128–191	2	2	255.255.0.0
C	192–223	3	1	255.255.255.0
D (Special)	224–239	-	-	-
E (Special)	240–255	-	-	-

8.8   What is TCP?

The Transmission Control Protocol (TCP) is a connection-based communication protocol that provides reliable two-way communication between hosts. It establishes a connection and makes sure that outgoing messages are divided into packets capable of being sent on the physical network. It also reassembles incoming packets in the correct sequence—error free to the layers above.

When IP transmits data, it is concerned with getting it from network A to network B and from machine A to machine B. The TCP protocol takes this process to the next step, making sure that the data gets to the correct application once it arrives at the correct machine. It does this using a port to identify the application the message is intended for. Each application on a server must have a unique 16-bit port number to identify itself. There are several well-known ports, such as those for FTP (21), HTTP (80), and Telnet (23). Your applications should stay away from these port numbers. A single machine can have several server applications listening on different ports. For example, a Windows NT server may be hosting IIOP for your Jaguar server on port 9000 and also be listening for HTTP (80), SMTP (25), FTP (21), and Telnet (23) clients. IP makes sure that the correct machine gets the data you are sending, and TCP makes sure that the message intended for the Jaguar server does not get sent to the SMTP service as shown in figure 8.3.

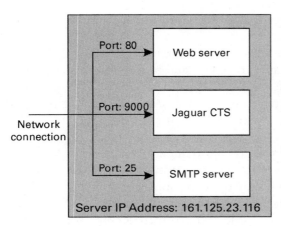

Figure 8.3 TCP/IP on a machine with several server applications

When a connection is established between two applications on a TCP/IP network it is called a socket. A socket is a unique connection formed by combining an IP address and a port number. There are numerous Request for Comments (RFC) documents that are available for more information on TCP (RFC 793), IP (RFC 791), and other Internet technologies. Check out the RFC search site at:

http://www.cis.ohio-state.edu/hypertext/information/rfc.html

DEFINITION UDP TCP/IP actually has two different transport protocols, TCP and UDP. The User Datagram Protocol (UDP) is a connectionless-based communication protocol that runs over IP. It is faster than TCP because it does not provide reliable communication between hosts. UDP does not guarantee that the data will get to its destination or will be error-free.

8.9 What is a dynamic web site?

Up to now we have looked at a basic web site, where a browser requested an HTML file from a web server. The web server receives the HTTP request for a document, retrieves the document from the local file system, and returns the document to the browser. The documents that the web server can retrieve and return at this point are static HTML pages. These HTML pages are fixed documents in which the content does not change without a developer editing the file and redeploying the document. Static web sites do not display real-time data or allow user interaction with the site.

As compelling as static web sites are, the real power is in providing a dynamic site that allows a user to interact with the site and access data in a database. A dynamic web site allows a web server to take a URL request from the browser (or another web server) and return a dynamic HTML page that is generated at runtime instead of returning a static document from the file system. A dynamic web page is generated each time it is accessed. Because dynamic pages are generated at run time, they can respond to input from the web browser, return data requested by the user, and access information real-time. A dynamic HTML page typically will run scripts that execute on the server. These scripts can access a component on an application server or data in a database.

In general web servers do not process logic or access databases. That is not part of the functionality that is required to receive and process HTTP requests for documents. However, as the Internet and Web expand, web servers are providing more features including CGI, API extensions (ISAPI, NSAPI), data encryption (SSL), and server authentication (digital certificates) that enable developers to build dynamic web sites.

In order for a web server to return a dynamic HTML page, an interface is required between the web server and the program or application server that executes the script. The most common web server interface is the Common Gateway Interface (CGI), which is also the industry standard. In addition to CGI, some web server vendors provide proprietary interfaces to their servers, the two most common are NSAPI (Netscape Application Programming Interface) and ISAPI (Internet Server Application Programming Interface). ISAPI is the API supported by Microsoft's web server—Internet Information Server (IIS). In addition to ISAPI, Microsoft IIS also has its own built-in script execution engine called Active Server Pages (ASP).

8.10 *What are CGI, NSAPI, and ISAPI?*

The Common Gateway Interface (CGI) was designed to allow web servers to access external programs to produce dynamic content. These external programs can be any type of executable file including DOS batch files, UNIX shell scripts, and more commonly, Perl programs. The external program can also be a dynamic page server like PowerDynamo. CGI handles all the nuances of communicating between the web server and other applications, defining how data is passed to and from the web server and the external application, as well as describing how to invoke functions. The output that is returned by the CGI program to the web server is typically an HTML document, but it may also be any content or information that a web server can handle, including an image or a reference to another document. A CGI program can do just about anything, but usually creates a dynamic HTML document based on some input from the client and accesses a data source.

CGI creates a new process for each request, making it slow and inefficient. It also uses environment variables and standard input/output to gather and return information. Most web server vendors provide a proprietary interface, which allows the web server to execute programs in the same process space as itself, which makes it much faster and more efficient. The two most common proprietary interfaces are NSAPI and ISAPI.

A CGI, NSAPI, or ISAPI program is invoked using a URL, similar to requesting a static HTML document. Instead of specifying an HTML document, a CGI program is specified. Most CGI programs are stored in a special directory called `cgi-bin` as shown below:

http://www.MySite.com/cgi-bin/cgi_program.exe

When the web server receives a URL that requests a CGI resource, the server calls upon the external application and passes off the request through the CGI interface. The results of the program are returned as an HTML document that is sent to the web server. The web server passes this document back to the browser as pictured in figure 8.4.

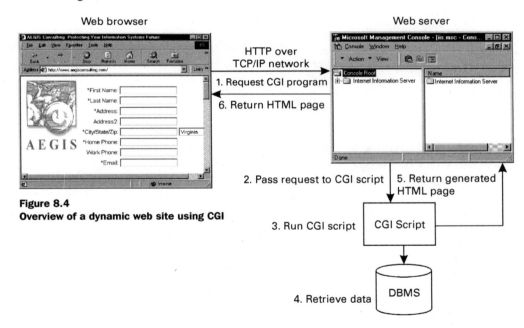

Figure 8.4
Overview of a dynamic web site using CGI

NOTE   Java servlets are Sun's answer to CGI, ISAPI, and NSAPI. Servlets allow a web server to call special server-side Java programs to perform similar tasks. The PowerDynamo server does not have a servlet container and cannot execute servlets; however, it could redirect requests to a Java servlet.

8.11 How do I access Jaguar components from the Web?

The Jaguar CTS server is a CORBA-compliant application server designed to execute components in a high speed, multithreaded kernel. Each Jaguar component is accessible to clients using the CORBA Internet Inter-ORB Protocol (IIOP), which is designed to allow any application servers that adhere to the CORBA 2.x specifications to communicate with each other and access components.

Now that you have built reusable business and data access components for the Jaguar CTS server, how can they be accessed over the Web? There are three different approaches to designing a web architecture that can be implemented with Jaguar CTS.

- Jaguar-Java applet (medium client)
- Jaguar-PowerDynamo (thin client)
- Jaguar-Java servlet (thin client)

The first is the Jaguar-Java applet approach, which allows a web browser to make an HTTP request to a web server for a web page or file. The web pages that are returned by the web server have Java applets embedded in the page, which are also downloaded to the browser over the HTTP protocol. After being downloaded, the Java applet is the primary client used to access the Jaguar server and invoke component methods over the IIOP protocol. This approach is illustrated in figure 8.5.

TIP   The Jaguar-Java applet approach can be implemented without a separate web server because Jaguar CTS supports HTTP requests and can serve static web pages and files (applets) to a web browser

REPORT CARD
Jaguar—Java applet

Pros	<ul><li>More robust GUI is possible with Java applets.</li><li>This method does not require an additional dynamic page server.</li><li>There is a direct persistent connection to Jaguar using IIOP.</li></ul>
Cons	<ul><li>Java applets require a Java-enabled browser and correct version of the JVM.</li><li>Java applets take longer to download then HTML pages.</li><li>Sandbox and firewall issues may make this unacceptable for Internet solutions.</li></ul>

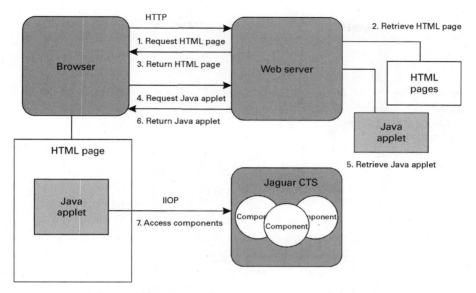

Figure 8.5   The Jaguar-Java applet architecture

An ultra-thin client application can be built by combining Jaguar CTS with PowerDynamo. PowerDynamo is a dynamic page server. PowerDynamo is based on templates that are files made up of a combination of HTML, PowerDynamo tags, and DynaScript. The DynaScript is executed by the PowerDynamo server and the results are used to build a dynamic web page at runtime. The script in the template can call Jaguar components, accessing them as a Java-CORBA client. The results from running the components can be used in the dynamic HTML page that is generated and returned to the client. This approach is illustrated in figure 8.6.

TIP   In addition to PowerDynamo, Jaguar CTS can be accessed by any web server or dynamic page server that can access COM or CORBA objects, including Microsoft ASP and Allaire's ColdFusion.

REPORT CARD
Jaguar—PowerDynamo

Pros	• There are minimal requirements on client machines (thin client). • HTML pages are typically small and download quickly.
Cons	• HTTP requests are stateless and require state management by the dynamic page server or Jaguar CTS. • PowerDynamo DynaScript is an interpreted language.

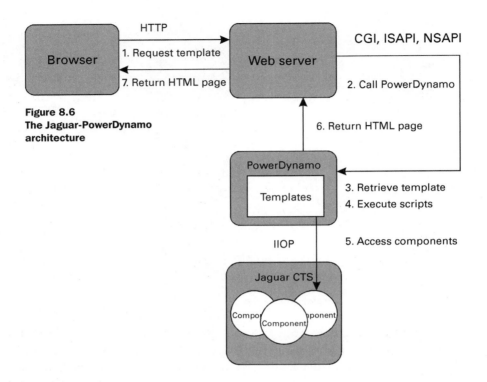

Figure 8.6
The Jaguar-PowerDynamo
architecture

A third approach is to have the browser access Java servlets that are deployed on the Jaguar CTS server. Java servlets are not Jaguar components; they are a special Java program that is designed to be called by an HTTP request. The Java servlet is similar to the PowerDynamo template in that it can access Jaguar components and use the results to build a web page or file. However, the Java servlet is 100 percent Java, so it may be easier to work with than DynaScript if the developers already know Java. In addition, the Java servlet is compiled into bytecodes, which are faster than the interpreted Dynamo templates. One of the major downsides to this approach is that the Jaguar CTS application server is now acting as a web server. The Jaguar server does not have all the capabilities that a web server like Microsoft IIS or Netscape Enterprise Server have. This Jaguar-servlet architecture is illustrated in figure 8.7.

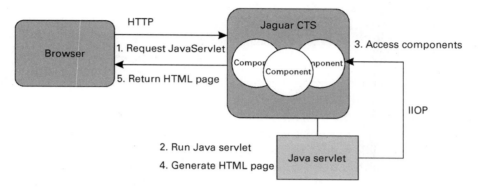

Figure 8.7   The Jaguar-Java servlet architecture

REPORT CARD
Jaguar—Servlet

Pros	<ul><li>There are few if any requirements on client machines (thin client).</li><li>This configuration allows Java classes to be called over HTTP.</li><li>Compiled Java is faster than interpreted pages.</li><li>HTML pages are typically small and download quickly.</li><li>Server-side coding is all done in Java.</li></ul>
Cons	<ul><li>HTTP requests are stateless and require state management by the servlet.</li><li>This method requires using Jaguar CTS as a web server to handle HTTP requests.</li><li>The Jaguar-servlet method requires HTML pages to be built in Java classes by concatenating strings of HTML and data. Note this is addressed with JSP.</li></ul>

It is important to point out that these three approaches are not mutually exclusive and can be combined to build a dynamic web application. In addition, there are other techniques that can be used to access a Jaguar CTS server over the Web; the ones presented here are the most straightforward and rely on industry standard practices and de facto standard technologies. The PowerDynamo approach is covered in this chapter and in chapter 9. The Java applet, servlet, and Sun's Java Server Pages (JSP) approaches are covered in chapter 10.

8.12   *What is PowerDynamo?*

Jaguar CTS is a component-centric application server, designed to host and run components. PowerDynamo is a page-centric application server, often referred to as a dynamic page server. It is designed to run HTML templates and scripts to generate dynamic HTML pages. It is similar to Microsoft's ASP, Sun's JSP, and Allaire's ColdFusion.

DEFINITION EAServer Enterprise Application Server (EAServer) is the name Sybase uses to refer to both Jaguar CTS and PowerDynamo

---

PowerDynamo generates dynamic HTML pages using a template. The template is a combination of HTML tags, Dynamo tags, and DynaScript. The Dynamo tags and DynaScript in the template are interpreted and run by the Dynamo server. The scripts can accept user input to determine which business logic and queries should be executed. The output of these scripts determines what the generated HTML page looks like to the person using the web browser. The process is illustrated in figure 8.8.

The steps below explain how PowerDynamo works:

1   The web server receives a URL request sent by a web browser.

2   The web server passes the request to PowerDynamo.

3   PowerDynamo retrieves the template from the database or file system.

4   PowerDynamo executes the scripts in the template to generate the HTML page.

5   PowerDynamo scripts may access a DBMS or application server for additional processing and data.

6   The generated HTML page is sent to the web server.

7   The web server returns the HTML page to the web browser.

PowerDynamo is a dynamic page server. It is not a web server and cannot receive HTTP requests directly. A web application built with PowerDynamo *requires* a separate web server. Web servers use extensions or gateways to interface with different programs and application servers. PowerDynamo supports CGI, ISAPI, and NSAPI and it is through these different interfaces that a web server can be configured to use PowerDynamo.

With PowerDynamo three different types of web applications can be built:

- Static content
- Dynamic content
- Dynamic content with components

PowerDynamo applications are built from various web resources including templates, scripts, HTML and XML pages, and images. These web resources can be deployed to a database or in a file system. Storing the web resources in a database can be a big advantage allowing the web site to be shared, backed up, replicated,

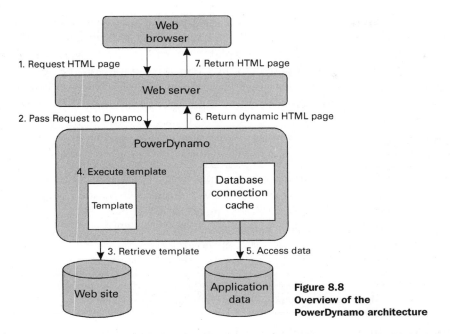

Figure 8.8
Overview of the
PowerDynamo architecture

and secured easily with database technology. The database used to store the Power-Dynamo web site resources does not have to be located on the same database or even use the same DBMS as the application data.

PowerDynamo is a high performance, extendable, page-based application server. It provides session management, access to application data on any DBMS that supports ODBC or Open Client (Sybase), and can cache dynamic pages and database connections. PowerDynamo is capable of supporting robust dynamic content web sites without another application server; however, it is not designed to run components, Java servlets, or provide access to non-Web clients.

PowerDynamo provides functionality that allows scripts to access both ActiveX (COM) and Java (Java, CORBA) objects. This lets the PowerDynamo scripts access Jaguar components. When PowerDynamo is teamed with Jaguar CTS, it enables all the power and advantages of the Jaguar server and the reusability of components to be moved to the Web. By placing logic and data access into components on Jaguar, a reusable set of business rules can be extended to any client or architecture. In addition, Jaguar has several features that PowerDynamo does not, including built-in load balancing and failover, transaction management, and support for several component languages and models.

The power of a PowerDynamo application is in the templates and scripts that are used to build a web site. The templates and scripts are written using HTML tags,

PowerDynamo tags, and PowerDynamo's own scripting language, DynaScript. The template scripts contain the business logic, database access logic, and HTML to generate dynamic HTML pages. The templates are run in the PowerDynamo interpreter on the server before it is sent to the client. This eliminates the need to worry about client-script compatibility issues. In addition, the client receives only the generated HTML, not the server-side scripts. Thus, application logic is protected.

REPORT CARD
PowerDynamo

Pros	▪ PowerDynamo supports session management.
	▪ There is a database deployment option to manage web resources.
	▪ PowerDynamo is easily managed through Sybase Central.
	▪ PowerDynamo supports CGI, Win-CGI, ISAPI, NSAPI.
	▪ Database connection caching is supported.
	▪ An interface to ActiveX, Java, and Jaguar objects is provided.
Cons	▪ Business logic is limited to web applications.
	▪ Database connectivity is limited to ODBC and Open Client.

8.13 How do I set up a web site in PowerDynamo?

When setting up a web site in PowerDynamo, there are two deployment options, deploying the web site resources into a database or deploying them as files. This is a deployment issue and it does not affect the development of the web site itself. One of the benefits of using a database is that a web site can easily be shared, backed up, or replicated to other servers.

Although PowerDynamo can access any database that supports ODBC for application data, PowerDynamo supports only Adaptive Server Anywhere (ASA) and Adaptive Server Enterprise (ASE) as the deployment database. In order to create a web site in PowerDynamo that uses an ASA database to store its web site resources, we need to follow these simple steps:

1   Create an ASA database to store the web resources.

2   Create an ODBC profile for the ASA database.

3   Create a connection profile for the web site in Sybase Central.

4   Connect to the web site using the connection profile to create system files/tables.

5   Create a mapping for the web site.

When using ASE, an ODBC profile is not required. Instead configure an Open Client profile, but otherwise the steps are the same. In order to create a web site in PowerDynamo that uses a file system to store resources, we need to follow these simple steps:

1 Create a directory to store the web site resources.

2 Create a connection profile for the web site in Sybase Central.

3 Connect to the web site using the connection profile to create system files.

4 Create a mapping for the web site.

8.13.1 *Creating a connection profile*

In order to create a connection profile for the PowerDynamo web site, open Sybase Central, which is listed as "Manage PowerDynamo" under the Windows Start Menu. Select the Tools | Connection Profiles... menu option as shown in figure 8.9. From the Connection Profile dialog, click on the New button to create the new profile. The next dialog will open and prompt you for the profile name and type. The profile name is used only in the Sybase Central tool and does not impact the Power-Dynamo web site. Make sure that you select PowerDynamo from the list of options listed for the Type field.

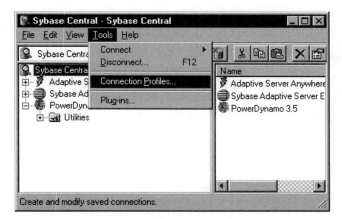

Figure 8.9
Creating a new
connection profile

Once the new connection profile is created, the properties need to be configured. The Properties dialog for a connection profile is pictured in figure 8.10. The connection type determines the deployment option for the PowerDynamo site. The choices are ODBC used for the ASA database option, Open Client used for the ASE option, and Dynamic file, which is used for the file option. The ODBC option will require the name of the ODBC profile and the database user ID and password. The

ODBC data source is the name of the ODBC profile created to connect to the ASA database that will store the PowerDynamo web site resources. The default user ID and password for an ASA database are *dba* and *sql* respectively. Once the connection profile is set up, it will appear in the list of available connection profiles as illustrated in figure 8.11.

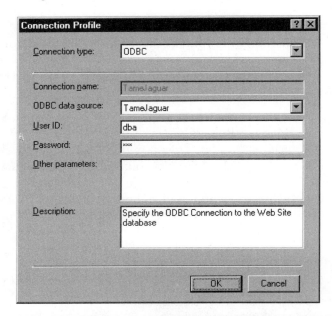

**Figure 8.10
PowerDynamo connection
profile properties**

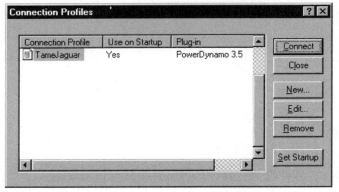

**Figure 8.11
PowerDynamo
connection profiles**

Now click on the Connect button to connect Sybase Central to the PowerDynamo web site. Because this is the first time that the web site is being accessed, there will not be a web site stored in the database. Sybase Central will prompt you to create the web site. Click the Yes button to create the web site tables and import the PowerDynamo system files. As the web site is created, Sybase Central will prompt you for the name of the root folder. This is the main folder for the web site from which all resources and subdirectories that will be available as part of the web site will be placed. The default name for the folder is Site. Once the web site is created and all the system files are imported, the PowerDynamo site setup is nearly complete and it can be managed through the Sybase Central application. Note that both the database and file deployment options manage the web site using a root folder and subdirectories that are under the root folder.

Figure 8.12 illustrates the PowerDynamo web site in the Sybase Central application. Notice the Site folder and the system and utils subdirectories. The system subdirectory contains all the system files and scripts that PowerDynamo needs to run the site. In general the system files and scripts should not be changed; however, there will be some exceptions. All application-specific files for the web site should be placed in the Site folder or in a separate subdirectory under the Site folder. Application-specific files should not be placed in the systems or the utils folder.

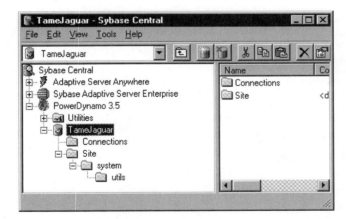

Figure 8.12
The PowerDynamo web site

8.13.2 Adding a mapping

Before the PowerDynamo web site can be accessed from a web server, it needs to have a mapping. The URL prefix specified in the mapping is used in the URL sent from the web browser or another web server to tell PowerDynamo which web site the request is meant for. The URL was explained in the sections 8.4 and 8.10.

When the web server receives an HTTP request, the server examines the URL to determine how to handle the request. The URL lets the web server know that the request should be passed on to PowerDynamo through the URL prefix, which is specified in the mapping. The PowerDynamo mapping name is placed after the host and port portion of the URL and before the path and file name portion of the URL as shown below:

protocol://host {:port}/PowerDynamo_Mapping/path/file_name

To add a mapping to a web site, click on the Configuration folder located under the Utilities folder for PowerDynamo. The available configuration utilities for PowerDynamo are listed as treeview items as illustrated in figure 8.13. Choose the Mappings folder to display all the mappings that are already set up for other PowerDynamo web sites. Now, click on the Add Mapping utility. The dialog shown in figure 8.14 will open.

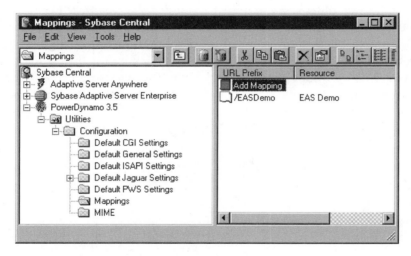

Figure 8.13   Creating a PowerDynamo mapping

In the URL prefix field, enter the name that will be used in the URL to access the PowerDynamo web site. The name must be prefixed with a backslash (/) as shown in figure 8.14. Once the mapping is created, a PowerDynamo web site that is running locally through the Personal Web Server with an HTML page named index.htm can be accessed from a web browser with the following URL:

http://localhost/safari/index.htm

The site type determines how the documents in the web site that the URL prefix points to are stored. The options are:

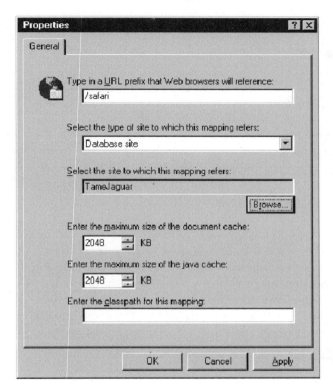

Figure 8.14
The PowerDynamo
mapping properties

- Database site: The documents are stored in a database and templates/scripts are executed.

- Dynamic file site: The documents are stored on disk and templates/scripts are executed.

- Static file site: The documents are stored on disk and templates/scripts are not executed.

The site location is where the name of the connection profile for the web site that is deployed to a database is specified. For the web site that is deployed using files, the site location is the path to the root directory of the site. The site location field is grayed out indicating that it is not editable; however, the field is editable and is required for the mapping to work.

The document cache size and the Java cache size settings indicate the maximum amount of memory that PowerDynamo should reserve for the document and Java caches respectively. The Java classpath is used to specify the class path for class files that are stored in the database.

> **TIP** In order for a new mapping to be recognized the web server/PowerDynamo must be stopped and restarted.

8.14 How do I configure a web server to use PowerDynamo?

PowerDynamo is a dynamic page server, it is not a web server. Once the PowerDynamo web site is set up, a web server must be configured to use PowerDynamo so that the web site is available over the Web. The Personal Web Server (PWS), which ships with EAServer, is automatically configured to use PowerDynamo. The PWS can be started from Sybase Central by clicking on the PWS icon under the Utilities folder for PowerDynamo.

Any web server that supports CGI, Win-CGI, ISAPI, or NSAPI can be configured to use PowerDynamo. The easiest way to configure the web server to use PowerDynamo is to install the web server before installing PowerDynamo. During the installation of PowerDynamo, the setup routine will detect the presence of the web server, edit the system path to include the PowerDynamo DLLs, and configure the web server automatically. Check out the PowerDynamo User's Guide for more information on how to configure CGI, Win-CGI, ISAPI, and NSAPI web servers.

> **TIP** When deploying a PowerDynamo web application, the web server and the PowerDynamo server must *always* be installed on the same machine.

8.15 How does a web server know to use PowerDynamo?

From a technical point of view, the web server receives a URL from a web browser or web server like the one listed below. The request is forwarded to PowerDynamo through either CGI, ISAPI, or NSAPI:

http://www.MySite.com/safari/StartPage.stm

The URL is initially sent as an HTTP request to the web server listening on port 80 that is on the machine specified by the address www.MySite.com. The web server, which is configured to use PowerDynamo, invokes the appropriate PowerDynamo ISAPI, NSAPI, or CGI program and sends the rest of the URL request to PowerDynamo. The URL prefix that corresponds to the mapping, in this case, */safari*, determines which PowerDynamo Web site gets the request (there could be more than one). The request that is passed to PowerDynamo is the path and name of the resource, which in this example is StartPage.stm. PowerDynamo looks for this document in the root folder and executes the document. The generated HTML page is returned to the web server.

The URL that the web browser or web server sends must specify the appropriate ISAPI, NSAPI, or CGI program as part of the URL. Which one and how this is done depends on the web server and the extensions that are being used. Web servers that use CGI have an executable directory where CGI programs are kept. This directory has an alias, typically, /cgi-bin, that can be used as part of the URL prefix. A URL call for PowerDynamo using CGI would look something like this:

http://www.MySite.com/cgi-bin/dycgi03.exe/safari/StartPage.stm

The dycgi03.exe file is the CGI program provided with PowerDynamo so that it can interface with a web server using CGI. In order for a web site to interface with PowerDynamo through CGI, the CGI Helper must also be running.

In order to make a call to PowerDynamo through ISAPI, the URL would look like this:

http://www.MySite.com/Scripts/dyisa03.dll/safari/StartPage.stm

The dyisa03.dll file is provided with PowerDynamo so that it can interface with a web server using ISAPI, and is usually placed in an executable directory with an alias, typically Scripts. An ISAPI filter can be used to hide the /Scripts/dyisa03.dll part of the URL, making it easier to call PowerDynamo. NSAPI is similar to ISAPI and also has a way to mask the internal process of routing the request to PowerDynamo from the web server.

8.16 *What is a PowerDynamo template?*

PowerDynamo templates are text files that are used to build the dynamic web site. PowerDynamo templates provide the simplicity of tag-based page design with the power and extensibility of the DynaScript language. Templates often have the file extension .stm.

A PowerDynamo template can contain one or more of the following:

- Static HTML
- Dynamo tags
- DynaScript

The static HTML is always presented to the client the same way each time the page is displayed, because it is sent without being changed by the PowerDynamo server. The Dynamo tags and the DynaScript are interpreted and run on the Power-Dynamo server before anything is sent to the client. The results of the scripts are used to generate the dynamic portion of the HTML page.

Templates often contain static HTML tags that define the basic layout of the page. The script on the template typically uses user input to run queries against a database or call components. The outcome of the queries and components is merged with the static HTML to form a completed HTML page.

8.17 What is a Dynamo tag?

Dynamo tags, like HTML tags, are used to create web documents. The difference between Dynamo tags and HTML tags is that the Dynamo tags are processed on the server by PowerDynamo, while HTML tags are processed on the client by the browser. Dynamo tags allow some functionality to be built into the web site without using DynaScript. There are several PowerDynamo tags including the following:

- <!--SQL-->
- <!--SCRIPT-->
- <!--INCLUDE-->
- <!--COMPONENT-->

Each Dynamo tag is embedded within an HTML comment, so they start with <!-- and end with a -->. The tag that is most commonly used is the SCRIPT tag, which is used to embed DynaScript in a template or script file. Most Dynamo tags have scripting equivalents, so some tasks can be accomplished with either a tag or a script. For example, the CreateComponent method on the java object can be used in place of the COMPONENT tag to access Jaguar components. The scripts are much more flexible than the tags. For more information on Dynamo tags, see the PowerDynamo User's Guide.

8.18 What is DynaScript?

DynaScript is PowerDynamo's server-side scripting language. It is a superset of ECMAScript, which is the standard that JavaScript is based on. As a result, much of the syntax is similar to JavaScript. This allows developers familiar with HTML and JavaScript to become proficient in writing PowerDynamo web sites very quickly.

DynaScript is used to write business logic, access components, and access data in a database. DynaScript is either embedded in a template (.stm) or stored in a separate script file (.ssc). Scripts can be written so that they generate an entire document including the HTML tags, or they can be combined with static HTML in a template to form a dynamic HTML document. Placing common scripts in a separate file allows the file to be included in other scripts or templates, making the code reusable throughout the site.

DynaScript is a language with its own set of literals, variables, expressions, statements, operators, functions, and objects. Some nuances of the DynaScript language include:

- script must be written within the SCRIPT tags
- language is case-sensitive
- variables do not need to be declared
- object-oriented, so developers can create their own objects

There are several predefined objects supported by DynaScript that make it easier to use to develop a web site. These objects provide important functionality such as session management, document redirection, and access to Java objects and Jaguar components. Some of the more common predefined objects include the following:

- document object
- java object
- session object
- site object

It is beyond the scope of this book to delve into all the nuances of DynaScript syntax and programming. Instead, this book will focus on the basics of generating dynamic HTML and how to access Jaguar components from a template script. Check out the PowerDynamo Reference for additional information.

NOTE   For those familiar with PowerSite, it has its own object model that is converted at deployment time into PowerDynamo syntax. This book will stick to using the PowerDynamo syntax as we are not directly covering the PowerSite IDE. PowerSite is a complete web application development tool and its scope lies outside of an advanced Jaguar book.

8.19 How do I create a PowerDynamo template?

PowerDynamo ships with Sybase Central, which is the management tool for PowerDynamo web sites. Sybase Central provides a basic interface for developing a template. In addition to the Sybase Central tool, PowerDynamo applications can be built with Sybase's PowerSite, a team-based web application development tool, which is fully integrated with the PowerDynamo product and can deploy web resources directly to the web site. At this point we will focus on Sybase Central and build a simple template.

In order to add a template to our web site, we need to open Sybase Central and connect to our PowerDynamo application through the connection profile. Click on the Site folder, which may be named differently depending on the name chosen for the root folder when the web site was connected for the first time. The right panel will display the utilities available for the web site as shown in figure 8.15. Select Add Template to open the New Template wizard.

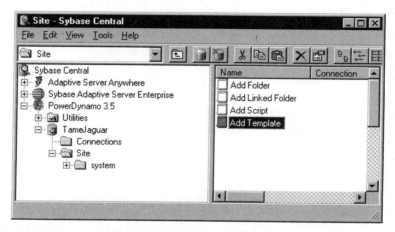

Figure 8.15   Add a template to PowerDynamo site

Figure 8.16   Editing the template in Sybase Central

The New Template wizard will prompt you for the name of the template. The wizard will also prompt you for information on which PowerDynamo database connection to use and what SQL query (if any) will be added to the template. (Because we will not be accessing data from this page, just accept the defaults.) Eventually you will arrive at a dialog where you can create an XML or HTML document. Choose HTML and click the Next button, and on the next dialog accept the default HTML document and then click the Finish button. After the wizard is finished, the Script editor will open with some basic HTML tags for a simple page. After some slight modifications, we have the page shown in figure 8.16. At this point we are building a simple HTML page without any special Dynamo tags or scripts.

Figure 8.17
Saving the template in
Sybase Central

Once the template changes are finished, we need to save the file. Using the File | Save menu option will prompt you to save the template as a file outside of the web site. When you want the changes to be effective in the web site, click the Save to Database toolbar button as pictured in figure 8.17 or the File | Save to Database menu option. Once the template is saved we will be able to see the file under the Site folder as part of the web site.

This file is now accessible by a web browser using the URL:

http://localhost/safari/StartPage.htm

Before running this test, be sure to start the Personal web Server.

8.20 *How do I turn off the directory listing?*

When a URL is sent to a web server and the name of the file or resource is not specified, the web server must determine which document to return to satisfy the request. The default document is the document that the web server displays when a document is not specified as part of the URL request.

When PowerDynamo uses the database to house the web site and no document is specified, the script Site/system/contview.ssc is run. This script is a system script, which is imported into the site when it is first created. The contview.ssc script will list all of the documents in the directory that is specified in the URL (or in the root directory if no directory is specified). For example, let's run the PowerDynamo site that we just created by typing the following URL in the browser:

http://localhost/safari

This URL will bring up the directory listing for the Site folder as shown in figure 8.18. In a web site, we typically do not want to show the user the listing of the directory. In order to turn this off, we need to make some changes to one of PowerDynamo's system files.

Figure 8.18
Directory listing of a
PowerDynamo site

One of the system files imported into the PowerDynamo web site is the Site/ system/autoexec.ssc script, which is automatically run when the web server is started. The autoexec.ssc file is used to initialize the PowerDynamo web site. One of the options that is set is the handling of requests for a directory. This is done with the site object. The site object in PowerDynamo is used to manage the web site. The OnEvent method of the site object is used to add an event handler to the web site. The Get event of the Directory item is triggered each time a directory is requested instead of a document, image, or some other resource. In the autoexec.ssc file, find the following line of script and remove it. You can do this by commenting out the line by prefixing it with a //:

```
site.OnEvent('Directory', 'Get', '', '', 'contview.ssc');
```

After making a change to the autoexec.ssc script, remember that the web server must be restarted before the changes take effect. At this point, trying to access the web site without specifying a document will result in a file-not-found error as shown in figure 8.19. In order to correct, this we will need to specify a default document.

Before moving on, it is important to point out that turning off the directory listing for PowerDynamo does not affect the web server itself. In order to handle a

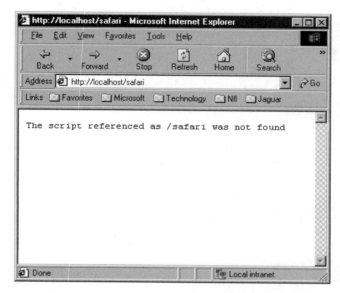

Figure 8.19
File-not-found error after
turning off directory listing

URL that does not specify a PowerDynamo mapping (http://www.MySite.com), the directory listing option will need to be turned off at the web server as well. How this is done depends on the web server.

8.21 *How do I set the default document?*

When a URL that does not specify a document or some other web resource is sent to PowerDynamo, the script contview.ssc is run. This script will display the file listing of the directory that is specified in the URL. In order to replace the directory listing with a default document, we need to change the autoexec.ssc file.

In the autoexec.ssc file, find the line shown below. If you are following along with this chapter, it is commented out:

```
site.OnEvent('Directory', 'Get', '', '', 'contview.ssc');
```

Replace the contview.ssc file name with the name of a default script or document, including the directory relative to the Site folder. An example is shown below:

```
site.OnEvent('Directory', 'Get', '', '', '/default.ssc');
```

Using a script file allows the default document page to be changed without changing the autoexec.ssc file. Therefore, stopping and restarting the web server will not be required. An example of the default document is listed below:

```
<!--SCRIPT
document.redirect="/safari/StartPage.stm";
-->
```

After making a change to the autoexec.ssc script, remember that the web server must be restarted before the changes take effect. At this point, trying to access the web site without specifying a document will result in the default document being returned to the web browser. This web document could be another script that generates an HTML page as well as a PowerDynamo template. In our example, let's run the Power-Dynamo site that we just created by typing the following URL in the browser:

http://localhost/safari

This URL will cause PowerDynamo to execute our default script, which will redirect the browser to the StartPage.stm template and return the generated HTML page as shown in figure 8.20.

Figure 8.20
StartPage.stm in a browser

Before moving on, it is important to point out that setting the default document for PowerDynamo does not specify the default document that the web server will return when only the domain name or IP address is specified. In order to handle a URL that does not specify a PowerDynamo mapping (http://www.MySite.com) the default document will need to be handled at the web server as well. How this is done depends on the web server.

TIP   With IIS, we can use ASP to set up the default document on the web server to redirect the web request to our PowerDynamo web site. This will allow a web browser to send requests to our PowerDynamo web site using just the web server domain name or address (http://www.MySite.com).

8.22 How do I add DynaScript to a template?

DynaScript is added to a template using the SCRIPT tag. All the script is then written between the <!--SCRIPT and --> tags. A simple example is shown below:

```
<HTML>
<TITLE>HelloWorld.stm</TITLE>
<BODY>
<!--SCRIPT
   document.Write( "<H1>Hello world</H1>" );
-->
</BODY>
</HTML>
```

The script in the example uses the document object to access the document being generated. The Write method of the document object is used to add the string "<H1>Hello World</H1>" to the document itself. The string that is added is a combination of HTML tags and text that will be sent to the web browser as follows:

```
<HTML>
<TITLE>HelloWorld.stm</TITLE>
<BODY>
<H1>Hello world</H1>
</BODY>
</HTML>
```

Notice that the actual script is not sent to the web browser. It is executed on the PowerDynamo server and the output is applied to the document.

8.23 How do I create a PowerDynamo script?

A PowerDynamo script is a file that contains only DynaScript. By placing common logic, functions, and class definitions into a separate script file, the code is reusable between templates because the script file can be imported. Scripts often have the file extension .ssc.

In order to add a script to our web site, we need to open Sybase Central and connect to our PowerDynamo application through the Connection Profile. Click on the Site folder, which may be named differently depending on the name chosen for the root folder when the web site was connected to for the first time. The right panel will display the utilities available for the web site. Select Add Script icon to open the New Script wizard. Type the name and the description of the script.

The script will be saved and placed in the web site under the Site folder. Open the script by double-clicking on it in Sybase Central. All the logic is written between the <--SCRIPT and --> tags. In this example, we will create a separate script file, GetDate.ssc, to get today's date. The code is shown below:

```
<!--SCRIPT GetDate.ssc
function getTodayDate()
{
    myDate = new Date();
    iMonth = myDate.getMonth();
    iDate = myDate.getDate();
    iYear = myDate.getFullYear();
    switch (iMonth) {
    case 0:
        sMonth = "January";
        break;
    case 1:
        sMonth = "February";
        break;
    case 2:
        sMonth = "March";
        break;
    case 3:
        sMonth = "April";
        break;
    case 4:
        sMonth = "May";
        break;
    case 5:
        sMonth = "June";
        break;
    case 6:
        sMonth = "July";
        break;
    case 7:
        sMonth = "August";
        break;
    case 8:
        sMonth = "September";
        break;
    case 9:
        sMonth = "October";
        break;
    case 10:
        sMonth = "November";
        break;
    case 11:
        sMonth = "December";
        break;
    }
    CurrentDate = sMonth + " " + iDate + ", " + iYear;

    return CurrentDate;
}

-->
```

This script can now be used in any template to display the current date.

8.24 How do I import a script into the template?

If we want to import the script GetDate.ssc we can add a SCRIPT tag to a template and use the import function. The import function takes a string argument that contains the name of the script file that is being imported. The script file needs to have the path specified in relation to the root of the web site. For the GetDate.ssc file which is in the root directory just prefix the name of the file with a / as shown in the code sample below:

```
<HTML>
<TITLE>StartPage.stm</TITLE>
<BODY>
<!--SCRIPT
// Import scripts
import('/getdate.ssc');
-->

<H1>Taming Jaguar</H1>
<P>
Welcome to the Safari Web Site - today is
<!--SCRIPT
// Write out the data
document.writeln(getTodayDate());
-->

</BODY>
</HTML>
```

The function getTodayDate can now be called from other scripts in the template.

8.25 How are page parameters passed?

A web application is built by passing information between the web client and the web server and also between HTML pages. This information can be user input from an HTML form or a hyperlink. This information can also be data previously collected and being forwarded to the new page due to the stateless nature of the Web.

Any information from the web browser is sent to the web server as part of the URL when a hyperlink (link) or a button on a form is clicked by the user. The address and the web resource portion of the URL described in section 8.4, "What is a URL," are separated from the arguments being passed to the page by a question mark to signify that a list of values follows. The arguments are listed in name/value pairs and are separated by an ampersand when passing more than one. The name/value pairs are in the format name=value where the argument name is followed by an "=" sign and the value being passed. The URL syntax is shown below:

http://www.MySite.com/Dynamo_Mapping/
template-name?arg1=value1&arg2=value2

This URL can be sent from an HTML *form* or *anchor* tag, so let's quickly examine these. If you are interested in learning more about these HTML tags and others, we recommend checking out additional HTML resources like *HTML the Definitive Guide,* published by O'Reilly.

The HTML form tag is the most common way to send requests to a web server. It allows the user to enter information in a variety of formats that are read by the browser and appended to the end of the URL automatically. The HTML form is delimited by the tags <FORM> and </FORM>. Everything in between the tags is considered part of the form. Anything outside the form tags will be ignored when the form is submitted.

The form tag has several attributes but the ACTION and METHOD are the most important. They determine the address and resource that will receive the request and how the request will be sent as described in table 8.2.

Table 8.2   FORM attributes

Attribute	Description
ACTION	This is the address and resource to send the URL to when the user submits the form.
METHOD	This specifies the way the request is sent. The valid values are GET and POST.

The GET and POST values of the METHOD attribute define how the data on the form is sent from the web browser to the web server and from the web server to the CGI, ISAPI, or NSAPI program. The GET method sends information in the URL, while the POST method passes data as a stream. The GET method has a limit as to the number of characters that can be sent, determined by the browser being used. This can be a problem with large forms and TEXTAREA tags (similar to multiline edit). The POST method does not have this limitation and is the preferred means of passing information. In addition to the limit on the size of the input that can be sent, GET and POST require different methods of reading in the data by the CGI program. However, PowerDynamo will automatically handle reading the input from the form based on the METHOD and pass the values to the template.

Another important aspect on passing information from an HTML form is that the GET value for the METHOD attribute passes information so that it can be seen in the address field of the browser, while the POST value does not as shown in figures 8.21 and 8.22. Although both the GET and POST methods pass the same information, they pass it differently. This is important when passing sensitive information like passwords or hidden information so that the values cannot be seen in the browser. The information, however, is not encrypted when passed over the network as this requires a secure socket using the Secure Socket Layer (SSL).

Figure 8.21 Address field of browser using the GET method

Figure 8.22 Address field of browser using the POST method

An example of a simple HTML form is an HTML page that requests a user ID and a password from the user. When the user clicks on the Submit button, the URL specified in the ACTION attribute is sent to the web server along with the data in the INPUT tags. Here is the template StartPage.stm, which has an HTML form tag added to it that collects the UserID and password of the user.

```
<HTML>
<TITLE>StartPage.stm</TITLE>
<BODY>
<!--SCRIPT
// Import scripts
import('/getdate.ssc');
-->

<H1>Taming Jaguar</H1>
<P>
Welcome to the Safari Web Site - today is
<!--SCRIPT
// Write out the date
document.writeln(getTodayDate());
-->

<P>
<FORM ACTION="_GetLogonParams.stm" METHOD=GET>
<TABLE>
<TR>
    <TD align=right>UserID:</TD>
    <TD align=left><INPUT TYPE=text NAME=UserID></TD>
</TR>
```

```
<TR>
    <TD align=right>Password:</TD>
    <TD align=left><INPUT TYPE=password NAME=PWD></TD>
</TR>
<TR>
    <TD align=center colspan=2><INPUT TYPE=submit VALUE=Logon></TD>
</TR>
</TABLE>
</FORM>

</BODY>
</HT\ML>
```

The HTML page is displayed in the browser as shown in figure 8.23. Once the user types in a user ID and password and clicks the Submit button, the following URL is generated and sent to the web server:

> http://localhost/safari/_GetLogonParams.stm?UserID=MIKE&PWD=PASSWORD

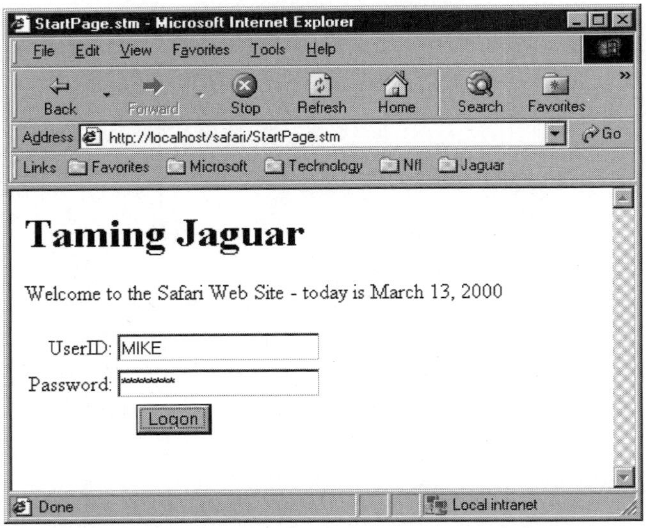

Figure 8.23
An HTML form in a browser

Notice that the argument names match the INPUT tag NAME attributes used in the HTML form. The INPUT tag is the basic building block of an HTML form. The INPUT tag specifies what elements make up the form. Several attributes of the INPUT tag are listed in table 8.3.

Table 8.3   Input tag attributes

Attribute	Description
CHECKED	Used by radio button and check box inputs to determine if the object is selected.
MAXLENGTH	Used by the text input to limit the number of characters that are accepted in the field.
NAME	Identifies the argument name that the name/value pair should be passed as.
SIZE	Used by the text input to determine the width of the field shown.
TYPE	Specifies the type of input object to be displayed.
VALUE	The initial value of the input (or for buttons the name shown on the button face).

The INPUT tag is quite versatile, allowing for several different input types. The type of input displayed is specified using the TYPE attribute. Valid values for the TYPE attribute of the INPUT tag are shown in table 8.4.

Table 8.4   Values for the TYPE attribute

Value	Description
TEXT	A single line edit field.
CHECKBOX	A checkbox.
RADIO	A radio button.
PASSWORD	A single line edit field, which hides each character the user types with a *.
HIDDEN	A hidden text field.
SUBMIT	The Submit button, which sends the URL specified by the action to the web server.
RESET	The Reset button, which clears all the elements in a form.
BUTTON	Creates a custom button.
IMAGE	Same as the Submit button, but an image can be used in place of the button.
FILE	A single-line edit that accepts a file name and uploads the actual file. Requires the FORM attribute ENCTYPE= "multipart/form-data".

The Submit button is required to trigger the action specified by the form. When the Submit button is clicked, the browser collects all the values from the form elements and appends them to the URL before sending the request to the web server. In addition to the INPUT tag, there is the text area (<TEXTAREA>) tag and the select (<SELECT>) tag. The text area tag is used to display a multiline edit field. The select tag is used with the option (<OPTION>) tag to create a drop down list.

The anchor tag <A> is used to create hyperlinks in an HTML document. These links can direct the browser to other portions of the same document or to other documents, images, or application programs that can reside on both the local machine or on a remote machine. Hyperlinks, defined by the anchor tag, are the basic way a user navigates around the web. HTML documents contain links to other documents, usually related to the information on the current page. The HTML page that contains the hyperlink is considered the source document. The document that is referenced by the URL in the anchor tag is the target document. The anchor tag has several attributes that can be used to control how the link will work as shown in table 8.5.

Table 8.5   Anchor tag attributes

Attribute	Description
HREF	Used to specify the URL of the target document.
NAME	Used to name a section of the current document as a hyperlink target so that other links can point to it.
TARGET	Used to direct the browser to display the target document in a specific frame.

The text between the <A> and </A> tags defines the text area that a user may click on to jump to the new URL or subsection. Most browsers show this text in a different color and underline it. A code sample of a hyperlink is shown below:

```
<HTML>
<TITLE>Sample.stm</TITLE>
<BODY>
<H1>Taming Jaguar</H1>
<H2>Sample<H2>
<P>
<A HREF="HelloWorld.stm">Go to HelloWorld</A>
</BODY>
</HTML>
```

This is displayed in a browser as shown in Figure 8.24.

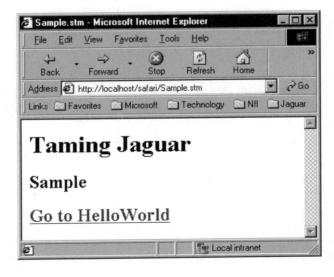

Figure 8.24
The Anchor tag in a browser

An anchor tag can also specify an image in between the <A> and </A> tags. This image is now a link that the user can click on to jump to another URL. The code sample for an anchor tag as an image is shown below:

```
<A HREF="HelloWorld.stm"><IMG SRC="JagHead.jpg" BORDER=0></A>
```

The NAME attribute is used to define a target for a hyperlink. The HREF attribute is used to define the URL of the new resource. The NAME and HREF attributes should not be used in the same tag. The URL can specify an absolute address or a relative address. An absolute address contains the protocol, domain name of the server and resource. The relative address is based off of the location of the current document, usually the HTML directory on the web server.

Here is an example of an anchor tag that uses an absolute address to point to a document on another web site:

```
<A HREF="http://www.sybase.com">Sybase Inc.</A>
```

An anchor tag that references a document on the same server could use a relative address as shown below:

```
<A HREF="about.stm">About Taming Jaguar</A>
```

The HREF in the example above will look for the about.stm page in the same directory that the current document was found. This makes HTML page management easier.

To include arguments in an anchor tag, they must be hard-coded onto the end of the URL using the same syntax as the <FORM> URL. The URL can be dynamically created in a Dynamo script. To add arguments to the URL, add a "?" after the document name followed by the arguments in name/value pair format. The argument values are listed one after the other and are separated by an ampersand (&) as shown below:

```
<A HREF="_GetLogonParams.stm?UserID=MIKE&PWD=PASSWORD">Logon</A>
```

In order to build this dynamically, the HTML must be constructed using Dyna-Script and written out to the document as shown in the code sample below:

```
<!--SCRIPT

// Get the values to be passed in Anchor Tag
UserName = "MIKE";
PassWord="PASSWORD";

// Build Anchor Link
Link='_GetLogonParams.stm?UserID=' + UserName + '&PWD=' + PassWord

// Write Anchor tag to document
document.writeln('<A HREF="' + Link + '">Logon</A>');

-->
```

This anchor tag will call the _GetLogonParams.stm page passing in the arguments UserID and PWD. When passing an anchor tag with information, it is important to note that the URL can be seen in the address field of the browser. This is similar to the GET method.

8.26 *How are page parameters received?*

The page parameters that are passed into a template can be accessed directly in HTML or in a script through the document object. The name of each page parameter is determined by the name of the argument passed in through the URL. The StartPage.stm HTML FORM will pass a URL to the web server as shown below after the user types in the information and clicks on the Submit button:

http://localhost/safari/_GetLogonParams.stm?UserID=MIKE&PWD=PASSWORD

The page parameters are named UserID and PWD with the values MIKE and PASSWORD respectively.

The value of a page parameter can be directly inserted into the HTML portion of a document by preceding the name of the page parameter with a dollar sign. For example, to show the UserID and Password passed to the _GetLogonParams page from the StartPage.stm form, we can code the following:

```
<HTML>
<TITLE>_GetLogonParams.stm</TITLE>
<BODY>
<P>
The UserID passed in is $UserID;
<BR>
The Password passed in is $PWD;
</BODY>
</HTML>
```

This template,—when returned to the browser after typing in a UserID of MIKE and a password of PASSWORD in the form supplied by the StartPage.stm—generates the output illustrated in figure 8.25.

Page parameters are accessed inside scripts through a property of the document object. The syntax to access a page parameter from the document property is as follows:

```
document.value.variable
```

The variable portion of the syntax is where the name of the page parameter is specified. This property of the document object is read-only. The following code sample

Figure 8.25   Displaying page parameters

illustrates how to use the document object to get the user input of UserID and PWD that were passed into the template. The code sample also illustrates how to write them out to the document:

```
<HTML>
<TITLE>_GetLogonParams.stm</TITLE>
<BODY>
<P>
<!--SCRIPT
var UserName= document.value.UserID;
var Password = document.value.PWD;

document.writeln('The UserID passed in is ' + UserName);
document.writeln('<BR>');
document.writeln('The Passoword passed in is ' + Password);

-->
</BODY>
</HTML>
```

This template will result in the same browser output as shown in figure 8.25. Sometimes a template that expects page parameters that are not passed in can cause errors when it attempts to access them. For example, type the following URL in a web browser:

http://localhost/safari/_GetLogonParams.stm

This will ask PowerDynamo to run the _GetLogonParams.stm template without passing in any page parameters. When this happens, the document.value.variable property is undefined and generates a web page with errors as shown in figure 8.26.

To avoid any errors or references to undefined variables, we can check for the existence of the page parameter first. Note the following code sample:

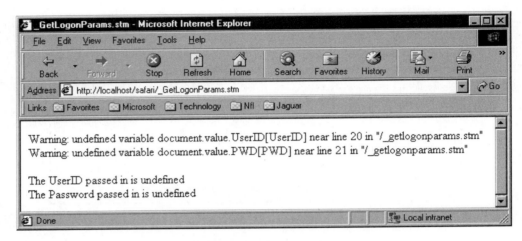

Figure 8.26 Error accessing undefined page parameters

```
// Check for UserID page parameter
if (exists(document.value.UserID)) {
   UserName= document.value.UserID;
}
else {
   UserName= "";
}

// Check for PWD page parameter
if (exists(document.value.PWD)) {
   Password= document.value.PWD;
}
else {
   Password= "";

}
```

8.27 How can I set URL page parameter case-sensitivity?

While DynaScript is case-sensitive, the page parameters passed in through the URL that PowerDynamo accepts can have case-sensitivity turned on and off. Under the PowerDynamo Utilities folder, click on the Configuration folder and highlight the Default General Settings folder. One of the available settings is "URL arguments case sensitive." The value can be set to *yes* to have case-sensitivity turned on and set to *no* to have case-sensitivity turned off.

For example, given the following code and a page parameter passed in as PWD=PASSWORD, we will get two different results based on the value of this PowerDynamo setting.

```
document.writeln('<P>');
document.writeln('The Password passed in is ' + document.value.PWD);
document.writeln('<BR>');
document.writeln('The Password passed in is ' + document.value.pwd);
```

When case-sensitivity is turned on, the page parameter document.value.pwd is considered undefined and we get the following result:

```
The Password passed in is PASSWORD
The Password passed in is undefined
```

When case-sensitivity is turned off, the page parameter document.value.pwd is considered the same as the page parameter document.value.PWD and we get the following result:

```
The Password passed in is PASSWORD
The Password passed in is PASSWORD
```

8.28 *How do I deal with special characters in a URL?*

When passing data back and forth in a URL, you will probably run across some characters that need to be handled specially in order to successfully pass them from a web browser to the web server. Some of these characters include the space character, colon, semicolon, backslash, equal sign, and double quote. These characters need to be encoded in a URL using their ASCII hexadecimal equivalents, prefixed by a % sign. For example, a space character is ASCII 20, so all space characters in a URL should be replaced with a %20.

PowerDynamo provides two system functions to handle encoding and decoding a URL. These are the escape and unescape functions. The escape function is used to encode special characters so they can be used in URLs. The unescape function is used to decode special characters from URLs.

So for example if I wanted to pass the value "TEST = 1:TEST% as part of my URL, I would code something like the following:

```
<!--SCRIPT

// Get the values to be passed in Anchor Tag
Value = escape('"TEST = 1:TEST%');

// Build Anchor Link
Link='URLTest.stm?URLArg=' + Value;

// Write Anchor tag to document
document.writeln('<A HREF="' + Link + '">Click to Send URL</A>');

-->
```

The value returned by the escape function and passed in the URL would be encoded with the following %22TEST%20%3d%201%3aTEST%25.

TIP	Only use *escape* on the value that you are trying to pass and not on the entire URL. Otherwise, the escape character will encode parts of the URL that should not be encoded, like the // in http:// or the "?" that separates the address and resource name from the page parameters.

8.29 *How are multiple values passed using the multiple SELECT tag or checkbox?*

When page parameters are passed from an HTML page to the web server, and ultimately, to PowerDynamo, the name of the page parameter often appears only once as a name/value pair in the URL. We have seen this in previous examples where we have looked at an HTML form used to log in to a web site. The form contains an input tag with the name UserID and another with the name PWD. Sometimes, however, the name of a page parameter can appear multiple times in an HTML form, which will show up as several name/value pairs with the same name in the URL as well. An example of this is seen when trying to collect information with a checkbox input tag or a multiple select statement.

An HTML form can be used to collect information with a checkbox or multiple select that indicates that more than one option applies for a given parameter. For example, if we were collecting information on the pets that visitors to our web site had, we might present a list of animals probably generated from a result set that was retrieved from a database. Each specific animal would have a unique ID and a description. Because some users might have more than one type of animal as a pet, we would need to allow them to enter more than one value. The HTML page below shows how this information could be collected with an HTML form and the checkbox input tag. Notice that each input tag has the same value for the NAME attribute, pets_id, but has a different value for the VALUE attribute associated with the unique pet ID stored in the database. This allows us to collect one or more pet ID values and store them in a table that associates pets with our web visitor. This technique is easier than generating a unique NAME attribute for each checkbox that is shown on the page, because managing the number of unique names for a large set of data could be cumbersome, especially when trying to process the page parameters in the script or template the HTML form calls.

```
<HTML>
<TITLE>CheckBox</TITLE>
<BODY>
<H1>Check all that apply</H1>
```

```
Which pets do you own?
<FORM ACTION=getmultivalue.stm METHOD=GET>
    <TABLE border=1>
        <TR>
        <TD>Select</TD>
        <TD>Pet</TD>
        </TR>

        <TR>
        <TD><INPUT TYPE=checkbox NAME=pets_id VALUE=1 ></TD>
        <TD>Dog</TD>
        </TR>

        <TR>
        <TD><INPUT TYPE=checkbox NAME=pets_id VALUE=2 ></TD>
        <TD>Cat</TD>
        </TR>

        <TR>
        <TD><INPUT TYPE=checkbox NAME=pets_id VALUE=3 ></TD>
        <TD>Bunny</TD>
        </TR>

        <TR>
        <TD><INPUT TYPE=checkbox NAME=pets_id VALUE=4 ></TD>
        <TD>Iguana</TD>
        </TR>

        <TR>
        <TD colspan=2 align=center><INPUT TYPE=submit VALUE=OK></TD>
        </TR>
    </TABLE>
</FORM>
</BODY>
</HTML>
```

The code sample below shows an HTML page that uses a multiple select tag to do the same thing as the HTML page that uses the checkbox. With the select tag, there is only one NAME attribute associated with the tag so a multiple select tag will always pass back the values chosen with the same name in the URL.

```
<HTML>
<BODY>
<H1>Check all that apply</H1>
Which pets do you own?
<FORM ACTION=getmultivalue.stm METHOD=GET>
    <SELECT NAME=pets_id multiple>
        <OPTION VALUE=1>Dog
        <OPTION VALUE=2>Cat
        <OPTION VALUE=3>Bunny
        <OPTION VALUE=4>Iguana
    </SELECT>
    <BR>
```

```
    <INPUT TYPE=submit VALUE=OK>
</FORM>
</BODY>
</HTML>
```

The HTML page above produces the output in a browser as pictured in figure 8.27.

Figure 8.27
A multiple select tag

Once the user selects the appropriate choices and clicks the Submit button, the HTML form generates a URL as shown below:

http://localhost/safari/getmultivalue.stm?pets_id=1&pets_id=3

Because two pets were selected, the URL contains the name/value pair for pets_id twice.

8.30 How do I get the values from a multiple SELECT tag or checkbox?

When page parameters are passed into PowerDynamo, they are accessed through the document object. The document object has a value property that has a variable property defined for each page parameter with corresponding names. For details on this, see section 8.26, "How are page parameters received." However, when a name appears more than once in the URL, PowerDynamo handles this in the document.value.variable, which is similar to an array.

```
document.value.variable[i];
```

So if only one item is selected or there is only one value passed in with the same name, the value is held in document.value.variable. When two or more items are selected, the values are stored in the document.value.variable as document.value.variable[0], document.value.variable[1], and so on.

This is easier to see in an example. The following URL was generated by either the checkbox or multiple select HTML pages described in the previous question and shown below:

http://localhost/safari/getmultivalue.stm?pets_id=1&pets_id=3

We would have the following in our document object:

```
document.value.pets_id[0] = 1
document.value.pets_id[1] = 3
```

Although the way PowerDynamo uses the document.value.variable to hold multiple values looks like an array, there is no length property. Thus, it is easier to work with the page parameters if the contents are copied into a PowerDynamo Array object first. A script that contains a function that converts a page parameter into a PowerDynamo array is shown below:

```
<!--SCRIPT
function PageParam_Array(PageParam)
{
    // convert a page parameter into an array
    // expects a page parameter with multiple values
    PDArray = new Array();
    i = 0;

    if( typeof( PageParam ) == "object" ) {
        while( exists( PageParam[i] ) ) {
            PDArray[i] = PageParam[i];
            i++;
        }
    }
    else {
        PDArray[i] = PageParam;
    }

    return PDArray;
}

-->
```

The script is designed to handle page parameters that have only one value as well as those that contain several. The PowerDynamo template that expects multiple values for a given page parameter name can import the script and use the PowerDynamo array to manage the values. A sample template that uses the script is shown below:

```
<HTML>
<TITLE>Get Multi Value</TITLE>
<BODY>
<H1>Your selections:</H1>
<!--SCRIPT
  import ArrayHelper.ssc;

  if (exists(document.value.pets_id)) {
    myArray = PageParam_Array(document.value.pets_id)

    for(var i=0; i<myArray.length; i++) {
        document.writeln( "value[" + i + "] = " + myArray[i] );
        document.WriteLn( "<BR>");
    }
  }
  else {
    document.writeln( "Page parameter document.value.pets_id does not exist.");
  }
-->

</BODY>
</HTML>
```

8.31 *How do I redirect a document in PowerDynamo?*

When a browser asks for a particular web page, it may be necessary to redirect the request to another web page that it did not ask for to satisfy the request. In addition, an application may have a standard web page to handle error reporting to the user. As a script processes, it may need to redirect the client to the error page when it encounters a problem. The PowerDynamo document object has a redirect property that allows the script to specify the URL to which the current request should be directed.

```
document.redirect=URL_String
```

Continuing with the login example, we can implement a simple validation routine that checks to see if the UserID is equal to the password passed in from the HTML form. Based on the success or failure of the login attempt, the web browser is directed to the next appropriate page. The client, however, did not directly request the page that was received.

```
if (UserID==Password) {
    // valid logon
    document.redirect="HelloWorld.stm";
}
else {
    // invalid logon
    document.redirect="LogonError.stm";
}
```

The redirect will load and run the page specified after the current script and all the scripts on the current page have been processed. In order to get the current page to immediately direct the request to the new URL, use the exit statement after the redirect. The exit statement stops processing the current document from that point forward.

```
document.redirect="StartPage.stm";
exit;
```

Using PowerDynamo, the redirect property can be used to direct the user of the web site to any valid URL. This includes other web resources stored in a PowerDynamo web site, or any other web site. The redirect property can even be used to call Java servlets as shown below:

```
document.redirect="/servlet/HelloWorld";
exit;
```

9

Jaguar and PowerDynamo

This chapter covers

- PowerDynamo and Jaguar CTS integration
- Accessing Jaguar components from PowerDynamo
- Dealing with PowerDynamo as a Java client to Jaguar

In chapter 8, we discussed PowerDynamo's capabilities to deliver a dynamic web site. In this chapter, we will continue the discussion looking at how PowerDynamo and Jaguar CTS can be used together to provide a complete solution to building and running enterprise web applications.

9.1 How is PowerDynamo 3.5 integrated with Jaguar CTS 3.5?

In PowerDynamo 3.0x and Jaguar CTS 3.0x, you needed a separate web server to deploy a web application built with PowerDynamo. In release 3.5 of these products, the HTTP capabilities of Jaguar can be used to route requests to the PowerDynamo server. PowerDynamo, however, must still use the java object, or one of the other techniques discussed in this chapter to call Jaguar components.

NOTE   PowerDynamo *must* be installed on the same machine as the web server. Because Jaguar would serve in that capacity now, PowerDynamo must be installed on the same machine as the Jaguar CTS installation that is acting as the web server. When using another web server product instead of Jaguar CTS, PowerDynamo can be run on a separate machine from the Jaguar server.

PowerDynamo access through Jaguar can be enabled from the Dynamo tab on the Server Properties dialog in the Jaguar Manager by checking the Enable Dynamo execution option as shown in figure 9.1.

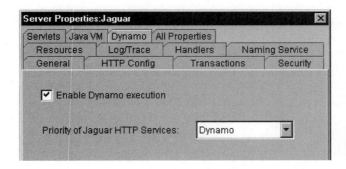

Figure 9.1
Enabling Dynamo execution from Jaguar

In addition to checking the Enable Dynamo option, you must modify either the system environment variables or the serverstart.bat file located in the %JAGAUR%\bin directory so that the Win32 directory under the PowerDynamo installation is in the PATH and the class03 directory is in the CLASSPATH. For example, if PowerDynamo were installed in D:\Program Files\Sybase, then the following directory should be placed in the PATH:

D:\Program Files\Sybase\PowerDynamo\win32

The serverstart.bat file would be modified as follows:

```
set PATH=.;%JDK_LATEST%\bin;%JAGUAR%\dll;D:\Program Files\Sybase\PowerDynamo\
    win32;%PATH%;
```

If PowerDynamo were installed in D:\Program Files\Sybase, then the following directory should be placed in the CLASSPATH:

D:\Program Files\Sybase\PowerDynamo\class03

The serverstart.bat file would be modified as follows:

```
CLASSPATH=.;%JAGUAR%\html\classes\powerjr.zip;
%JDK_LATEST%\lib\classes.zip;%JAGUAR%\html\classes\ldap.jar;
%JAGUAR%\html\classes\providerutil.jar;
%JAGUAR%\html\classes\jsdk.jar;
%JAGUAR%\html\classes\datawindow.jar;%JAGUAR%\java\classes;
%JAGUAR%\html\classes;
D:\Program Files\Sybase\PowerDynamo\class03;%CLASSPATH%
```

Note that Jaguar by default listens to HTTP requests on port 8080. A web browser would be able to access a PowerDynamo web site with a mapping of safari and a resource named StartPage.stm using the following URL:

http://localhost:8080/safari/StartPage.stm

In order to change the HTTP listener to listen on port 80, use the Jaguar Manager to change the Listener port property on an http listener. Note that there should not be any other web services running on the same machine as Jaguar CTS if this change is made because web servers listen for HTTP requests on port 80 by default, resulting in a conflict.

9.2 *How does PowerDynamo access Jaguar CTS?*

The PowerDynamo dynamic page server allows components executing on Jaguar to be made accessible through a web architecture. To do this, PowerDynamo is a client to Jaguar CTS calling methods on components and uses the results to generate dynamic web pages. Jaguar CTS supports IIOP and Open Client requests directly, and it also provides an interface to allow ActiveX clients to access Jaguar components. The PowerDynamo server can use any of these protocols to access Jaguar CTS components and invoke methods as shown in figure 9.2. PowerDynamo can access Jaguar through: Java (CORBA, EJB) ActiveX (COM,DCOM), and MASP (Methods As Stored Procedures).

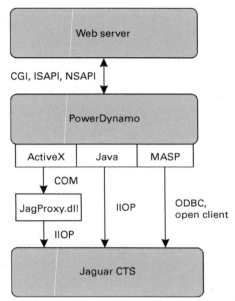

Figure 9.2
Overview of PowerDynamo access
to Jaguar CTS

PowerDynamo provides all of these options to allow developers the flexibility to use the techniques that best suit their needs and expertise. It also allows PowerDynamo to be used with other application servers.

NOTE   ActiveX clients rely on Microsoft's Distributed Component Object Model (DCOM) to access Jaguar components. DCOM is available on Microsoft operating systems. DCOM has also been ported to UNIX as well, but the authors have no experience with the UNIX implementations and cannot comment on how well DCOM/UNIX operates in production applications.

Depending on the protocol used to access a Jaguar component, PowerDynamo has several different options that can be utilized in DynaScript to invoke component methods. Table 9.1 summarizes them.

Table 9.1   PowerDynamo component access options

Access	Option
MASP	Dynamo SQL tag
MASP, Java, ActiveX	Dynamo COMPONENT tag
MASP	connection.CreateQuery
MASP	connection.CreateComponent

Access	Option
Java (CORBA)	java.CreateComponent
Java (EJB)	java.GetHomeInterface
ActiveX	CreateObject

NOTE   When PowerDynamo calls Jaguar components using MASP, only result sets can be returned.

PowerDynamo allows you to create instances of Java classes in scripts using the java object as shown in figure 9.3. The java object represents the Java class running in the JVM and allows scripts to use the instance of the class. Figure 9.4 illustrates how the java object allows PowerDynamo to access Jaguar CTS components through Java stubs as if it were a Java CORBA or Java EJB client. This book will focus on using the java object in Power-Dynamo, because Java works across all platforms, allows the greatest flexibility in the data types a component can accept and return, and uses IIOP to communicate with Jaguar.

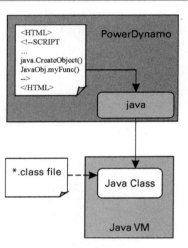

Figure 9.3   PowerDynamo accessing a Java class

9.3   *How do I configure PowerDynamo to use Jaguar CTS through Java?*

PowerDynamo can access Java classes including a CORBA ORB and Jaguar stubs through the java object. Before PowerDynamo can use Java classes to access Jaguar CTS, it must be properly configured.

The following list details the steps required to configure PowerDynamo to use Jaguar CTS:

1   Enable the Java VM.

2   Set the PATH.

3   Set the CLASSPATH.

4   Set up the Jaguar client.

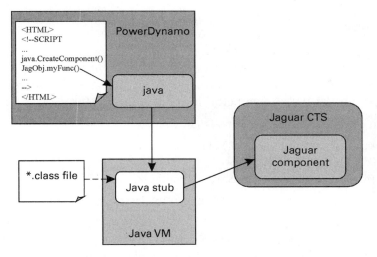

Figure 9.4   Accessing Jaguar through the java object

TIP   The Jaguar client (JagClient.exe) does not need to be installed and set up if PowerDynamo is running on the same machine as Jaguar CTS.

Before going into details on how to perform each step, it is important to point out that any changes made to the PowerDynamo server under the Utilities | Configuration folder are specific to the current machine. An administrator cannot use Sybase Central to log into a remote PowerDynamo site and change settings under the Configuration folder and expect them to be applied to the remote machine. All changes must be applied locally. Once the changes are made to the settings, they will not take effect until PowerDynamo has been stopped and restarted.

The first step is to enable the Java Virtual Machine (JVM). To set the JVM for PowerDynamo, use Sybase Central. Click on the Utilities folder under the Power-Dynamo icon. Then select the Default General Settings option under the Configuration folder and use the Java VM setting. Select File | Properties from the main menu (or double-click Java VM) to access the Configuration dialog.

PowerDynamo has the following Java VM support:

- None
- Microsoft Java VM
- Sun Java VM
- Sun Debug Java VM

In order for PowerDynamo to access Jaguar CTS through the java object, the Java VM must be set to the Sun Java VM. Note that PowerDynamo cannot use Java classes in a template or script if the Java VM is set to None.

The second step is to set the PATH system environment variable so that the proper JDK bin directory is available. To use the Sun VM that Sybase installs, place the bin directory for the JDK shown below in the system PATH variable:

C:\Program Files\Sybase\Shared\Sun\JDK11x\bin

The next step is to set the CLASSPATH system environment variable so that it points to the Java classes. To use the Sun Java classes that Sybase installs, place the following directory in the system CLASSPATH variable:

C:\Program Files\Sybase\Shared\Sun\JDK11x\lib\classes.zip

In addition to the Sun Java classes, the CLASSPATH must point to the location of the Jaguar stubs that are generated and compiled as Java classes (more information on stubs follows). The default location for the placement of Java stubs when PowerDynamo and Jaguar CTS are installed on the same machine is %JAGUAR%\html\classes. When PowerDynamo and Jaguar CTS are installed on separate machines, the Java stubs must be copied to the PowerDynamo machine so the location of the Java classes may differ. The base path to the stubs is the only directory that must be added to the CLASSPATH. The class files are actually located in the subdirectories that are under the base path. The subdirectories are named after the packages that each component is deployed to in Jaguar. These subdirectories do *not* need to be included in the CLASSPATH.

The final step is required only when PowerDynamo is installed on a separate machine from the Jaguar server. Copy the JagClient.exe file located in the %JAGUAR%\client directory to the PowerDynamo machine. Install the Jaguar Java client classes by running the executable and selecting the Java Runtime. To use the Jaguar Java runtime classes, place the following directory in the system CLASSPATH variable:

C:\Program Files\Sybase\Shared\Jaguar CTS 3.5\JagClient.zip

TIP   When changing the CLASSPATH, make sure that the . (period) is in the path. This tells Java to look in the current directory.

After changing the environment variables, PowerDynamo must be stopped and restarted.

PowerDynamo controls the connections to the Jaguar CTS server through both default settings and a manager. These settings are found under the Utilities | Configuration | Default Jaguar Settings folder. These settings allow different ORB classes to be specified. Jaguar clients should use the class com.sybase.CORBA.ORB. The Retry Count and Delay settings, which specify how many times PowerDynamo should attempt to connect to the server and how long it should wait between each try in milliseconds, can be set here as well. The Proxy Host and Port properties can also be set if required. Jaguar uses the default settings if a particular Jaguar manager is not set up in Sybase Central or it cannot find the Manager settings based on the URL specified when a connection with Jaguar is attempted.

9.4 How does PowerDynamo handle Jaguar connections?

In order to maximize both performance and server resource usage, PowerDynamo caches Jaguar connections. This is pictured in figure 9.5. PowerDynamo manages the actual establishment of the connection to the Jaguar server. It also acquires the connection for a script and returns it to the cache automatically after the script finishes. Thus, the developer doesn't need to worry about handling this.

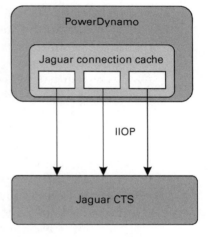

Each template or script that is run, at the request of a client, that needs to access Jaguar, is given a Jaguar connection from the cache by PowerDynamo. However, because the web is stateless after the template is finished processing and the client request is satisfied, its connection to the web server/PowerDynamo is disconnected. This results in the Jaguar connection for

Figure 9.5 Jaguar connection caching in PowerDynamo

that particular client being returned to the cache. The next request by the same client to the web server/PowerDynamo that uses a Jaguar component will probably result in a different Jaguar connection being utilized. This is illustrated in figure 9.6.

Jaguar manages client sessions for each connection. Because a web client cannot guarantee that it will get the same Jaguar connection each time it makes a request and it cannot stop another client from using the connection it just finished using, it cannot rely on any information held by the client session in Jaguar. This includes the SessionID, which is often considered a strong candidate for storing and managing state in a stateless object. (See the discussion on state management in chapter 2 for more details.) The web client also cannot rely on any stateful objects being available or having a set of state values that it will recognize between web requests.

When an object instance is activated, it is bound to a client session and remains attached to that session until it is deactivated. When the Jaguar component is stateless, by enabling Auto Demarcation/ Deactivation, we don't have much of a problem because the component is deactivated after each method call. Even if a script makes several method calls in the same script to a stateless object, the object instance will be activated at the beginning of every method call and deactivated at the end of every method call. In fact, several different instances of the component class may end up being used to satisfy the numerous requests. When the component is stateful, however, we can run into some interesting situations. If a component is stateful, but the PowerDynamo template or script deactivates the instance before processing of the script is completed, then this is an acceptable use of a stateful object.

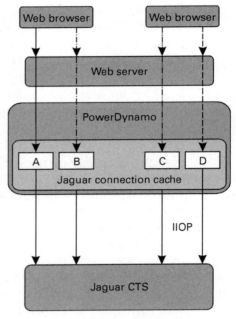

Figure 9.6 Clients use different Jaguar connections with each request

A good example of this is a script that uses a stateful Customer object and calls several methods to set up the state. The Customer object stores the state in instance variables and is available while the script is running. After setting the state using setXXX methods, the script calls the saveCustomer method. This method updates the database and then uses SetComplete/completeWork or SetAbort/rollbackWork to vote on the transaction and deactivate the component when the transaction is completed. The script sample below illustrates this:

```
...
JagObject = java.CreateComponent("JaguarJungle/Customer");
JagObject.setFirstName("Mike");
JagObject.setLastName("Barlotta");
...
rc = JagObject.saveCustomer();
if (rc==1) {
   document.redirect="SaveOK.stm";
}
else {
   document.redirect="SaveError.stm";
}
```

If the stateful component instance is not deactivated (either directly by the script calling a deactivate method on the component or by calling a function that votes on a transaction), the component instance hangs around, bound to the client session. However, the object reference to it is no longer valid because PowerDynamo will have removed it when the script finished executing. This results in component instances being "stranded" in Jaguar. The only way to get rid of them is to perform a manual refresh of the server or use the Component Timeout property.

In addition, the client will not get the expected results trying to use a stateful object over multiple PowerDynamo requests because the state data stored in one script is no longer accessible in calls to subsequent scripts. Let's look at our earlier example with the Customer object. In this case, the script is divided in two. The client calls the first script, which uses the Jaguar Customer component and stores some values using the setXXX methods.

```
...
JagObject = java.CreateComponent("JaguarJungle/Customer");
JagObject.setFirstName("Mike");
JagObject.setLastName("Barlotta");
...
```

This works fine and the Customer object stores the data in instance variables as before. However, when the script finishes, the object reference to the Customer object is removed, the connection to Jaguar is returned to the cache, and the client is disconnected from PowerDynamo. When the browser follows this up with a call to another script, which calls the Jaguar Customer component and attempts to save the values using the saveCustomer method, a new connection is established to PowerDynamo and a Jaguar connection is taken from the cache. A new object reference is created and an instance of the Customer object on Jaguar is either created or taken out of the instance pool. A script sample is shown below:

```
...
JagObject = java.CreateComponent("JaguarJungle/Customer");
rc = JagObject.saveCustomer();
if (rc==1) {
   document.redirect="SaveOK.stm";
}
else {
   document.redirect="SaveError.stm";
}
...
```

However, instead of saving the values stored in the previous script, the component will not have any state in its instance variables. It will either detect that there is no data to be saved or save an empty row depending on the function logic.

FYI   For more information on the Jaguar component life cycle, check out the book *Jaguar Development with PowerBuilder 7*. This book explains the fundamentals of developing Jaguar components for Jaguar CTS. While the examples are based on PowerBuilder, the concepts are applicable to all development tools.

A stateful object should not be used in PowerDynamo unless it is deactivated at the end of the script in which it was called. In order to use a stateful object instance between two or more client requests to separate Dynamo scripts, the component will need to be able to handle early deactivation and restore any state that either Power-Dynamo will need to pass to it or the component will need to manage. Because a stateless component has the same requirements to manage its state between requests, it is recommended over a stateful component that uses early deactivation.

9.5   How do I store state between requests in PowerDynamo?

The web uses HTTP, a stateless communication protocol, meaning that the client application connects and disconnects from the web server and PowerDynamo with each request. That means that all of our PowerDynamo templates and scripts are essentially stateless objects (actually stateless pages). Any information that is generated during the execution of a script is lost when the script is finished. If there is any information that we want to store between requests it will need to be specifically stored, managed, and restored when needed. An excellent example of this is logging into a web site. Once a user has logged into the site they will not want to have to reenter their user ID and password for every page they request, but unless their user ID and password are stored somewhere the page will have no way of verifying who the user is. Another example is selecting items to purchase as users navigate through a site. Once items are selected, users should not have to reselect them as they move through the site. In order to do this, the application needs to maintain this information across the requests. Unless they are stored, however, each new request will have no way of knowing what items were selected. Even if these items are stored in a database, each page must at a minimum know who is logged in so that they can re-retrieve the proper customer's selected items in the shopping cart.

Let's quickly review some of our options on how to store state for our web pages.

- Pass state data as page parameters.
- Use the session object.
- Store the data in the database.
- Store the state in the object instance.

9.5.1 *Passing page parameters*

One way that state can be preserved across requests is by passing the information as page parameters. This is a form of client-side caching of state data discussed in chapter 2. At first glance, this seems like a valid approach and for a limited number of data items, it is. For large sites, this can be difficult to manage as information accumulates. The problem is that as we collect a large number of data items that we need to maintain between requests, we increase the number of items that are passed across the wire. This increases network traffic and decreases performance. In addition, we need to pass all the information to each page even if it does not need it, so that the values are preserved for the pages that do need them on subsequent requests. This is usually done with hidden INPUT tags in a FORM or attaching them to the end of the URL specified in the HREF property of an Anchor tag. This requires each page to be able to handle all the page parameters that will ever be passed in the system. This is tough to develop and probably impossible to maintain. As more data items are added to the application, each page will need to be updated.

9.5.2 *The session object*

The session object is a predefined object in PowerDynamo that is used to store information between requests. The session object is implemented using a cookie, so it also uses a form of client-side caching to maintain state across page requests. The cookie is stored on the client machine. The client, in this case, is the client to PowerDynamo, which is the machine where the web browser is making requests. The cookie is automatically sent and received by the web browser and PowerDynamo server so there are no extra development issues required to handle the passing of the data. The state information is saved as name/value pairs in the cookie. When the PowerDynamo server receives the cookie, the values are loaded into the session object making them easy to access in a script. Session values are accessed inside scripts in a manner that is similar to the document.value.variable property. The syntax to access a session value from the session object is as follows:

session.variable

The variable portion of the syntax is where the name of the state data is specified. The following code sample illustrates how to use the session object to store the user input of UserID and PWD passed into the template:

```
<!--SCRIPT
// Get page parameters
var UserName= document.value.UserID;
var Password = document.value.PWD;

// Processing - to check for valid login
      if (UserName == Password) {
```

```
   // OK so save values
   session.UserID = UserName;
   session.PWD = Password;

   document.redirect="HelloWorld.stm";
}
else {
   // invalid logon
   document.redirect="Logon.stm";
}
-->
```

The user ID and password used to log into the application are now stored in the session object. The user ID value is stored with the name UserID and the password value is stored with the name PWD. The following code sample illustrates how to use the session object to get the user ID out of the session object. To avoid any errors or references to undefined variables, we can check for the existence of the session properties first as shown in the following code sample:

```
// Check for UserID in session
if (exists(session.UserID)) {
   UserName= session.UserID;
}
else {
   UserName= "";
}

// Check if logged in
if (UserName == "") {
   // not logged in
   document.redirect="Logon.stm";
   exit;
}

// logged in so process script
...
```

The session object is stored as a cookie. To ensure that old state is not used, the cookie is given an expiration. If the cookie expiration has not been updated within the specified timeout period, then the cookie is no longer valid. The cookie expiration is updated with each request to PowerDynamo, so it will be invalidated only if the client is idle for a time that exceeds the timeout period. The timeout period is specified by the cookie timeout setting under the Utilities | Configuration | Default General Settings folder in Sybase Central. The default setting is five minutes.

WARNING   The session object does not work when using the Jaguar CTS server as the web server to a PowerDynamo application. Jaguar CTS does not handle the cookie used to implement the session.

9.5.3 *Storing state in a database*

To avoid the increase in network traffic caused by storing state on the client, Power-Dynamo can store state information in a database table that it can directly access. This takes advantage of the database connection caching technique discussed in chapter 2, which minimizes the network traffic between the web client and the web server/PowerDynamo. Using this technique, PowerDynamo can retrieve only the state required for each request and either use it for processing in a script or pass the data to a Jaguar component as illustrated in figure 9.7. This technique, however, requires the requested script to know which client is accessing the page at a given point in time so that it can retrieve the correct state data from the database. Giving each client a uniquely generated session ID that its state is stored under accomplishes this. At a minimum, this requires the client to maintain the session ID across requests. This can be done with page parameters or with the PowerDynamo session object. However, all the remaining state that needs to be managed can be stored in a database table.

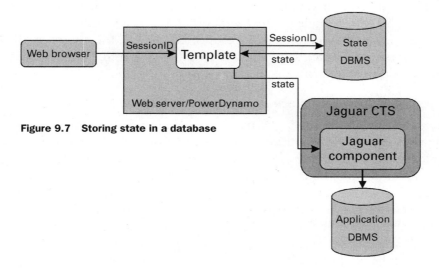

Figure 9.7   Storing state in a database

WARNING   Using the SessionID retrieved with the getSessionID function on the CtsSecurity::SessionInfo component in Jaguar, is not a valid primary key to store state under for web clients like a PowerDynamo application. Each request by a web client can use a different Jaguar connection to satisfy a request for an object and thus get a new SessionID value each time.

9.5.4 *Storing state in an object instance*

Storing state information using the database technique, the session object, or the page parameter approach discussed above all require the state information to be managed by PowerDynamo scripts. Because all the state data is managed in a PowerDynamo script, the data required by a Jaguar component will need to be passed to the component instance as needed through method arguments.

Another approach is using the object instance on Jaguar to manage the state so that PowerDynamo does not have to. The Jaguar component, whether stateless or stateful, can store state using any of the techniques described in chapter 2. However, each of these techniques requires the client (PowerDynamo) to notify the object instance who is accessing the instance at a given point in time so that it can retrieve the correct state. This is usually done with a uniquely generated session ID that is generated and given to the client during the login process. The client is required to maintain the session ID across requests, which can be done with page parameters or with the PowerDynamo session object. It also requires each method on a stateless object to accept the session ID as an argument. A stateful component can handle this with a single method setSessionID, which sets the session ID value in an instance variable and restores the proper state. Using this approach, the management of the state (except for the session ID) is removed from PowerDynamo and given to the component.

9.5.5 *Another look at storing state in an object instance*

We have discussed in section 9.4 that state stored in an object instance is valid only during the script that it is running. After the script is finished executing, PowerDynamo loses contact with the object instance because it loses the object reference. However, you can pass object references using the session object to maintain access to an object instance and continue to use its state values, assuming it is stateful and has not been deactivated. Let's look at this technique using our earlier example with the Customer object. In this case the script is divided into two scripts. The client calls the first script, which uses the Jaguar Customer component and stores some values using the setXXX methods. The only difference between this script and the last one we used is that the object reference is stored with the session object.

```
...
JagObject = java.CreateComponent("JaguarJungle/Customer");
JagObject.setFirstName("Mike");
JagObject.setLastName("Barlotta");
...
session.JagCust = JagObject;
...
```

The second script will also need a minor change. Instead of using CreateComponent to get an object reference to the Customer object, it will use the object reference stored in the session object. When the browser follows the call to the first script with a call to this second script, the same Jaguar Customer component instance is used so the attempt to save the values stored in the component using the `saveCustomer` method will work as expected. The state information stored with the `setXXX` methods will be saved. A script sample is shown below:

```
JagObject = session.JagCust;
...
rc = JagObject.saveCustomer();
if (rc==1) {
   document.redirect="SaveOK.stm";
}
else {
   document.redirect="SaveError.stm";
}
...
```

Although this technique is useful to store state between requests, it is not recommended. Maintaining the object reference to the stateful object instance locks up server resources that are idle by continuing to keep the instance activated. Because there is no guarantee on when or if the client will respond, this resource is held up indefinitely. If this technique is used, be sure to set a Component Timeout property to ensure that component instances are not left hanging in memory.

9.6   *How does a script access a Jaguar component using Java and CORBA?*

PowerDynamo can access Jaguar as a Java CORBA client using the java object. PowerDynamo uses the CosNaming API to locate objects and get remote references to object instances running on Jaguar. Each Jaguar component that will be accessed from a PowerDynamo script as a CORBA object must have a Java stub generated and compiled. The Java stubs must be placed into a directory that is in the CLASSPATH.

FYI   For an in depth discussion on CORBA, IDL, and stubs. see *Jaguar Development with PowerBuilder 7.*

To generate Java stubs for a component, use the Jaguar Manager. Select the package that contains the component. Highlight the component and select the File | Generate Stub/Skeleton menu option. The Generate Stubs & Skeletons dialog will open as shown in figure 9.8. Enable the Generate Stubs checkbox and select

Generate Java Stubs. Make sure to choose the CORBA 2.2 and JDK 1.1 options. The stubs are placed by default in a subdirectory under the %JAGUAR%\html\classes directory that has the same name as the package the Jaguar component is installed with. Java stubs can be placed in a separate directory by typing the base path in the Java Code Base field. Once the options are entered, click on the Generate button to generate the stubs.

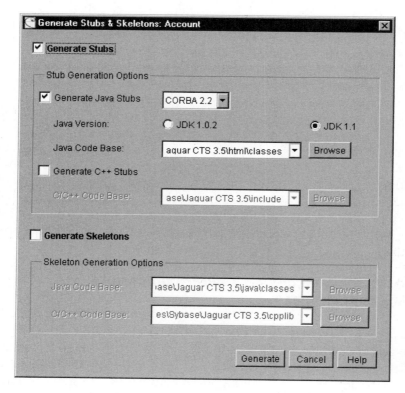

Figure 9.8
Generating Java
CORBA stubs

NOTE   The generation of Java stubs is required to access a Jaguar component via the java object in PowerDynamo. However, this does *not* mean that the Jaguar component is written in Java. In fact, the component can be written in any language that Jaguar supports. The Java stubs are required because PowerDynamo is a Java client to the Jaguar CTS server when the java object is used. A Java client requires Java stubs to use a Jaguar component.

After generating the stubs, they need to be compiled. Compiling Java stubs is done through the command prompt. Open a command prompt window and navigate to the location of the base directory where the Java stubs are located. The default location is %JAGUAR%\html\classes. From this directory, navigate to each subdirectory that has stubs needing to be compiled. For example, the Account object deployed to the JaguarJungle package in Jaguar would have its generated stubs placed in %JAGUAR%\html\classes\JaguarJungle. Once in this directory, type javac *.java at the command line to compile the stubs. This process is shown in figure 9.9.

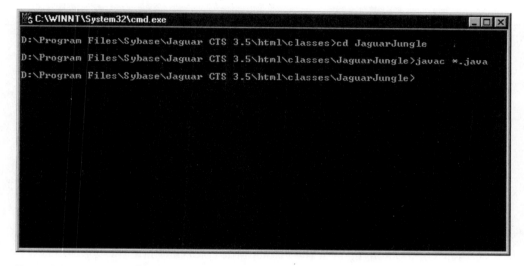

Figure 9.9 **Compiling the Java stubs**

NOTE   When the compilation of the Java stubs fails, it often is indicative of an incorrect CLASSPATH.

Once the Java stubs are generated for a component, PowerDynamo can use them to access the object in Jaguar. The stubs will not need to be generated and compiled again unless a new method is added, or the method signature for an existing method is changed or removed. Changing the Java stubs requires PowerDynamo to be stopped and restarted to flush the Java cache. Once the Java stubs are compiled and the PowerDynamo server has been stopped and restarted, we can create a template to access the Jaguar components.

TIP To simplify the compilation of the Java stubs, a batch file like the one shown below can be used:

```
@echo off
if "%1" == "" goto sethelp
D:
CD %JAGUAR%\html\classes
title Compiling Jaguar Stubs for %1
@echo on
CD %1
JAVAC *.JAVA
@echo off
goto end
:sethelp
echo Invalid option.
echo Usage: jagcompile [package_name]
:end
PAUSE
```

Save this as jagcompile.bat and run at the command line as follows:

```
C:>jagcompile JaguarJungle
```

The java object has a `CreateComponent` method that is used to create an instance of a Jaguar component through Java using the CORBA naming services. The syntax of the method is shown below:

```
java.CreateComponent( component_name, [JagURL, JagUser, JagPassword,
    narrowing_component] )
```

The component_name is the name of the component on the Jaguar server using the Package/Component naming convention (i.e., SVU/SVULogin). The rest of the arguments are optional. The JagURL argument has a default value of iiop://localhost:9000. In order to specify a Jaguar server on a separate machine (or to use a different port number) this parameter must be given using the URL format to identify the IIOP protocol, Jaguar server address, and the port Jaguar is using to listen for IIOP requests. The JagUser and JagPassword arguments are used to specify a particular Jaguar user. These arguments are required if the Jaguar server is using Operating System authentication or if the package, component, or method that will be accessed through the java object is protected with a Role. The Narrowing_Component argument is used to specify the component class to narrow or cast the object to. The Jaguar server returns a component instance that must be narrowed or cast to an interface that the component supports. The default interface is the name of the component that is being called. A sample script to illustrate how to access a Jaguar component is shown below. The script is accessing a Jaguar CORBA component named jagloginPB, which is deployed to the JaguarJungle package and has a method called `validatelogin`, which accepts two strings.

```
<!--SCRIPT
if (exists(document.value.UserID)) {
   UserName= document.value.UserID;
}
else {
   UserName= "";
}
if (exists(document.value.PWD)) {
   Password= document.value.PWD;
}
else {
   Password= "";
}
JagLogin=java.CreateComponent("JaguarJungle/jagloginPB");
if (JagLogin == null) {
   document.writeln(site.GetErrorInfo());
}
else {
    rc = JagLogin.validatelogin(UserName, Password);
    if (rc==1) {
        // valid logon
        document.redirect="HelloWorld.stm";
    }
    else {
        // invalid logon
        document.redirect="StartPage.stm";
    }
}
-->
```

9.7 How does a script access a Jaguar component using Java and EJB?

PowerDynamo can access Jaguar as a Java EJB client using the java object. Power-Dynamo uses JNDI to locate EJB objects and get access to Home interfaces. The Home interface allows a script to get a Remote reference to the remote interface of the EJBObject, which is used to access the instance of an EJB running on Jaguar. Each Jaguar component that will be accessed from a PowerDynamo script as an EJB object must have generated and compiled Java stubs. The Java stubs must be placed into a directory that is in the CLASSPATH.

FYI   For more details on the EJB specification, check out chapter 3.

Use Jaguar Manager to generate Java stubs for a component. Select the package that contains the component. Highlight the component and select the File | Generate Stub/Skeleton menu option. The Generate Stubs & Skeletons dialog will open as shown in figure 9.10. Enable the Generate Stubs checkbox and select Generate Java Stubs. Make sure to choose the EJB 1.0 and JDK 1.1 options. The stubs by default are placed in a subdirectory under the %JAGUAR%\html\classes directory that has the same name as the package the Jaguar component is installed with. Java stubs can be placed in a separate directory by typing the base path in the Java Code Base field. Once the options are entered, click on the Generate button to generate the stubs.

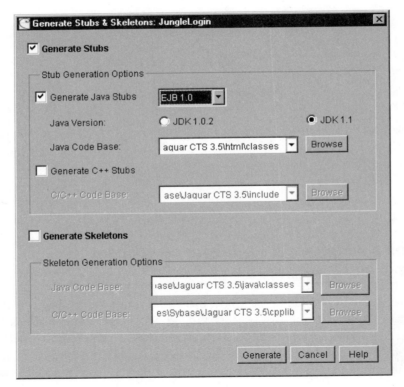

Figure 9.10
Generating Java EJB stubs

Once the stubs are generated, they must be compiled just like the Java CORBA stubs. See section 9.6 for details.

The java object has a `GetHomeInterface` method that is used to get a reference to a Home interface (EJBHome) of an EJB component on Jaguar through Java using JNDI. The reference to the Home interface allows an instance of an EJB Jaguar component to be created.

The syntax of the method is shown below:

```
java.GetHomeInterface( component_name, [JagURL, JagUser,
JagPassword] )
```

The component_name is the name of the Bean Home Name specified for the component on the Jaguar server. The Bean Home Name is one of the component properties for an EJB component that has been deployed to Jaguar CTS and is shown in figure 9.11.

The rest of the arguments for the `GetHomeInterface` method are optional. The JagURL argument has a default value of iiop://local-host:9000. In order to specify a Jaguar server on a separate machine or use a different port number, this parameter must be given using the URL format to identify the IIOP protocol, server address, and the port Jaguar is using to listen for IIOP requests. The JagUser and JagPassword arguments are used to specify a particular Jaguar user. These arguments are required if the Jaguar server is using Operating System authentication or the package, component, or method that will be accessed through the java object is protected with a Role.

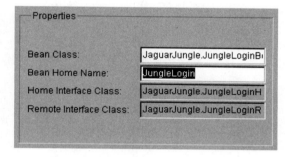

Figure 9.11   The EJB Bean Home Name

A sample script to illustrate how to access an EJB component on Jaguar is shown below. The script is accessing a Jaguar EJB component named JungleLogin that is deployed to the JaguarJungle package It has a method validateLogon, which accepts two strings.

```
<!--SCRIPT

if (exists(document.value.UserID)) {
   UserName= document.value.UserID;
}
else {
   UserName= "";
}

if (exists(document.value.PWD)) {
   Password= document.value.PWD;
}
```

```
else {
   Password= "";
}

EJBHome=java.GetHomeInterface("JungleLogin");
if (EJBHome == null) {
   document.writeln(site.GetErrorInfo());
}
else {
   EJBRemote = EJBHome.create()
   if (EJBRemote == null) {
       document.writeln(site.GetErrorInfo());
   }
   else {
       rc = EJBRemote.validateLogon(UserName, Password);
       if (rc==1) {
           // valid logon
           document.redirect="HelloWorld.stm";
       }
       else {
           // invalid logon
           document.redirect="StartPage.stm";
       }
   }
}

-->
```

9.8 *How are Java properties accessed using the java object?*

The java object lets PowerDynamo interact with Java classes. However, a limitation to the java object is it inability to directly access the fields or properties of a Java class using dot notation. This makes dealing with Java class properties, Holder objects, and structures difficult in PowerDynamo scripts.

DEFINITION   FIELD   A field is the Java term used to describe the data members or instance variables that hold the state of an object.

Let's look at an example of this using a Java class named Customer that has a property LastName declared to be of the type String (java.lang.String). The code to implement the class is shown below:

```
class Customer {
   String LastName;
}
```

If we wanted to access the String value of the field LastName in a PowerDynamo script, we might try using the code sample below:

```
myJavaObject = java.CreateObject("Customer");
myValue = myJavaObject.LastName;
```

As we already stated, however, this code will not work. In order to get the value from the field on the Java class, we are going to have to do a bit more work and take advantage of a Java object's ability to describe itself at runtime. All classes in Java are derived from the Object class (java.lang.Object). The Object class has a property defined as a Class class (java.lang.Class). The Class class represents the running Java class or interface. A reference to the Class class is returned by the getClass method on the Object class. Using the Class class, we can get information on the Java class including its methods and fields. This is what we are looking for: another way to access the field on the instance of our Java class. Using the getField method of the Class class, we can get a reference to a Field object (java.lang.reflect.Field) for a specific field of the class. The getField method takes a String argument, which is the name of the field for which we are trying to get an object reference. The Field class provides information on a single property field of a class or an interface and allows access to its value via get and set methods. This is exactly what we need to access the value of our LastName property on our Customer Java class. We can access the String value of the property using the code sample below:

```
// Instantiate Java class "Customer"
myJavaObject = java.CreateObject("Customer");
// Get Class Object from Java Object
myClass = myJavaObject.getClass()
// Get Field Object from Class for property named "LastName"
myField = myClass.getField("LastName");
// Get Object from Field (in this case a String object)
myValueObj = myField.get(myJavaObject);
// Get the value from the String object
myValue = myValueObj.toString();
```

Dave Wolf of Sybase Inc. has already created a PowerDynamo script with a Power-Dynamo object JavaFieldHelper that encapsulates all of this logic. It has methods to handle accessing and converting each Java data type. The script is named javawrappers.ssc and is available from the SDN site (www.sybase.com/sdn). The rest of the examples in this chapter use the javawrappers.ssc script.

9.9 *How are data types passed by reference using the java object?*

CORBA IDL allows arguments to be passed in one of three modes: in, inout, and out. CORBA arguments passed as in parameters are passed by value. CORBA arguments passed as inout or out parameters are passed by reference. Java, however, passes data types only by value. Java cannot pass data types by reference-only objects. In order to handle passing Java data types by reference, the CORBA IDL to Java mapping defines special Holder classes. A Holder class is a container or object wrapper for a data type. By wrapping the value of the data type in an object, Java will pass it by reference. There is a separate Holder class for each IDL data type in the org.omg.CORBA package provided by the ORB. The Jaguar application server generates Holder classes for user-defined data types like structures when the Java stubs are generated. The code sample below illustrates what a Holder class looks like for a String:

```
final public class StringHolder
{
   public String value;
   public StringHolder() {}
   public StringtHolder(String initial_value)
   {
      value = initial_value;
   }
}
```

The Holder class has an instance variable named value, which is declared to be of the same data type as the data type the holder is wrapping. The instance variable holds the data value for the data type. The Holder class can be initialized with no value or a default value through one of the two constructor methods defined.

When a component is listed in the Jaguar Manager on the Component Properties dialog, the arguments to a method are shown with the CORBA IDL data type. However, as you can see from table 9.2, the Java data type that corresponds to the CORBA IDL type will actually be different depending on whether the parameter is passed by value (in, return) or passed by reference (inout, out). So when a component has a method with an argument that is listed in the Jaguar Manager as a string passed as inout, the Java stub will be expecting a StringHolder object, *not* a Java String object to be passed.

Table 9.2   A sample of CORBA IDL—Java data types

Java class	CORBA IDL	Mode
java.lang.String	string	In, return
org.omg.CORBA.StringHolder	string	Inout / out
Int	long	In, return
org.omg.CORBA.IntHolder	long	Inout / out

FYI   Appendix A lists all of the Jaguar-CORBA IDL data types and the corresponding Java and PowerBuilder data types.

In order for a Java client application to pass values by reference to a CORBA component, they must first instantiate an instance of the Holder class of the proper data type and pass that object to the method instead of the actual data type variable. To illustrate this, let's take our validatelogin function on our JaguarJungle/jagloginPB component and add a third argument that is passed by reference. This argument is used to pass an error message back from the component to the client application. The script to implement this function call is shown below:

```
<!--SCRIPT
   var RespMsg = "";
   JagObject = java.CreateComponent("JaguarJungle/jagloginPB");
   RespMsgHolder = java.CreateObject("org.omg.CORBA.StringHolder",
RespMsg);
   rc = JagObject.validateuser(UserID, Password, RespMsgHolder);

   ...

-->
```

The `CreateComponent` method, as we have already seen, is used to access components on the Jaguar application server using Java stubs. The `CreateObject` method of the Java object is used to instantiate a local Java class. The Java class files that implement the Holder classes are stored locally (on the same machine as PowerDynamo) so the `CreateObject` method is used to instantiate them. The `CreateObject` method takes the Java class name and an optional list of parameters that are passed to the constructor method of the Java class specified.

Once the Jaguar component method is finished, the Holder class is returned with the new value stored inside. However, as we mentioned earlier, the Java object in PowerDynamo cannot access instance variables on a Java class via dot notation. In order to get the new value returned by the method call out of the Holder class, we will need to use the javawrappers.ssc file. A code example using this JavaField-Helper object in the javawrappers.ssc file is shown below:

```
import javawrappers.ssc
…
        rc = JagObject.validateuser(UserID, Password, RespMsgHolder);

jHelper = new JavaFieldHelper(RespMsgHolder);
RespMsg = jHelper.getString("value");
```

The examples shown here focused on a String data type, but this same technique is used for all of the Java data types when they are passed by reference.

9.10 *How are binary, decimal, and date/time data types handled?*

Passing data types by reference is not the only time the data type of a parameter specified in the Jaguar Manager (CORBA IDL) will differ from the data type that Java uses. When passing binary data (blobs), decimal values, and date, time, or date/time values between Jaguar and a Java client, the data types need to be converted between the IDL data type (BCD::x or MJD::x) and the Java data type (BCD.* or MJD.*). The Java BCD and MJD data types are usually converted into another Java class that provides a useful API to access the values. Table 9.3 lists the CORBA IDL data types and the corresponding Java classes for the date, time, and date/time data types.

Table 9.3 The CORBA IDL–Java date, time, date/time data types

Java class	CORBA-Java	CORBA IDL	Mode
java.sql.Date	MJD.Date	MJD::Date	In, return
java.sql.Date	MJD.DateHolder	MJD::Date	Inout/out
java.sql.Time	MJD.Time	MJD::Time	In, return
java.sql.Time	MJD.TimeHolder	MJD::Time	Inout/out
java.sql.Timestamp	MJD.Timestamp	MJD::Timestamp	In, return
java.sql.Timestamp	MJD.Timestamp	MJD::Timestamp	Inout/out

To convert between the IDL data types and the Java classes Jaguar ships with the com.sybase.CORBA.jdbc11 package. This packages contains two classes: the SQL class, which is used to convert IDL types into java.* classes; and the IDL class, which is used to convert java.* classes into IDL types.

To illustrate this, we will look at how to handle a date data type. In our example, we will pass a date value collected in a PowerDynamo script as three separate values (month, day, and year) to a Jaguar component as an in parameter. The script shown below illustrates this:

```
// create a java.sql.Date object and initialize it with the date
jDate  = java.CreateObject("java.sql.Date", parseInt(year),
```

```
parseInt(month), parseInt(day));

// convert the java.sql.Date object into an MJD.Date object
mjdDate = java.CallStaticMethod("com.sybase.CORBA.jdbc11.IDL",
"getDate", jDate);

// Pass the MJD.Date object as a parameter
JagObject.passDate(mjdDate);
```

When an object returns an MJD.Date value as either a reference argument or a return value, the value needs to be converted into a java.sql.Date object as shown in the following script:

```
mjdDate = JagObject.getDate();
jDate = java.CallStaticMethod("com.sybase.CORBA.jdbc11.SQL",
 "getDate", mjdDate);
```

Once the IDL type is converted into a Java object, the data value can be accessed using the Java API of the object. Note that passing a date or any of the other values by reference requires a Holder class.

9.11 How is a structure passed from PowerDynamo to Jaguar (Java)?

The Java language does not support structures as a separate data type like Power-Builder or C++ do. In order to mimic a structure in Java, a class is created with the same name as the structure. The class contains instance variables that match the fields in the structure. It also contains two constructor methods: one to handle initializing all the instance variables and the other that sets all of the values to null. Because NULL values cannot be passed in CORBA, all of the class/structure fields need to be initialized before the structure is passed as an argument to a method on a Jaguar component.

When a Jaguar component has a structure defined as part of its interface, the Jaguar server generates the Java class that mimics the structure as well as Helper and Holder classes when the Java stubs are generated. Let's look at this with an example using the Customer structure and the Customer component built in PowerBuilder for our fictitious company Safari Shipping. Our example will show how to pass a structure by reference to the getCustomer method. The first thing that needs to be done in a PowerDynamo script is to define and initialize variables that match the fields in the structure.

```
import javawrappers.ssc;

// Get Customer ID
...

// Create Jaguar component
...
```

```
// Initialize Customer Structure elements
CustID = document.value.CustID;
Name = "";
Address = "";
City = "";
State = "";
Zip = "";
Phone = "";
Email = "";
UserID = session.UserID;
```

The next step is to instantiate the Java class that mimics the structure. It is always a good idea to check and make sure that the Java class was successfully created. There is usually a problem creating the class when the stubs for the component have not been generated or compiled yet. There may also be a mismatch in data types.

```
// Create Customer Structure
str_customer = java.CreateObject ("JaguarJungle/str_customer",
parseInt(CustID), Name, Address, City, State, Zip, Phone, Email, UserID);

// determine if object is OK
if (str_customer == null) {
   document.writeln(site.GetErrorInfo());
}
```

In order to pass a structure by reference, the Holder generated by the Jaguar Manager needs to be used. The name of the Holder class is the name of the structure with Holder tacked on the end of it.

```
// Create Customer Structure Holder
str_customerHolder = java.CreateObject("JaguarJungle/
str_customerHolder", str_customer);
```

After the Holder class is created, the structure can be passed in as an argument to a method that expects the structure passed as an inout or out parameter (by reference).

```
// Get Customer Info
rc = JagCust.getcustomer(CustID, str_customerHolder);
```

Once the method is finished, the Java class is returned with the data we want. Because the Java class/structure is in the Holder class, we need to get this out before we can access the instance variables in the Java class that implements the structure.

```
// Get the Structure out of the Holder
jHelper = new JavaFieldHelper(str_customerHolder);
str_customer = jHelper.getObject("value");
```

Working with the Java class that implements the structure is hampered by the limitation we mentioned earlier with the java object in PowerDynamo: the inability to access instance variables on a Java class via dot notation. In order to get the values of the structure out of the Java class (structure), we will need to use the javawrappers.ssc file. A code example using this JavaFieldHelper object in the script file is shown below:

```
// Get Data from Customer Structure
jHelper = new JavaFieldHelper(str_customer);
CustID = jHelper.getInt("customer_id");
Name = jHelper.getString("name");
…
Email = jHelper.getString("email");
```

The string specified in the `getString` and `getInt` methods of the JavaFieldHelper object in javawrappers.ssc must match the names of the structure fields used to generate the names of the instance variables in the Java class.

9.12 How is a Java array handled in PowerDynamo?

When dealing with arrays in PowerDynamo, it is important to keep in mind that the PowerDynamo array and the Java array are not compatible. PowerDynamo arrays must be converted into a Java array in order to pass them into a Jaguar component through the java object. PowerDynamo scripts can use Java arrays, but they cannot access a Java array using the standard array index syntax, so it is probably easier to convert a Java array into a PowerDynamo array before using it in a script. In order for a PowerDynamo script to access a Java array, the java.lang.reflect.Array class must be used. This class allows an array's members be accessed using `get` and `set` methods. A script sample is shown below that converts a PowerDynamo array of string values named PDArray into a Java array of String (java.lang.String) values named Java Array using the java.lang.reflect.Array class.

```
// Java Array - CORBA sequence
// 1. Create datatype for array
JavaString_Class = java.CallStaticMethod("java.lang.Class",
"forName", "java.lang.String");

// 2. Create Java array
JavaArray = java.CallStaticMethod("java.lang.reflect.Array",
"newInstance", JavaString_Class, PDArray.length);

// 3. Populate Java array with PowerDynamo array
for (var i=0;i<PDArray.length;i++) {
   java.CallStaticMethod("java.lang.reflect.Array", "set",
JavaArray, i, PDArray[i]);
}

// 4. Call Jaguar Component method
JagData.sendarray(JavaArray);
```

In order to get elements out of the Java array, use the `get` method as shown below:

```
myString=java.CallStaticMethod("java.lang.reflect.Array", "get",
```

```
JavaArray, 0);
document.writeln("JavaArray[0]:" + myString.toString());
```

It is important to point out that in CORBA IDL, a sequence is a variable-sized one-dimensional array. An array, however, is a fixed-size multidimensional array. Both can contain members that are of any IDL-defined type. In the CORBA IDL to Java mapping, a CORBA sequence is mapped to a Java array. The Jaguar server generates a CORBA sequence IDL definition as well as Helper and Holder classes when Java stubs are generated for a class that contains an array in its interface. In order to pass an array by reference, the Holder class is required.

WARNING A limitation in Jaguar CTS 3.5 does not allow an array to be passed from PowerDynamo to Jaguar CTS.

9.13 How is a Tabular ResultSet used in PowerDynamo and the java object?

Passing a result set is an excellent way for a component to return a set of data, especially when dealing with rows of data. Jaguar CTS has a special CORBA IDL data type that is used to pass back result sets–the TabularResults::ResultSet. When a Tabular ResultSet object is returned by a Jaguar component, the PowerDynamo script needs to convert the IDL object into a java.sql.ResultSet object that it can work with. The java.sql.ResultSet object has its own set of methods and properties that allow the result set data to be manipulated.

Converting from the TabularResults::ResultSet CORBA IDL object into the java.sql.ResultSet object is handled by the com.sybase.CORBA.jdbc11.SQL class. The SQL class contains a method called `getResultSet`, which accepts a Tabular-Results::ResultSet CORBA IDL object and converts it into a java.sql.ResultSet object. The PowerDynamo script to do this is shown below:

```
// Call Jaguar component that returns a result set
IDL_RS = JagOrderStatus.getorderstatuslist();

// Convert result set into a java.sql.ResultSet object
jQuery = java.CallStaticMethod( "com.sybase.CORBA.jdbc11.SQL",
"getResultSet", IDL_RS );
```

In addition to manipulating the java.sql.ResultSet object directly with the Java API for the object, PowerDynamo ships with a utility script containing the definition of a PowerDynamo object called JavaQuery. The JavaQuery object definition is contained in the javaqry.ssc file in the System | Utils folder under the web site root folder. In addition to wrapping the code to convert a TabularResults::ResultSet CORBA IDL object, the JavaQuery object contains methods to manipulate the result set data. The script to wrap an IDL result set object with the PowerDynamo JavaQuery object is shown below:

```
// Call Jaguar component that returns a result set
IDL_RS = JagOrderStatus.getorderstatuslist();

// Convert result set into a JavaQuery object
jQuery = new JavaQuery(IDL_RS);
```

The methods that are implemented on the JavaQuery object are listed in table 9.4.

Table 9.4   JavaQuery methods

JavaQuery method	Description
GetColumnCount()	Get number of columns in the result set.
GetColumnIndex(name)	Get the index number for a particular column.
GetColumnLabel(index)	Get the column label for a particular column.
MoveNext()	Move the cursor pointer ahead one row.
GetValue(index)	Get the value for a particular column.

The java.sql.ResultSet cursor pointer starts ahead of the first row so it must be moved to the first row before values can be accessed. The MoveNext method is used to do this. The MoveNext method returns true as long as the cursor pointer points to a valid row. Once the cursor pointer has moved past the last valid row, the MoveNext method returns false. Here is a script that illustrates how to use the JavaQuery object by walking through a result set and generating the HTML for a drop down list (SELECT tag). The function in the script accepts the IDL Result Set and coverts it into a JavaQuery object. The function also accepts the name of the SELECT tag and the column names that should be used for the display value and the data value. The function also accepts the value that should be shown as selected in the list. The selected value is compared against all the values in the data column.

```
function getDropDownList(select_name, IDLResultSet,
display_column, data_column, selected_value)
{
// Convert result set into a java.sql.ResultSet object
jQuery = new JavaQuery(IDLResultSet);

display_col_idx = jQuery.GetColumnIndex(display_column);
data_col_idx = jQuery.GetColumnIndex(data_column);

HTMLString="<SELECT NAME=" + select_name + ">";

while (jQuery.MoveNext()) {
   disp_value = jQuery.GetValue(display_col_idx);
   data_value = jQuery.GetValue(data_col_idx);

if (data_value == selected_value) {
HTMLString+="<OPTION SELECTED VALUE=" + data_value + ">" +
```

```
disp_value + "</OPTION>";
    }
    else {
HTMLString+="<OPTION VALUE=" + data_value + ">" + disp_value +
  "</OPTION>";
    }
}// end while loop

HTMLString += "</SELECT>";

return HTMLString;

}//end of function
```

The function walks through the result set, getting the values for the specified data and display columns and generating the appropriate HTML. This function was saved in a script named ResultSetHelper.ssc. In order for a script to use this function, it must import both the ResultSetHelper.ssc and the javaqry.ssc files. An example is shown below:

```
import ResultSetHelper.ssc;
import system/utils/javaqry.ssc;

JagOrderStatus = java.CreateComponent("JaguarJungle/order_status");
IDL_RS = JagOrderStatus.getorderstatuslist();
HTMLString=getDropDownList("OrderStatusID", IDL_RS, "description",
  "status_id", "");
document.writeln(HTMLString);
```

Another useful function in the ResultSetHelper.ssc file converts all the values for a given column name into a PowerDynamo array. This makes the values for a column in a result set very easy to work with in a script.

```
function getColumnValues(IDLResultSet, column_name)
{
  // Returns an array

  var column_values = new Array();
  var i = 0;

  // Convert to java.sql.ResultSet
  jQuery = new JavaQuery(IDLResultSet);

  column_idx = jQuery.GetColumnIndex(column_name)

  // Loop through the rows
  while (jQuery.MoveNext()) {
    column_values[i] = jQuery.GetValue(column_idx);

    // Advance array
    i += 1;

  }// end while loop

  return column_values;

}//end of getColumnValues
```

9.14 How does a PowerBuilder component generate a Tabular ResultSet?

The PowerBuilder data type ResultSet is equivalent to the TabularResults::ResultSet CORBA IDL object. The ResultSet object can be generated from a DataStore using the GenerateResultSet method. This allows Jaguar components written in PowerBuilder to generate a CORBA IDL result set, which can be used by other Jaguar components. The code sample below illustrates how a method on a Jaguar component written in PowerBuilder would generate a ResultSet object that is passed back to the client application as the return value of the method.

```
// GetOrderStatusList
// Returns:
// resultset

long ll_rows
resultset lrs
datastore lds_data

lds_data = CREATE datastore
lds_data.DataObject = "d_order_status_list"
lds_data.SetTransObject(SQLCA)
ll_rows = lds_data.Retrieve()
IF ll_rows >= 0 THEN
   lds_data.GenerateResultSet(lrs)
END IF

RETURN lrs
```

WARNING The DataStore should not be destroyed before returning the ResultSet object, otherwise the data in the ResultSet object will not be passed back correctly.

9.15 How does a PowerJ component generate a Tabular ResultSet?

Java uses Java Database Connectivity (JDBC) to connect to and communicate with a database using SQL statements. The JDBC classes are contained in the java.sql package. In order for a JDBC result set (java.sql.ResultSet) class to be passed as a IDL compliant return value from a component, the com.sybase.CORBA.jdbc11.IDL class needs to be used to convert it into a TabularResults.ResultSet class. The com.sybase.CORBA.jdbc11.IDL class has a getResultSet method that has the following method signature:

```
public static TabularResults.ResultSet getResultSet(java.sql.
ResultSet rs)
```

The following code sample illustrates how the `getResultSet` method is used.

```
public TabularResults.ResultSet getAccounts() throws java.rmi.
RemoteException, JException, SQLException
{
   String JagCache="BTFBank_JDBC";
   JCMCache _cache = null;
   Connection conn = null;
   Statement stmt  = null;
   ResultSet rs= null;
   TabularResults.ResultSet CORBA_rs = null;

      // Get a JDBC connection cache handle from Jaguar Connection
Manager.
   try {
      _cache = JCM.getCacheByName(JagCache);
   }
   catch (Exception e) {
      Jaguar.writeLog(true, "getAccounts:getCacheByName() exception" + e.get-
   Message());
      _cache = null;
   }

   if (_cache == null) {
      Jaguar.writeLog(true, "getAccounts:Could not access connection
cache (" + JagCache + ").");
   }

   // get JDBC Connection class
   conn = _cache.getConnection(JCMCache.JCM_FORCE);

   // Create a Statement instance and send query
   stmt = conn.createStatement();
   stmt.execute("SELECT id, last_name FROM account");
   // get result set
   rs = stmt.getResultSet();
   // convert result set
   CORBA_rs = com.sybase.CORBA.jdbc11.IDL.getResultSet(rs);

   return CORBA_rs;
}
```

Java and Jaguar
on the Web

10

This chapter covers:

- Accessing Jaguar components from a Java applet
- Using Java servlets on Jaguar CTS
- A preview of Java Server Pages (JSP)

279

We have taken a detailed look at how a dynamic page server, specifically PowerDynamo, can extend a Jaguar application to the Web. However, this is not the only technique available. In this chapter, we will take a look at how Java technologies such as applets, servlets, and Java Server Pages (JSP) all extend the reach of Jaguar to the Web.

10.1 *What are Java applets?*

Java applets are small client-side programs written in Java that are run in a web browser or an applet viewer. Java applets cannot run on their own because they are not Java applications. Applets are used to create dynamic web sites by extending the capabilities of the browser with the Java language. Java applets are Sun's answer to client-side ActiveX controls and Netscape plug-ins. The browser itself can be thought of as an applet container. It provides the process and the thread in which the applet will run. The browser also controls the applet life cycle and provides information to the applet through methods on the applet interface.

What makes applets interesting in a web architecture is the fact that the client-side program is downloaded when it is executed, thereby allowing the user to have a richer graphical experience without the deployment issues often found in client/ server applications. In a web based *n*-tier application, applets also allow a persistent connection to be established with the Jaguar application server eliminating some of the problems dealing with the statelessness of HTTP. However, the solution is more of a hybrid web application because the applet and Jaguar communicate using IIOP instead of HTTP.

In order for an applet to work, the web browser must be Java-enabled. While browsers have been Java-enabled for some time (Netscape Navigator since version 2.0 and Microsoft Internet Explorer since version 3.0), there are still issues regarding the version of the Java Virtual Machine (JVM) that the browser uses and whether it supports all or just some of the Java core class libraries.

FYI Sun Microsystems Inc. (Sun) provides a Java plug-in that can be used with a web browser that allows an external JVM from Sun instead of the browser's internal JVM to be used to run a Java applet. The Java plug-in must be downloaded, installed, and configured on each client workstation. Visit www.javasoft.com for more information.

A Java applet is embedded into an HTML page using special HTML tags. This is similar to embedding graphics in an HTML page with the IMG tag. When the browser interprets the HTML tags, the resource that is specified is requested from the web server and downloaded. Once the resource is downloaded, the tag tells the browser what to do with it. In the case of a Java applet, the class file is the resource that is downloaded. When a Java applet class is received, a JVM is started on a thread in the browser process and the class is instantiated.

The Java applet architecture is illustrated in figure 10.1.

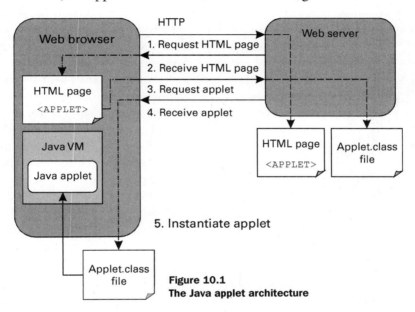

Figure 10.1
The Java applet architecture

The Java class extends the java.applet.Applet class. The Applet class specifies methods that are used by the web browser to let the Java applet know about particular events during the applet instance's life cycle. The applet does not have control over the thread that it runs in, the web browser does. If an applet needs to perform any time-intensive processing, particularly graphic animation, it should spawn its own thread.

The Applet class has four methods that are used by the web browser to indicate to the Java Applet class where in the life cycle it is. They are listed below:

```
public void init()
public void start()
public void stop()
public void destroy()
```

The `init` method of an applet is called when the class is first loaded into the browser. This method is used to initialize the applet, usually by accessing any initialization parameters specified in the HTML page. Once the applet is loaded and initialized, the start method is called. This method lets the applet know it is visible and can do whatever it was designed to do. The init and start methods are guaranteed to be called by the browser in that order as the class is instantiated. The init method is called only once. The start method can be called multiple times as the applet is made invisible and visible. Whenever the applet is made invisible, the stop method is called. The destroy method is called right before the Applet class is unloaded, giving the class a chance to clean up any resources before it is destroyed.

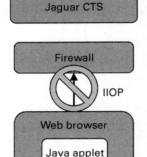

Figure 10.2   Java applets requests cannot get through a firewall

Once a Java applet is running on the client through the web browser, it can communicate with the Jaguar application server just like any Java application. On the Internet, however, web sites are often protected by firewalls. Firewalls can be implemented with software or hardware and are used to protect web sites from attack. One of the ways that firewalls can prevent many types of attacks is by blocking out all traffic directed to the web site that does not use the HTTP protocol. When a firewall prevents non-HTTP traffic from getting through, a Java applet cannot access the Jaguar application server since they communicate over IIOP.

TIP   The Jaguar CTS ORB uses HTTP tunneling to bypass firewalls that do not allow IIOP traffic. The ORB wraps the IIOP request in an HTTP request to let it through the firewall. The ORB handles this automatically after the IIOP request is rejected. In order to have the ORB automatically use HTTP-tunneling instead of waiting for a failed IIOP request, set the ORB-Http property to true.

Java applets were extremely popular when Java was first introduced. However they have lost much of their appeal for Internet applications due to the larger downloads, firewall issues, sandbox problems, and browser incompatibilities with JVMs and Java releases. They are much better suited for Intranet applications where the client workstation environment can be controlled and the network bandwidth is larger.

10.2   *What is the Java sandbox?*

A Java class is not run directly by a CPU; instead, it is run within a JVM. The JVM interacts with the CPU, interpreting the bytecodes into appropriate machine code and giving Java its platform independence. The JVM not only interprets the bytecodes of a Java class; it also provides a controlled environment for the class to run in. The browser takes advantage of this fact, implementing a Security Manager that monitors a Java applet and keeps it from compromising the system by enforcing stringent security policies. Because the applet is controlled by the JVM and the JVM is controlled by the browser, these policies are always enforced. Given that the Java applet is run in such a controlled environment, this environment is often called a *sandbox.*

Each browser can implement different restrictions on a Java applet. Here is a list of some of the restrictions imposed on applets that are downloaded:

- The applet cannot run local programs.
- The applet cannot read or write to local files.
- The applet cannot read system properties.
- The applet can make a network connection only to the host that it was downloaded from.

The restriction that hampers a Java applets' viability on the Internet is the inability to access a machine other than the one that the Java class was downloaded from, as pictured in figure 10.3. This makes load balancing difficult and failover impossible. It also makes partitioning an application onto several Jaguar servers impossible. Load balancing can be implemented by having clients use different Jaguar servers to load their Java applet from, but the sandbox will prevent the applet from accessing another host, thus preventing successful failover.

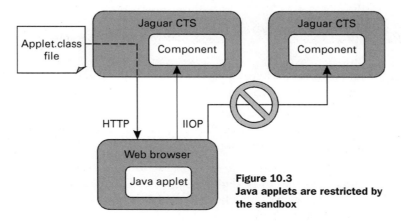

**Figure 10.3
Java applets are restricted by
the sandbox**

The sandbox can be turned off in a web browser, but for Internet users this is an unsafe option given the large number of viruses and hackers roaming the Internet. On an Intranet site, however, turning off the sandbox is a completely valid option, allowing the user to safely surf the Internet and still use Java applets with few restrictions.

To disable the sandbox for Intranet applications in Internet Explorer 5, follow these steps:

- Choose the Tools | Internet Options menu option.
- Select the Security tab and highlight the Intranet zone icon. Click the Custom Level... button to open the Security Settings dialog shown in figure 10.4.

Figure 10.4
Internet Explorer Security Settings

- Under the Java permissions item check the Custom option and than click the Java Custom Settings... button. This will open up the dialog shown in figure 10.5.
- On the Edit Permissions tab under Unsigned Content | Run Unsigned Content choose the Enable option as shown. This will allow the Java applet to run without the sandbox restrictions.

TIP   Java allows JAR files to be digitally signed and verified. This gives the user that trusts your web site the flexibility to allow your Java applet more privileges than unsigned applets.

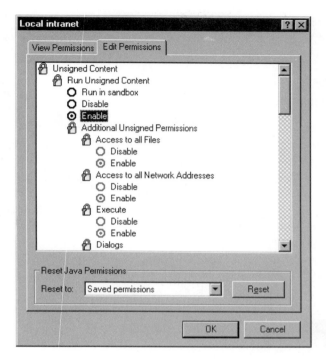

Figure 10.5
Internet Explorer: Java permissions

10.3 How do I write a Java applet?

In this section we will look at how to build a Java applet in PowerJ. The applet we will build will use a Jaguar component that is deployed as a CORBA object that is written in PowerBuilder to get an account balance. The CORBA object is deployed to Jaguar under the Jaguar package BTFBank with the component name Account. The BTFBank/Account component has a method called `getbalance`, which has the following method signature in Jaguar:

```
decimal getbalance(integer<16> in, string inout)
```

This method signature translates to a Java stub method signature as follows:

```
BCD.Decimal getbalance(short, StringHolder)
```

In order for a Java applet to use a CORBA-compliant Jaguar component, the Java class must have access to the CORBA Java stubs. Generating CORBA Java stubs from the Jaguar Manager was covered in detail in chapter 9, section 6. Once we ensure that the Java stubs are generated and compiled so that our Java applet class will have access to them, we can look at how to call methods on the Jaguar component.

Open PowerJ and create a New Workspace by selecting File | New Workspace from the menu. This Workspace is a collection of one or more targets. To create a new applet, there are two basic steps:

1 Create a New Target—Java applet.

2 Build the Java applet.

That second step is a bit vague, but it really depends on what the applet will do. In PowerJ, there are two different wizards that will help a developer create a Java applet. When a new target is created for the applet, the first choice is to decide whether or not to use the PowerJ framework. If you choose not to use this framework, you are required to implement the paint method on your own. The paint method determines what graphical components are used and where they are drawn. The framework provides a drag-and-drop palatte to design the applet form and some additional Java classes.

In this example we will use the framework. To create a new target select File | New from the menu. The New dialog will open. Select the Target tab and highlight the Java Applet icon as shown in figure 10.6.

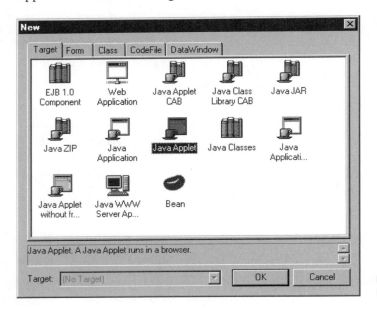

Figure 10.6
New Target—Java Applet

After choosing the Java Applet target, you are prompted for the target name and the location where PowerJ will store the application files as shown in figure 10.7.

The name of the target is the name that is given to the Java class that will be downloaded by web clients. In our example we will call it the BTFBankApplet.

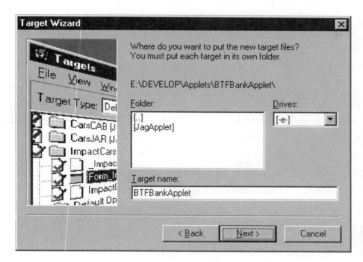

Figure 10.7
Java applet target name

PowerJ offers us another big choice in how we build our Java applet at this point. There are two kinds of applets, the Applet and the JApplet as shown in figure 10.8. The Applet uses the original AWT classes that are most widely supported by web browsers. The JApplet uses the newer Swing classes. Most browsers do not have the Swing classes; therefore, they will have to be included with the Java applet when it is deployed.

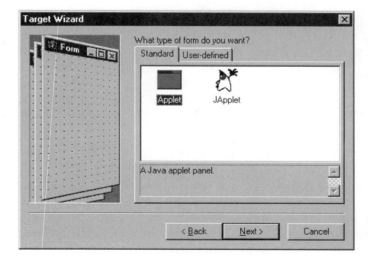

Figure 10.8
Choosing between AWT and Swing classes

WARNING   The Java Swing class files used with the JApplet target are not supported by most browsers. In order for the Java applet to work correctly, the Swing classes will need to be included with the Java applet when it is deployed and downloaded. Sybase provides a file swingall.jar in the %JAGUAR%\html\classes directory. To include the Swing classes make sure the following line of code appears in the HTML:

    <APPLET ... CODEBASE="classes/" ARCHIVE="swingall.jar" ...>

    This code assumes that the Java applet class is deployed to the %JAGUAR%\html\classes directory as well. Downloading the swingall.jar file will significantly impact the Java applet since it is over 2MB.

The next wizard will prompt us for the name of the form (or window) that the Java Applet class will implement. The Java class generated by the form wizard in PowerJ actually extends the java.applet.Applet class. Once you type in the name of the form, click the Finish button.

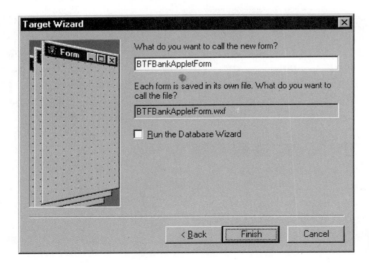

Figure 10.9
Naming the Java Applet form

PowerJ will generate class files based on our selections. The class hierarchy is illustrated in figure 10.10.

TIP   When creating the Java applet the form and the target cannot have the same name because the custom Java Applet class (BTFBankApplet) is named after the target and will extend the Java class (BTFBankApplet-Form) that extends java.applet.Applet, which is named after the form.

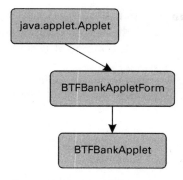

Figure 10.10 The BTFBankApple
class hierarchy

Now we can start coding our applet. On the BTFBankAppletForm class import the following files so that we can access the Jaguar server using CORBA:

```
import java.util.*;
import SessionManager.*;
import org.omg.CORBA.*;
```

We will need some data members (instance variables) to hold the Jaguar URL and the object reference to the BTFBank/Account object. Add the following data members:

```
BTFBank.Account jagAccount;
String JagURL  = " iiop://localhost:9000";
```

Create a protected user function, connectJag, to handle the connection to the Jaguar server on the BTFBankAppletForm class. The code for the connectJag function that connects to Jaguar using the SessionManger interface is listed below:

```
int myResult = 0;
short myAccount=0;
String myResponse = "";
org.omg.CORBA.StringHolder myResponseHolder;
java.math.BigDecimal myBalance = new java.math.BigDecimal(0);
BCD.Decimal myBCDBalance;

// setup properties to initialize ORB
Properties props = new Properties();
props.put("org.omg.CORBA.ORBClass", "com.sybase.CORBA.ORB");

// initialize ORB and get ORB object
ORB orb = ORB.init((String[]) null, props);

// get IOR for SessionManager/Manager
org.omg.CORBA.Object ior = orb.string_to_object(JagURL);
Manager manager = ManagerHelper.narrow(ior);

// create session on Jaguar & get Session object
Session session = manager.createSession("", "");

// lookup component
org.omg.CORBA.Object factObj = session.lookup("BTFBank/Account");
Factory factory = FactoryHelper.narrow(factObj);
jagAccount = BTFBank.AccountHelper.narrow(factory.create());
```

This code is covered in detail in section 10.15. In the BTFBankApplet class, open the `init` method and add the following line of code:

```
connectJag();
```

On the Object tab of the View dialog in PowerJ open the form and build the graphical user interface that the user will use to access the Jaguar component. Use AWT controls if you chose the Applet target and Swing controls if you chose the JApplet target.

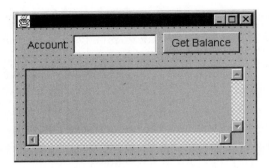

Figure 10.11
The BTFBankAppletForm

Add the event cb_getbalance_actionPerformed for the button. This event will invoke the getBalance method on the Account component and report the balance in the TextArea. The code is listed below:

```
short myAccountID=0;
String myResponse = "";
org.omg.CORBA.StringHolder myResponseHolder;
java.math.BigDecimal myBalance = new java.math.BigDecimal(0);
BCD.Decimal myBCDBalance;

texta_statusarea.setText("Getting balance...");
String myAccount = textf_account.getText();

try {
   myAccountID = (short) Integer.parseInt(myAccount);
   texta_statusarea.setText("Getting balance for account " +
myAccount.valueOf(myAccountID) + "...");

   myResponseHolder = new StringHolder(myResponse);

   try {
     // invoke methods on component
     myBCDBalance=jagAccount.getbalance(myAccountID, myResponseHolder);

     // convert BCD.Decimal to java.math.BigDecimal
     myBalance = com.sybase.CORBA.jdbc11.SQL.getBigDecimal(myBCDBalance);

     // Get String value out of Holder class
     myResponse = myResponseHolder.value;
     if (myBalance.floatValue() >= 0) {
        texta_statusarea.setText("Account Balance:" + myBalance.
toString());
     }
```

```
    else {
       texta_statusarea.setText(myResponse);
    }
  }
  catch(Exception e){
     texta_statusarea.setText("Exception encountered getting
balance...");
    }
}
catch(Exception e) {
  texta_statusarea.setText("Please enter a valid account
(all numbers)");
}
```

After the code is written, build the applet in PowerJ and run it in the applet viewer. The default runtime settings in PowerJ will run the applet in the applet viewer. The applet viewer simulates running in the browser and allows the applet class to be tested.

10.4 *How are applets embedded in HTML pages?*

The APPLET tag is used to embed a Java applet into an HTML page. The APPLET tag has a beginning tag, <APPLET> and an ending tag </APPLET>. The APPLET tag tells the web browser to reserve space in the document for the Java applet based on the HEIGHT and WIDTH attributes. The APPLET tag also tells the browser which Java class to download, where the class file is located, and if any additional files are required. Additional files and classes are stored in a Java Archive (JAR) file to make deployment and downloading easier.

The CODE attribute of the APPLET tag specifies the Java class file that extends java.applet.Applet and will be loaded in the browser JVM. Using our BTFBankApplet example, the class that is specified here is the one that has the same name as the target, BTFBankApplet. The CODEBASE attribute specifies the location of the Java Applet class as a URL or as a relative path to the document's base URL. If no CODEBASE is specified, the document's base URL is used as the default. The ARCHIVE attribute specifies any JAR or ZIP files that contain the additional classes that are required to run the applet. The location of these files is relative to the CODEBASE.

The HTML page that will allow our BTFBankApplet to be downloaded and run is listed below:

```
<HTML>
<TITLE>BTFBank</TITLE>
<BODY>
<H1>BTFBank Applet</H1>
<HR>
```

```
<APPLET CODE="BTFBankApplet.class" CODEBASE="classes/" ARCHIVE="BTFBankApplet-
   JAR.jar" width="361" height="197" >
</APPLET>
<HR>
</BODY>
</HTML>
```

An APPLET tag can have <PARAM> tags added between the <APPLET> and </APPLET> tags. The PARAM tag can be used to specify initialization information inside the HTML page for the Java applet. The initialization information in the PARAM tag is defined in name/value pairs. The NAME attribute specifies the name that the applet can use to access the value. The VALUE attribute defines the value associated with a name. An example of adding PARAM tags is shown below:

```
<APPLET CODE="BTFBankApplet.class" CODEBASE="classes/" ARCHIVE="BTFBankAp-
   pletJAR.jar" width="361" height="197" >
<PARAM NAME="TEST" VALUE="HELLOWORLD">
<PARAM NAME="JagURL" VALUE="iiop://localhost:9000">
</APPLET>
```

Building the JAR file for the Java applet and deploying the HTML page and the JAR file are covered in section 10.6.

10.5   *How do I access PARAM values in a Java applet?*

The PARAM tag values are processed in the `init` method of the Java applet class. The Applet class provides the `getParameter` method, which has the following method signature:

```
java.lang.String getParameter(name)
```

The `getParameter` method returns the value of a PARAM tag as a String. It returns a null if the request parameter does not exist. The `getParameter` argument is case-sensitive and needs to match the NAME attribute of the PARAM tag exactly. In order to change the Jaguar application server that a Java applet will try to access, we can add a PARAM tag as follows:

```
<APPLET …>
<PARAM NAME="JagURL" VALUE="iiop://localhost:9000">
</APPLET>
```

In the `init` method of the BTFBankApplet class we can access this parameter with the following line of code:

```
JagURL = getParameter("JagURL");
```

Make sure that the call to `getParameter` is placed before the call to the `connect-Jag` function otherwise the value will not be used.

TIP	If the web browser is using the sandbox to handle Java applets, then the Jaguar host name specified *must* be the same as the web server host name otherwise the connection to Jaguar will be denied. This is because Java applets can only access the host were it originated.

10.6 How do I deploy a Java applet to Jaguar?

Jaguar CTS does not run Java applets, but it can be used to deploy them to web browsers via an HTTP request. Java applets can also be deployed to any other web server using the same techniques we will discuss here. Before discussing how to deploy the files for our Java applet lets look at some of the files we will need:

- Java applet class.
- Supporting Java classes used by Java applet class.
- HTML file with an APPLET tag to download the Java applet.

The easiest way to deploy a Java applet that is made up of more than one Java class file is to collect them all and place them into a Java JAR file. To create the JAR file in PowerJ, create a new target. On the new dialog, select the Java JAR icon. We will build a target named BTFBankAppletJAR. Continue through the rest of the wizard. Once the target is generated, right click on it to access the popup menu. Select the Add Target Dependency option to open the dialog shown in figure 10.12.

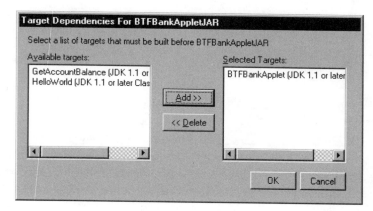

**Figure 10.12
Adding a target
dependency**

Select the BTFBankApplet target under the Available targets list and click the Add>> button. This tells the JAR target that the Java classes associated with this target should be included with the JAR file. Click OK to save.

Our Java applet uses a lot of additional Java classes to perform its tasks. These include org.omg.CORBA and SessionManager classes to access Jaguar and the

BTFBank/Account stubs to get an object reference to the Account component. These classes must be made available in the folder specified in the CODEBASE attribute of the APPLET tag or included in the JAR file in order for the Java applet to work correctly. Deploying the Java applet to Jaguar under the %JAG-UAR%\html\classes directory and using the following CODEBASE="classes/" will provide the applet with the access it needs to these additional classes. If the applet is deployed to another web server or a different directory in Jaguar, then the referenced classes should be included in the JAR file. To include the referenced classes in the JAR file, access the Build Options menu option for the JAR target. The Build Options dialog shown in figure 10.13 will open. On the Referenced Classes tab select the Deploy referenced classes option.

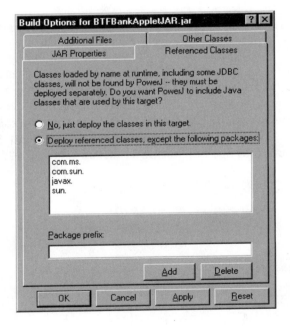

Figure 10.13
Build Options for the JAR target

Once this is done, click OK to save and then build the JAR file. Once the JAR file is built we need to deploy the HTML file and the JAR file to Jaguar CTS. Jaguar CTS can be used as a web server, but in order to do so it must have an active HTTP listener. The default HTTP listener when Jaguar is installed has a host name of local-host and listens on port 8080. In order to accept web requests from remote clients, the host name of the HTTP listener must be changed to either the IP address or computer name of the machine that Jaguar is installed on. In addition the port should be changed to 80 so that Jaguar can accept HTTP requests on the standard HTTP port, although this is not a requirement.

The default root directory for HTTP requests on Jaguar is %JAGUAR%\html. All HTML documents should be placed in this folder or a subdirectory under this folder. The JAR file can also be placed in the %JAGUAR%\html directory. If it is placed in this directory a CODEBASE attribute is not required. However, the JAR file will need to have all the referenced classes included in with it.

It is recommended that, when installing Java applets on the Jaguar server, the class and/or JAR files be placed in the %JAGUAR%\html\classes directory. This allows the applet to find any additional Java classes it may need. The CODEBASE attribute is required whenever the Java applet class and the HTML document are in separate directories. When the Java applet cannot find Java classes it needs locally it will attempt to find them in the directory specified by the CODEBASE. If the Java applet requires additional Java classes that are not already in the %JAGUAR%\html\classes directory, they can be added so that they are accessible when they are needed. See the Warning for an example of when additional classes may need to be added to the %JAGUAR%\html\classes folder.

WARNING Microsoft Internet Explorer does not include the Java RMI classes. In order for an applet to be able to communicate with the Jaguar CTS server, these classes are required. Class libraries that the applet does not find locally on the web browser are automatically requested from the same location where the applet was downloaded. The %JAGUAR%\html\classes directory does not include the Java RMI classes, so they must be added.

Running the applet in Internet Explorer with the Java console on will show misleading errors that are not indicative of the problem. The Java console reports that the Security Manager of the browser has thrown a SecurityException.

Special thanks go to Greg Douglas of Sybase Inc. for pointing this out on the Sybase SDN site. A zip file named JavaRMIclasses.zip contains the necessary RMI class files. Simply unzip this file in the %JAGUAR%\html\classes directory or equivalent directory on your web server to fix the problem.

Once the HTML document and the JAR file are deployed, and any additional classes are also correctly setup the Java applet can be accessed through a web browser, as shown in figure 10.14.

**Figure 10.14
Running the applet in
a browser**

10.7 What are Java servlets?

Java servlets are small server-side programs written in Java that are used to create dynamic web sites by extending an HTTP server. Java servlets are Sun's answer to CGI and allow developers to write Java programs to respond to HTTP requests. Servlets are designed to be faster than CGI because they run in the same server process as the HTTP server on a separate thread similar to ISAPI and NSAPI, rather than starting a new process for each request. The Java class that implements the servlet is loaded in memory once and remains in memory after use ready to process additional requests. Java servlets can even handle several requests simultaneously as long as they are thread-safe.

Java servlets are used to dynamically create web content, just like CGI programs, PowerDynamo, and Microsoft's ASP. Since Java servlets are Java programs, they can use all the rich functionality provided by the Java API to process requests and generate an HTML document. Figure 10.15 illustrates how a basic Java servlet responds to an HTTP request from a web browser. The HTTP server analyzes the URL notices that the URL is requesting a servlet and passes the request to the Java servlet engine. The Java servlet engine runs the Java servlet and the response, usually a dynamically generated HTML document, is returned to the web browser. A URL specifies a Java servlet by using a URL alias, which is similar to the PowerDynamo mapping covered in chapter 8. The default URL alias for servlets is /servlet, which is followed by the Java servlet name as shown in the URL below:

http://localhost:8080/servlet/JavaServlet_Name

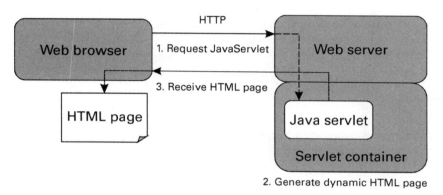

Figure 10.15   The basic Java servlet architecture

Java servlets, like all Java programs, are platform-independent. Java servlets are also server-independent, allowing them to be run on any application server that implements a servlet container. The servlet container receives the HTTP request and passes it off to the Java servlet instance. The container is a coordinator between the web server and the Java servlet instance, managing any input from the request and the generated output from the servlet, ensuring that they are handled correctly. In order for an HTTP server to run Java servlets, they need to have a servlet engine that implements a servlet container to handle the requests. The servlet container that the servlets run in must adhere to the Java servlet API and specification.

Jaguar CTS can act as a web server handling HTTP requests and has a built-in servlet engine allowing it to run Java servlets. Running on the Jaguar server, the Java servlet can also use Jaguar database connection caches or call Jaguar components to handle data processing. Using Java servlets as a wrapper, Jaguar components can be extended to handle HTTP requests. An HTML page can submit data through a hyperlink or an HTML FORM. The servlet receives the information submitted by the web browser and calls Jaguar components, supplying the data as function arguments. The Jaguar component can process the information and initiate the transactions passing the results back to the servlet, which can generate an appropriate HTML response. Figure 10.16 illustrates an extended Java servlet architecture using Jaguar CTS.

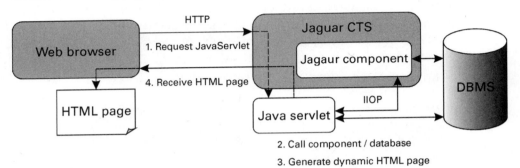

Figure 10.16 Using Java servlets to extend Jaguar to the Web

10.8 *How do Java servlets work?*

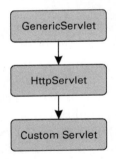

**Figure 10.17
The Java servlet
class hierarchy**

Java servlets that respond to HTTP requests extend the Http-Servlet class, which has a special interface defined by the Java Servlet API that is used by the servlet container. The HttpServlet class is located in the javax.servlet.http package. The Http-Servlet class is descended from the GenericServlet class, which is located in the javax.servlet package. The GenericServlet class defines an abstract Servlet class that is protocol-independent. The HttpServlet class is a specialized abstract servlet class that provides HTTP specific capabilities that are useful when writing a Java servlet that responds to HTTP requests. The Java class that implements the Java servlet extends the HttpServlet class as shown in figure 10.17.

The GenericServlet class provides several methods, three of which are essential to controlling the life cycle of the Java servlet. They are the init, destroy, and service methods and are listed in table 10.1. When a Java servlet container loads the Java Servlet class for the first time, the init method is invoked. This lets the Java servlet know that it is being put into use and allows the Java class to initialize itself. The servlet container only calls the init method once, when the Java class is initially instantiated. After that, the Java class instance is used to service incoming HTTP requests. The Java servlet cannot be accessed until the init method has completed. The init method accepts the servlet configuration object, ServletConfig. The ServletConfig object is used by the servlet container to pass configuration information to the Java servlet. The ServletConfig object contains the ServletContext object and any initialization parameters that might be provided. The ServletContext object provides information on the server the servlet is running on and defines a set of methods to allow a servlet to communicate with the container. The initialization parameters provide initialization values and are stored in name/value pairs. The initialization parameter values are used in the init method to initialize the Java class properly.

Table 10.1 The main GenericServlet method signatures

GenericServlet method signatures
public void init(ServletConfig config) throws ServletException
public void service (ServletRequest req, ServletResponse resp) throws ServletException, java.io.IOException
public void destroy()

A single Java servlet instance handles all the incoming HTTP requests. This sounds like a potential bottleneck for large systems. But a single Java servlet instance can handle all the HTTP requests quickly because the requests themselves are run on separate threads. The HTTP requests call the service method on the Java servlet instance causing the method to be executed on several threads concurrently as illustrated in figure 10.18. However, running a Java servlet like this requires it to be thread-safe.

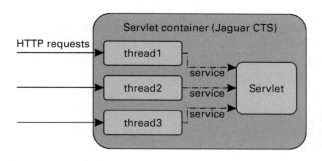

**Figure 10.18
Java Servlet handling
several requests.**

The service method is where the Java servlet handles responses to HTTP requests. The HttpServlet class has additional methods that are used to service an HTTP request that are listed in table 10.2.

Table 10.2 The main HttpServlet method signatures

HttpServlet method signatures
public void service (ServletRequest req, ServletResponse resp) throws ServletException, java.io.IOException
protected void service (HttpServletRequest req, HttpServletResponse resp) throws ServletException, java.io.IOException

HttpServlet method signatures (continued)
protected void doGet (HttpServletRequest req, HttpServletResponse resp) throws ServletException, java.io.IOException
protected void doPost (HttpServletRequest req, HttpServletResponse resp) throws ServletException, java.io.IOException

In the HttpServlet class the public service method on the GenericServlet class is overridden and it invokes the protected service method. The public service method should not be overridden on the custom Java class that extends HttpServlet. The protected service method routes HTTP requests to doXXX methods based on the type of HTTP request, for example a POST request is routed to the doPost method. The HttpServlet class defines doGet, doPost, doDelete, doPut, doTrace, and doOptions methods. It is easier to override the protected service method in the custom Java class and code the handler for the HTTP request once than it is to implement each individual doXXX method. This is due to the fact that an Anchor tag and an HTML FORM using the GET method send HTTP GET requests and an HTML FORM using the POST method sends HTTP POST requests resulting in two different doXXX methods being called. It is unlikely that these requests will require different responses.

The public service method accepts two arguments, the ServletRequest object and the ServletResponse object, which are provided by the Servlet container. These objects allow the Java Servlet to access information sent with the request and send a response. The public service method on the HttpServlet object not only invokes the protected service method but it converts the ServletRequest and ServletResponse objects into the HttpServletRequest and HttpServletResponse objects respectively. These are the arguments that the protected service method expects. The HttpServletRequest object encapsulates the information sent in the HTTP request including page parameters, content type, and remote address. It also allows access to the HttpSession object. The HttpServletResponse object provides methods for sending an HTTP response to the client. The protected service method is where the logic that the Java servlet class implements is written. It uses the HttpServletRequest and HttpServletResponse objects to handle the HTTP requests appropriately. This process is illustrated in figure 10.19.

When a server unloads the Java class that implements the Java servlet, the destroy method is invoked. This gives the Java class a chance to clean up any resources before it is removed from memory. The destroy method is only called once on any Java servlet instance.

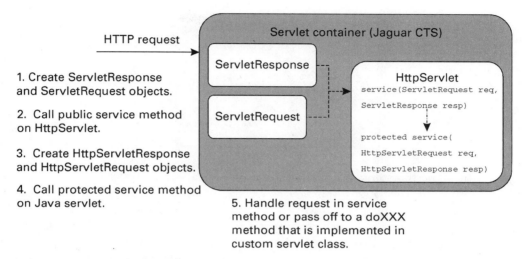

1. Create ServletResponse and ServletRequest objects.

2. Call public service method on HttpServlet.

3. Create HttpServletResponse and HttpServletRequest objects.

4. Call protected service method on Java servlet.

5. Handle request in service method or pass off to a doXXX method that is implemented in custom servlet class.

Figure 10.19 Overview of calling the service methods

10.9 How are Java servlets that are not thread-safe handled?

By default only a single instance of a Java servlet class is loaded into memory to handle all the HTTP requests. This single instance receives calls to the service method from multiple threads, representing multiple clients, at the same time so the servlet must be able to handle concurrent requests running at the same time on a single instance. In order for a servlet to handle concurrent requests, it must be thread-safe and must synchronize access to shared resources. Shared resources include instance variables, files, database connections, and remote object references. Figure 10.18 illustrates how a single servlet instance handles multiple requests simultaneously. It is run in separate threads that represent a different HTTP request.

If an instance of a Java servlet cannot be executed in several threads at the same time, it must let the servlet container know that it must be run single threaded. Java classes can implement the SingleThreadModel interface. This interface does not add any methods or functionality to the servlet; instead, it is used to indicate to the server that the Java servlet class is single threaded. When the Java servlet class is single-threaded, only one thread can call the service method on a single instance of the servlet at a given point in time. All additional requests to the servlet instance are serialized or queued until the service method has completed processing and is ready for the next request. This is pictured in figure 10.20.

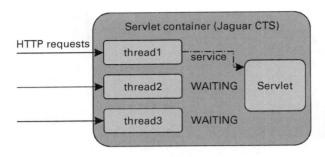

Figure 10.20
A Java servlet that implements the
SingleThreadModel interface

The threading of a Java servlet that is installed on Jaguar CTS can be configured through the Jaguar Manager as well. However, any Java servlet class that implements the SingleThreadModel interface will be run single-threaded regardless of the Jaguar threading property settings. To set the threading of a Java servlet installed on Jaguar CTS, highlight the servlet and choose the File | Servlet Properties menu option. The Servlet Properties dialog will be opened. Choose the Threading tab as shown in figure 10.21.

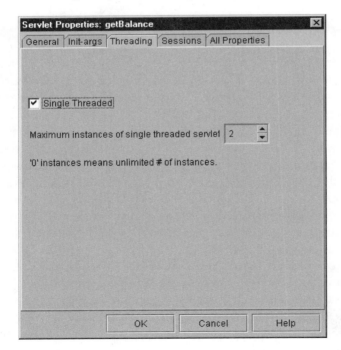

Figure 10.21
The Servlet Properties
Threading tab

Enable the Single Threaded option to tell Jaguar CTS to serialize calls to the Java servlet. This allows only one request to the service method to run at a given point in time in a Java servlet instance. Since trying to handle a large volume of serialized requests with a single instance of a Java servlet will not do anything to increase an application's performance or a user's overall experience with the web site, Jaguar allows multiple instances of the Java servlet to be created. Jaguar CTS allows several instances of the same Java servlet to be run in memory to increase performance and eliminate the waiting time for other threads. The Maximum instances field allows the administrator to configure how many Java servlet instances Jaguar should be allowed to create at any point in time.

When there is more than one instance of the Java servlet running, Jaguar directs incoming requests to the next available instance. If all the instances of the servlet are in use and Jaguar has already instantiated the maximum amount of classes, the remaining requests will need to wait until a service method finishes running on one of the instances. Only a single request will be run on any one instance of the Java servlet at a single point in time. However, at a single point in time, several instances of the same Java servlet class may be processing calls to the service method at once as shown in figure 10.22. Using multiple single-threaded instances of a Java servlet class can guarantee that each individual instance is thread-safe, protecting instance variables and other internal resources, It does not, however, guarantee access to external resources, like a file, will be thread-safe between instances running at the same time.

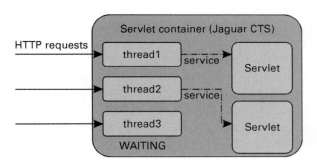

**Figure 10.22
A single-threaded servlet with
multiple running instances**

In general, writing thread-safe Java servlets should be the goal whenever possible. There are many techniques that can be used to make a Java class thread-safe, including using synchronized blocks of code and eliminating storage of state information in instance variables. For additional techniques check out the book *Java Threads,* published by O'Reilly.

10.10 When do I use Java servlets over Jaguar components?

Java servlets run on the Jaguar CTS server and can be used to write dynamic web applications. Although Java servlets can use the Java API to process business logic and access databases they do *not* and should *not* replace Jaguar components. Both servlets and Jaguar components have their appropriate uses and together form a powerful web application architecture. However, Java servlets can only be invoked by HTTP clients, typically web browsers, and return all of their output, typically HTML or XML pages, through the ServletOutputStream. Because of these limitations, any processing or business logic placed in the Java servlet will be "locked" into a web-only solution. Although Java servlets can use Jaguar database connection caches and can invoke methods on Jaguar components, they *cannot* participate in Jaguar transactions. On the other hand, a Jaguar component allows business logic to be extended to a wider variety of clients and can return complex objects and data types in their natural format. Jaguar components can also participate in Jaguar-managed transactions. Because logic placed in Jaguar components can run in a Jaguar managed transaction and be executed by several different clients (COM, CORBA, EJB) they offer more flexibility in how they can be used and are therefore better suited for implementing business and transaction logic.

Java servlets are ideal for handling web page specific processing eliminating this "presentation logic" from the middle-tier business components. They are also an ideal way to make Jaguar components available over the web. In order to make Jaguar components available over the web, they must be made available over HTTP requiring either PowerDynamo pages or Java servlets. By wrapping Jaguar component calls in a PowerDynamo page or a Java servlet, the Jaguar component becomes accessible to any client. Table 10.3 summarizes the differences between the Java servlet and the Jaguar component. Note that the Jaguar component does not need to be written in Java.

Table 10.3 Comparing the Java servlet and the Jaguar component

Task	Servlet	Component
Implement business logic	Yes	Yes
Access Jaguar database connection cache	Yes	Yes
Access Jaguar components on same or different server	Yes	Yes
Participate in a Jaguar transaction	No	Yes
Require a stub on the client	No	Yes
Available to HTTP request	Yes	No
Available to IIOP request	No	Yes

10.11 *How do I write a Java servlet?*

In this section we will look at how to write a simple Java servlet in PowerJ. Our first servlet example will simply walk us through the process of building a Java servlet, covering various aspects of servlet development. Our first Java servlet will return an HTML page that returns the message HelloWorld. We will build more complex servlets throughout the chapter.

Open PowerJ and create a New Workspace by selecting File | new Workspace from the menu. This Workspace is a collection of one or more targets. To create a New servlet there are three basic steps:

  1 Create a New Target: Java Classes.

  2 Create a New Class: Standard Class.

  3 Implement the service method.

The new target is used to collect the Java classes that will implement our HelloWorld servlet. To create a new target, select File | New from the menu. The New dialog will open. Select the Target tab and highlight the Java Classes icon as shown in figure 10.23. The remaining wizard dialogs will prompt you for the name of the target and where it should be placed. Name the target HelloWorld.

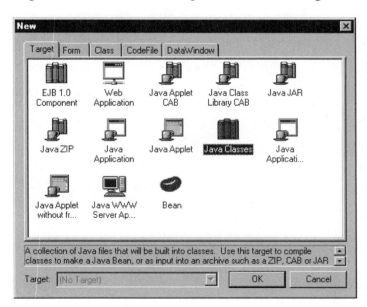

Figure 10.23
The Java Classes target

After the target is created, we will need to create a new Java class. To create a new Java class, select File | New from the menu. The New dialog will open. Select the Class tab and highlight the Standard Class icon as shown in figure 10.24. Notice that this class is being attached to the HelloWorld target we just created. In order to write a Java class in PowerJ, it must be associated with a target. Click OK to open the Class wizard shown in figure 10.25. On the Class wizard dialog specify the Java package name, the Java class name, and the class that the Java class extends. A custom Java servlet class extends the javax.servlet.http.HttpServlet class. Once the dialog is completed click the Finish button to generate the Java class.

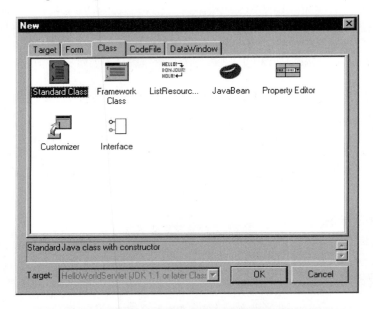

Figure 10.24
The Standard Java class

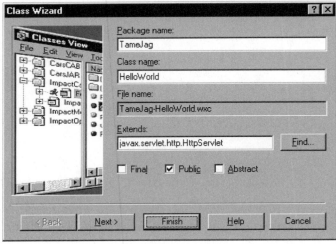

Figure 10.25
The Java Class wizard

Our Java class doesn't do much right now. Let's add the following import statements to get it started:

```
import java.io.*;
import javax.servlet.*;
import javax.servlet.http.*;
```

The java.io package contains the IOException that the service method throws plus the PrintWriter object (more on that soon). The remaining two packages contain classes that are needed by the Java servlet. After coding the import statements, let's override the protected service method of the HttpServlet class. To add a new method, highlight the Java class and choose Insert | Method as shown in figure 10.26. The Method wizard will open. Type the name of the method in the Name field and enter the function prototype as shown below and in figure 10.27.

```
protected void service(HttpServletRequest req, HttpServletResponse resp)
throws ServletException, IOException
```

Click the Finish button to generate the method prototype in the Java class.

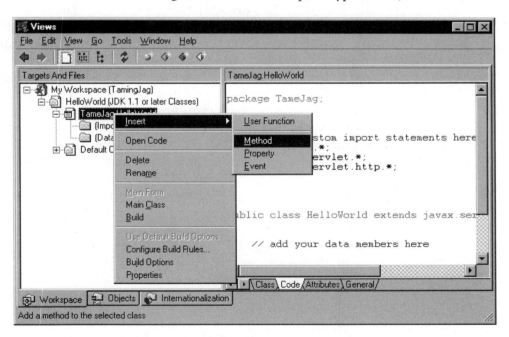

Figure 10.26   Adding a new Method to the Java class

Now that we have our method prototype we can look at how to write our service method to return a simple dynamically generated HTML page. The output for

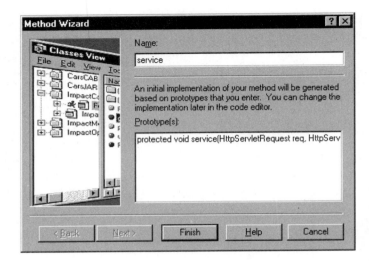

Figure 10.27
Overriding the service
method on HttpServlet

a Java Servlet is managed by the HttpServletResponse object. The output stream can be produced through the ServletOutputStream object or the java.io.PrintWriter object. To use the ServletOutputStream object, call the getOutputStream method of the HttpServletResponse object. To use the java.io.PrintWriter object, call the getWriter method of the HttpServletResponse object. The PrintWriter object is useful for returning character-encoded text like dynamically generated HTML pages. To send raw binary data use the ServletOutputStream.

The output from a servlet must specify the status, content type, and content that is being returned through the HttpServletResponse object. The HttpServletResponse object has methods to set the status (setStatus, sendError) and content type (setContentType). The default status is an HTTP 200 status code (SC_OK), so nothing needs to be done unless there is an error condition. The content type determines the character encoding used by the PrintWriter object and must be set using the setContent method before the PrintWriter object is obtained using the getWriter method. The content type for an HTML page is text/html. Other content types will require a different setting. The HTML page is built using the print and println methods to write to the PrintWriter object or ServletOutputStream object. The code sample below illustrates how our HelloWorld Java servlet service method is implemented.

```
protected void service(HttpServletRequest req, HttpServletResponse
resp) throws ServletException, IOException
{
    // override HttpServlet service method
    // allow a servlet to handle a GET and POST request the same way
```

```
    // set the content type for an HTML page
    resp.setContentType("text/html");

    // get the PrintWriter
    PrintWriter out = resp.getWriter();

    // generate the HTML page
    out.println("<HTML><HEAD><TITLE>HelloWorld</TITLE></HEAD>");
    out.println("<BODY>");
    out.println("<H1>Hello World - Servlet demo</H1>");
    out.println("</BODY></HTML>");

    // close the PrintWriter
    out.close();
}
```

Writing the function listed above in the doGet method instead of the service method would leave the doPost method without an implementation. Failure to implement a doXXX method will result in an HTTP bad request error (400) if it is actually called. Implementing the code in the protected service method over the doXXX methods has the advantage of being able to handle GET and POST requests the same way. Now we don't have to worry about an HTML FORM that changes the METHOD attribute between GET and POST or whether the servlet is called from an Anchor tag or a FORM using the POST method. Implementing the servlet in the protected service method also blocks all calls to the doXXX methods because the HttpServlet class implementation of the service method handles the redirection and it is overridden by the custom Java class.

10.12 How are Java servlets deployed to Jaguar?

Once the Java servlet class has been created and compiled, here are the steps to deploy a Java servlet to Jaguar:

1 Copy the class file to the Jaguar server.
2 Add a New Servlet through the Jaguar Manager.
3 Start the Java servlet.
4 Test the servlet via a web browser.

When the Java class used to implement the Java servlet is compiled in PowerJ, the class file is placed in either a Release or a Debug directory under the Target folder. If a release build was done, the class file is placed under the Release directory in a sub-directory named after the Java package. In the case of the HelloWorld servlet, the HelloWorld.class file is located under the HelloWorld\Release\TameJag folder.

On the Jaguar server, create a subdirectory under the %JAGUAR%\java\classes directory with the same name as the Java package for the Java servlet class. In our

example, this is TameJag. Copy the class file and place it in the new %JAGUAR%\java\
classes\TameJag directory.

TIP   The Java servlet class file does not have to be placed in the %JAGUAR%\ja-
va\classes path. It can be placed anywhere in the CLASSPATH as long as it
is in a subdirectory named after the Java package. It is important to note
that only Java servlet classes placed in the %JAGUAR%\java\classes path can
be refreshed.

In the Jaguar Manager, highlight the Jaguar server. Select the Installed Servlets
folder and right click to open the popup menu. Choose Install Servlet… as shown
in figure 10.28. When the next dialog opens, choose Create and install a New Servlet option. The New Servlet wizard will prompt you for a new servlet name. The
servlet name is the name that the Java servlet will appear under in the Jaguar Manager and the name that must be used in the URL to access the Java servlet class.
Type HelloWorld and click the Create New Servlet button. The Servlet Properties
dialog will open. On the General tab, enter the Servlet's fully qualified class name,
which is the Java package name followed by the Java class name separated by a "/"
as shown in figure 10.29. The Load during Startup option tells Jaguar whether the
Java servlet class instance should be instantiated when the Jaguar server starts up or
on the first request to the Java servlet. Because the init method is called when the
Java Servlet is instantiated, it is a good idea to have this done while the Jaguar
server is starting up, sparing the first request from having to wait for the class to be
instantiated and the init method to be run.

After the servlet is initially installed, the Java servlet must be started by highlighting the servlet name under the Installed Servlets folder and right clicking to
access the popup menu. Select the Start menu option. The Java servlet needs to be
refreshed when an existing Java servlet is redeployed by copying an updated class
file to the Jaguar server or making any changes to servlet properties. This is done by
highlighting the servlet name under the Installed Servlets folder and right clicking
to access the popup menu. Select the Refresh menu option. This stops the Java
servlet and restarts it.

Once the Java servlet has been started, it can be accessed through a web
browser. The default URL alias for servlets on the Jaguar server is \servlet\. The
URL to access the HelloWorld servlet is shown below:

http://localhost:8080/servlet/HelloWorld

The output from the Java servlet is shown in figure 10.30.

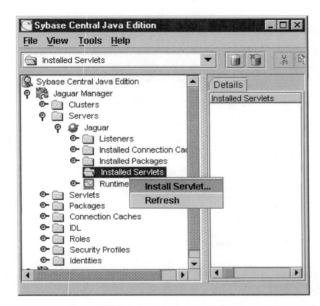

Figure 10.28
Installing a Java servlet

Figure 10.29
The Servlet Properties—
General tab

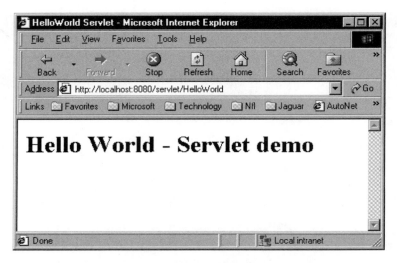

Figure 10.30   A dynamically generated HTML page from the Java servlet

WARNING   A HTTP return code of 400 (Bad Request) means there was a problem with the servlet. It usually means that Jaguar could not find the Java class or the service method was incorrectly coded.

10.13 How is a Java servlet initialized?

The HelloWorld Java servlet is a good example of a simple Java servlet, but it does not provide much in the way of functionality. Our next Java servlet will provide more functionality by accessing a Jaguar CORBA object. The CORBA object is a PowerBuilder component that returns account balances. In PowerJ, create a new target named GetAccountBalance. Create a new standard Java class TameJag.getAccountBalance that extends the javax.servlet.http.HttpServlet class.

In this section, we will look at how to initialize the Java servlet using initialization arguments. Initialization arguments are similar to an .ini file or using component properties to define initialization information the servlet needs. This information includes which database connection cache name to use or which Jaguar server to look in for a component. When the Jaguar server loads the Java servlet class for the first time, the init method is invoked. The init method is passed in the ServletConfig object as an argument from the servlet container. The ServletConfig object provides a method, getInitParameter, which allows the servlet to access initialization arguments. The syntax for the getInitParameter is listed below:

```
java.lang.String getInitParameter(java.lang.String Param_Name)
```

The Param_Name is the name of the initialization argument. The getInitParameter method returns a String value if the initialization parameter is found, otherwise it returns a null value. It is up to the Java servlet class to cast the value to the proper data type as required.

To access initialization arguments, we need to override the init method of the GenericServlet class. Create a new method on the getAccountBalance Java class with the following method signature:

```
public void init(ServletConfig conf) throws ServletException
```

TIP   When overriding the init method, make sure that the first line of code calls the ancestor init method so that the ServletConfig object is obtained from the servlet container. The line of code shown below will do the trick:
```
super.init(conf);
```

Declare three String data members (instance variables), which will be used to hold the initialization argument values as follows:

```
String JagURL = "";
String JagUser = "";
String JagPwd = "";
```

The code sample below shows how a Java servlet can use the getInitParameter method of the ServletConfig object to read in initialization argument values.

```
public void init(ServletConfig conf) throws ServletException
{
super.init(conf);

  JagURL = conf.getInitParameter("JagListener");
  if (JagURL == null) {
    log("init: Error getting JagListener configuration
parameter.");
  }
  else {
    log("init: JagListener:"+JagURL);
  }

  JagUser = conf.getInitParameter("JagUser");
  if (JagUser == null) {
    log("init: Error getting JagUser configuration parameter.");
  }
  else {
    log("init: JagUser:"+JagUser);
  }

  JagPwd = conf.getInitParameter("JagPwd");
  if (JagPwd == null) {
```

```
   log("init: Error getting JagPwd configuration parameter.");
}
else {
   log("init: JagPwd:"+JagPwd);
}

}
```

After coding the init method, build the Java Servlet and deploy it to the Jaguar Server. Name the servlet getBalance.

In order to define initialization arguments for a Java servlet, highlight the servlet name under the Installed Servlets folder in the Jaguar Manager. Choose the File | Servlet Properties… menu option. Select the Init-args tab on the Servlet Properties dialog as shown in figure 10.31.

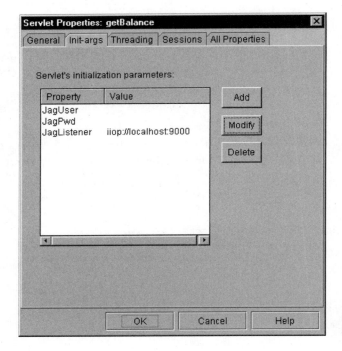

Figure 10.31
Servlet Properties—Init-args tab

The initialization arguments are listed on this tab. To add an initialization argument, click on the Add button. The New Property dialog shown in figure 10.32 will open. Specify the name of the initialization argument in the Property Name field and enter the value in the Property Value field. Click OK to save. The value typed in the Property Name field is the same name that the Java servlet must use as an argument to the getInitParameter method.

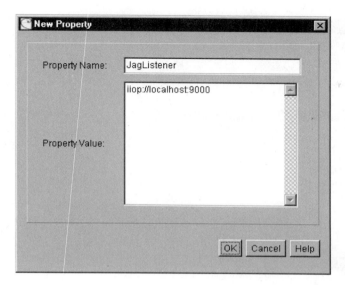

Figure 10.32
Adding an initialization argument

Once all the initialization arguments are added, refresh the Java servlet so that the init method gets executed and the values of the initialization arguments are accessed. Initialization arguments can be used to specify anything that the Java servlet needs to control, such as how it should handle requests from database connection cache names to debug options. If the Java servlet does not need to be initialized, this method does not need to be overridden and nothing needs to be specified on the Init-args tab. This is similar to the HelloWorld Java servlet.

WARNING After disconnecting from and reconnecting to Jaguar CTS through the Jaguar Manager, the initial arguments in the Init-args tab (figure 10.31) that were set are no longer listed. They are placed in the com.sybase.jaguar.sevlet.init.args property and are still available in the All Properties tab (figure 10.33). In addition, adding a new Init-arg value to the tab will overwrite the com.sybase.jaguar.sevlet.init.args property unless all the Init-arg values are also added again.

10.14 *How do I access input data in a Java servlet?*

The HttpServletRequest object extends the ServletRequest interface and provides methods that extend the Java Servlets ability to access information on an HTTP request it is processing. A Java servlet will typically need to access the page parameters that are being passed into it. Page parameters are passed in through the URL.

Figure 10.33
Servlet Properties—All
Properties tab

The ServletRequest object provides the getParameter method, which has the following method signature:

```
java.lang.String req.getParameter(name)
```

The getParameter method returns the value of a request parameter as a String. It returns a null if the request parameter does not exist. For an example of how this method can be used in a Java servlet, see the next section.

10.15 How do Java servlets access Jaguar components using CORBA?

A Java servlet can be used to perform a lot of complex business processing all by itself. It has the entire Java API at its disposal. However, a Java servlet can be accessed only by an HTTP request, so a better use would be to call methods on a Jaguar component that implements the business logic we are interested in running—rather than implementing it in a Java servlet.

We will continue working on the Java servlet TameJag.getAccountBalance that was started in the last section. This servlet will call a CORBA object that is written in PowerBuilder to get an account balance. The CORBA object is deployed to Jaguar under the Jaguar package BTFBank with the component name Account. The

BTFBank/Account component has a method getbalance, which has the following method signature in Jaguar:

```
decimal getbalance(integer<16> in, string inout)
```

This method signature translates to a Java stub method signature as follows:

```
BCD.Decimal getbalance(short, StringHolder)
```

In order for a Java servlet to use a CORBA-compliant Jaguar component, the Java class must have access to the CORBA Java stubs. Generating CORBA Java stubs from the Jaguar Manager was covered in detail in chapter 9, section 6. Once we ensure that the Java stubs are generated and compiled (so that our Java servlet class will have access to them), we can look at how to call methods on the Jaguar component. There are three techniques we can use to get a remote object reference to the Jaguar component: the Interoperable Reference (IOR), the CORBA CosNaming API, and the SessionManager interface provided by Jaguar CTS.

Getting the remote object reference using an IOR is the easiest way to access a CORBA component from a Java servlet. The IOR is part of the CORBA standard and it defines syntax for representing an object reference as a string. A standard CORBA IOR is a hex-encoded text string that describes how to connect to the server hosting the object. However, to access components on the same server, the string_to_object method on the ORB can be used with an IOR string defined as Package/Component. Using this IOR will access the Jaguar component on the same Jaguar server as the Java servlet. The code sample to implement this is listed below:

```
Properties props = new Properties();
props.put("org.omg.CORBA.ORBClass", "com.sybase.CORBA.ORB");
ORB orb = ORB.init((String[])null, props);
BTFBank.Account jagAccount=
BTFBank.AccountHelper.narrow(orb.string_to_object("BTFBank/Account"));
```

The only downside to using the IOR technique described above is that the Jaguar component must exist on the same Jaguar server as the Java servlet. If this is not the case, the Jaguar naming services could be used through either the CORBA CosNaming API or the SessionManager interface. Using the SessionManager interface, the Java servlet uses a URL-formatted IOR and the string_to_object method to get a reference to the Manager object. The URL-IOR is not a standard IOR and is not supported across all ORBs. The URL string is specified as follows:

```
iiop:// host:iiop_port
```

The string_to_object method returns an IOR that can be narrowed to the Manager object. This IOR does not force the Java servlet to use a Jaguar component on the same Jaguar server on which the servlet class is running Using the Manager object, a session can be created using the createSession method. The Session object that is returned by the createSession method allows us to look up the CORBA component using the method by supplying the Package/Component name. The lookup method uses the Jaguar naming services and returns a factory object that can be used to create the object reference to the CORBA object we want to use, in this case BTFBank/Account.

```
// setup properties to initialize ORB
Properties props = new Properties();
props.put("org.omg.CORBA.ORBClass", "com.sybase.CORBA.ORB");

// initialize ORB and get ORB object
ORB orb = ORB.init((String[]) null, props);

// get IOR for SessionManager/Manager
org.omg.CORBA.Object ior = orb.string_to_object(JagURL);
Manager manager = ManagerHelper.narrow(ior);

// create session on Jaguar & get Session object
Session session = manager.createSession(JagUser, JagPwd);

// lookup component
org.omg.CORBA.Object factObj = session.lookup("BTFBank/Account");
Factory factory = FactoryHelper.narrow(factObj);
BTFBank.Account jagAccount = BTFBank.AccountHelper.narrow
(factory.create());
```

Notice in the code above that the instance variables that were initialized in the init method with values supplied by the initialization arguments were used. The initialization arguments were covered in section 10.13.

    The entire service method using the IOR technique (it's shorter) is listed below. The only change that needs to be made to the method to use the SessionManager interface is to replace the code between the comments *// Get CORBA component using IOR* and *// invoke methods on component* with the code section above.

```
protected void service(HttpServletRequest req, HttpServletResponse resp)
 throws ServletException, IOException
{
  int myResult = 0;
  short myAccount=0;
  String myResponse = "";
  org.omg.CORBA.StringHolder myResponseHolder;
  java.math.BigDecimal myBalance = new java.math.BigDecimal(0);
  BCD.Decimal myBCDBalance;

  try {
    myAccount = new Short(req.getParameter("account_id")).shortValue();
    myResponseHolder = new org.omg.CORBA.StringHolder(myResponse);
    try {
      // Get CORBA component using IOR
      Properties props = new Properties();
```

```
      props.put("org.omg.CORBA.ORBClass", "com.sybase.CORBA.ORB");
      ORB orb = ORB.init((String[])null, props);
      BTFBank.Account jagAccount=
    BTFBank.AccountHelper.narrow(orb.string_to_object("BTFBank/Account"));

      // invoke methods on component
      myBCDBalance=jagAccount.getbalance(myAccount,
       myResponseHolder);

      // convert BCD.Decimal to java.math.BigDecimal
myBalance =
        com.sybase.CORBA.jdbc11.SQL.getBigDecimal(myBCDBalance);

      // Get String value out of Holder class
      myResponse = myResponseHolder.value;
      myResult = 1;
    }
    catch (Exception e) {
      myResult = -1;
      log("Exception:" + e.getMessage());
    }
  }
  catch(java.lang.NumberFormatException e) {
    myResult = -1;
    log("NumberFormatException thrown.");
  }

  // Generate HTML response
  resp.setContentType("text/html");

  // get PrintWriter
  PrintWriter out = resp.getWriter();
  out.println("<HTML  ><HEAD><TITLE>BTFBank online</TITLE></HEAD>");
  out.println("<BODY>");
  out.println("<H1>Account Balance</H1>");
  if (myResult == 1) {
    if (myBalance.floatValue()>0) {
      out.println("<P>Account balance:" +  myBalance.toString() + "</P>");
    }
    else {
      out.println("<P>"+myResponse+"</P>");
    }
  }
  else {
    out.println("<P>the account was not specified.</P>");
  }
  out.println("</BODY></HTML>");

  out.close();
      }
```

The Java servlet expects to receive a page parameter named account_id as part of the request. The value of the request parameter account_id is obtained using the getParameter method on the HttpServletRequest object. The code sample below lists the appropriate line of code from the service method:

```
myAccount = new Short(req.getParameter("account_id")).shortValue();
```

The rest of the code handles the cases where an account_id value is passed in, as well as when it is not passed in, and generates the HTML page accordingly.

10.16 How do Java servlets access Jaguar components using EJB?

Servlets can use JNDI classes in the javax.naming packages to access cached database connections in Jaguar. This is covered in detail in chapter 3, sections 13 and 14.

10.17 How do servlets log messages?

Java servlets can use the log method in the GenericServlet class to write messages to the Jaguar servlet log file. The Jaguar servlet log file is named httpservlet.log and is located in the %JAGUAR%\bin directory. The log method of the GenericServlet class has the following method signature:

```
public void log(java.lang.String msg)
```

> **TIP** The Jaguar servlet log file name can be changed by accessing the sybase.jaguar.server.http.servletlogname property under the All Properties tab of the Server Properties dialog.

In addition to using the log method on the GenericServlet class, the Java servlet can also use the writeLog method on the Jaguar object in the com.sybase.jaguar.server package to write messages to the standard Jaguar log file. The default standard Jaguar log file is srv.log. The writeLog method has the following method signature:

```
public static native void writeLog(boolean use_date, java.lang.
String msg)
```

10.18 How is state managed in a Java servlet?

The Web uses a stateless communication protocol resulting in a disconnection from the web server after each request. Like our PowerDynamo templates, a Java servlet—due to the nature of the Web—is essentially a stateless object. Any information that is generated during the execution of the service method of a servlet for a client session will be lost when the request is finished. This is even more important with servlets that do not serialize requests.. Unlike our PowerDynamo templates, a single Java servlet instance can be accessed by several client requests concurrently. Any state stored in instance variables that are specific to a particular client session are going to be corrupted by other requests within the same method call. Even if the servlet instance is single-threaded, the state stored in instance variables is valid only during a single method call. Any subsequent calls to the same servlet can result in a different instance being used to satisfy the request or an instance that has been used to satisfy requests for other clients in the interim. Like any web application, it is important to be able to save state between requests for a single client session. A Java servlet is essentially a PowerDynamo script, especially when dealing with state management. It can use any of the same state management options that were discussed in chapter 9, section 5.

In general, the best way to manage state is to pass a unique session ID to a client session that it maintains between requests. This session ID allows a Java servlet to either get the remaining state values from a database or it can pass this value to a Jaguar component that is managing its own state. The javax.servlet.http.HttpSession object is defined in the Java servlet API to help a Java servlet maintain state between requests for a particular client session. The HttpServletRequest object has a method, getSession, which allows the Java servlet to access the HttpSession object. The getSession method has the following method signature:

```
HttpSession getSession(boolean new_session)
```

The new_session argument is used to tell the HttpServletRequest object how to handle a situation where an HttpSession object does not exist. Passing in true will create a new HttpSession object if one does not already exist. Passing a value of false will return a null value if there is not already an HttpSession object.

The servlet container assigns a unique session ID to the client. This session ID must be passed back to the client so that it can be passed back on later requests so the correct state information can be retrieved. The session ID and any other session values are stored in a cookie. The session ID can be retrieved from the HttpSession object using the getID method. Additional information can be stored and retrieved using the putValue and getValue methods.

```
java.lang.String getID()
java.lang.Object getValue(java.lang.String name)
void putValue(java.lang.String name, java.lang.Object value)
```

It is probably a better overall design to use the session ID to store additional state in a database that is accessible by the Java servlet. You can also use the session ID as an argument to a component that manages state storage and retrieval on its own. It is not recommended to store vast amounts of state data in the HttpSession object.

WARNING The Java servlet 2.2 specification deprecates getValue and putValue, replacing them with getAttribute and setAttribute, respectively. Both functions have the same method signature, and only the names have changed.

The Java servlet can use the isNew method of the HttpSession object to determine if the client request has a current session or is using a newly created session. The isNew method returns true if it is a new session and false otherwise.

If your Java servlet will use session tracking, it must be enabled on the Sessions tab of the Servlet Properties dialog as shown in figure 10.34. When enabling session tracking, the time-out field specifies in seconds how long the session will be kept between requests. If the specified time in the time-out field has elapsed between requests, the session is discarded.

Figure 10.34
Enabling session tracking

Using the HttpSession object, we can track the number of times particular clients check their account balances, which demonstrates how to use session tracking in a Java servlet. The code sample that can be added to the service method of the getAccountBalance Java class is shown below:

```
// Track number of times a particular client checks account balance
Integer visit_counter;
HttpSession mySession = req.getSession(true);

if (mySession.isNew()) {
visit_counter = new Integer(1);
}
else {
   visit_counter = (Integer)
   mySession.getValue("getbalance.visitcounter");
   if (visit_counter == null)
      visit_counter = new Integer(1);
   else
      visit_counter = new Integer(visit_counter.intValue() + 1);
}
mySession.putValue("getbalance.visitcounter", visit_counter);
```

Because we are tracking the number of times a particular client is checking an account balance, we can report that in the HTML page as well by adding the following line of code:

```
out.println("<P>You checked an account balance " + visit_counter.
toString() + " time(s).");
```

10.19 How do Java servlets use database connection caches?

Servlets can use the com.sybase.jaguar.jcm.JCM and com.sybase.jaguar.jcm.JCM-Cache classes to access cached database connections in Jaguar. This is covered in detail in chapter 3.

10.20 What do the Java servlet properties on Jaguar do?

The Jaguar server has several servlet properties that affect how or whether a Java servlet can run. The Jaguar server-wide properties that govern servlets are listed on the servlets tab of the Server Properties dialog pictured in figure 10.35.

The Enable Servlet execution option allows servlets to be executed on the Jaguar CTS server. This is enabled by default. If this checkbox is not checked and servlet execution is disabled, Java servlets will not be executed and all attempts will generate a HTTP 400 Bad Request response.

The Enable Class-Name request option allows a servlet to be accessed by its class name as well as its servlet name. To access the Java servlet getBalance, which is implemented by the Java class TameJag.getAccountBalance, the following URL could be typed:

http://localhost:8080/TameJag.getAccountBalance

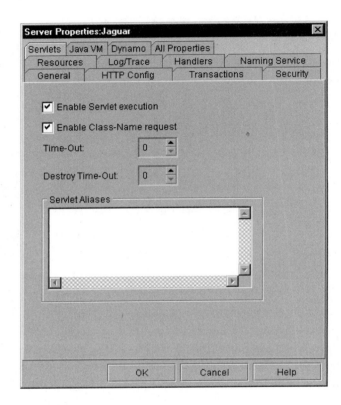

Figure 10.35
Jaguar Server-servlet properties

The Time-Out option tells the Jaguar server how long the init method of a servlet should be allowed to execute in seconds. The default is zero (0), which allows the init method to run for as long as it needs to. If the Time-Out option is set and the init method does not finish in the allotted time, the servlet is unavailable and must be refreshed or restarted.

TIP   An individual Java servlet can override the server time-out setting by adding the com.sybase.jaguar.servlet.init.timeout property under the All Properties tab of the Servlet Properties dialog. The value is measured in seconds.

When a servlet is refreshed or stopped, the destroy method is called. The Destroy Time-Out option tells the Jaguar server how long to wait in seconds before calling the destroy method of a servlet after a refresh or stop has been requested. The default is zero (0), which allows the destroy method to be called immediately.

An individual Java Servlet can override the server destroy time-out setting by adding the com.sybase.jaguar.servlet.desroy.wait-time property under the All Properties tab of the Servlet Properties dialog. The value is measured in seconds.

The Servlet Aliases option allows URL path prefixes to be set up. The URL path prefixes notify the Jaguar server that it should look for a servlet and work similarly to the PowerDynamo mapping. The default servlet alias is */servlet/*. To override the default servlet alias, enter each prefix in the box provided, each on a separate line. When adding a servlet alias, add a "/" to the beginning and the end of the alias name, or it will not work as expected. You must also add /servlet/ to the list of aliases. If you don't, it is overridden with the new values and will not work at all.

After adding /myJava/ to the servlet alias list and restarting the Jaguar server, the URL listed below will allow the getBalance servlet to be called:

http://localhost:8080/myJava/getBalance?account_id=100

If the alias were added as /myJava, the URL above would not work. Interestingly enough, leaving off the last "/" allows a URL typed as follows to call the servlet getBalance servlet:

http://localhost:8080/myJavagetBalance?account_id=100

TIP Any changes to the Servlets tab on the Server Properties dialog requires the Jaguar server to be stopped and restarted in order to take effect.

10.21 What are Java Server Pages?

Java Server Pages (JSP) is a new technology defined by the J2EE specifications. JSP is similar to PowerDynamo or Microsoft ASP. It allows page-centric development of a dynamic web site combining HTML or XML tags and Java. JSP relies on Java as the "scripting" language replacing DynaScript in PowerDynamo, and VBScript in ASP. This allows the full power of Java to be exploited on the Web. Java code is embedded in special tags: The symbol <% indicates the beginning of Java code and %> marks the end of Java code. Everything in between these tags is run on the server. A sample JSP page is shown below:

```
<HTML>
<BODY>
<%@ page language="java" import="" %>
<H1>JSP Sample Page</H1>
```

```
<%

String myPageParam = request.getParameter("page_param_name");
out.println(myPageParam);

%>
</BODY>
</HTML>
```

A JSP page is deployed as a page or document, but is executed as a Java servlet. When a request for a JSP page is made, Jaguar checks to see if the file has changed since the last time it was compiled, if it has the JSP page is compiled as a servlet and executed. If the page has not changed since the last compile, the existing servlet class is executed.

FYI   Sybase showcased this technology in the recent J2EE Whistle-stop Tour. However, the beta versions of Jaguar 3.6 and PowerJ 3.6 were not made available at the time of this writing so the details of how this technology works cannot be provided. Check the Manning web site (www.manning.com) and Author Online forum for updates.

The JSP page has special server-side tags to handle things like including other files or scripts, defining variables, and directing requests. JSP also allows custom tags to be defined. JSP, like the Java servlet, has a request, response, and session object to manage incoming and outgoing information and state. JSP pages can make calls to other Jaguar components and EJB objects similar to PowerDynamo pages. Like PowerDynamo or Java servlets, it is recommended that most (if not all) business and transactional logic be placed in a Jaguar component and called from a JSP.

JSP, like PowerDynamo, allows web pages to be laid out and developed by the web team in HTML and XML. Web pages can also be enhanced with dynamic content by the development team with embedded scripts. One of the benefits that JSP will offer over PowerDynamo is the ability to code "scripts" in Java instead of the DynaScript scripting language. This increases the learning curve (if you already know Java) and it should add a performance boost because the JSP will be compiled (at least into bytecodes). In addition, development of the JSP can be done in the PowerJ environment.

While the JSP will be executed as a Java servlet, it also offers some advantages over writing Java servlets directly. Java servlets embed HTML within Java, making it difficult to change the web page unless you are proficient in Java. It also requires a recompile and deployment to the Jaguar server followed by a refresh of the servlet for every change. JSP allows the code to be maintained and deployed as pages, which are easier to write and deploy.

JAGUAR data types

A

Table A.1 Mapping Jaguar/CORBA data types to PowerBuilder and Java data types

PowerBuilder data type	Java data type	CORBA IDL	Jaguar data type	Mode
integer	short	short	integer<16>	In, return
integer	org.omg.CORBA.ShortHolder	short	integer<16>	Inout / out
long	int	long	integer<32>	In, return
long	org.omg.CORBA.IntHolder	long	integer<32>	Inout, out
-	long	long long	integer<64>	In, return
-	org.omg.CORBA.LongHolder	long long	integer<64>	Inout, out
real	float	float	float	In, return
real	org.omg.CORBA.FloatHolder	float	float	Inout / out
double	double	double	double	In, return
double	org.omg.CORBA.DoubleHolder	double	double	Inout / out
boolean	boolean	boolean	boolean	In, return
boolean	org.omg.CORBA.BooleanHolder	boolean	boolean	Inout / out
char	char	char	char	In, return
char	org.omg.CORBA.CharHolder	char	char	Inout / out
string	java.lang.String	string	string	In, return
string	org.omg.CORBA.StringHolder	string	string	Inout / out
-	byte	byte	octet	In, return
-	org.omg.CORBA.ByteHolder	byte	octet	Inout / out
blob	byte[]	BCD::Binary	binary	In, return
blob	BCD.BinaryHolder	BCD::Binary	binary	Inout / out
decimal	BCD.Decimal	BCD::Decimal	decimal	In, return
decimal	BCD.DecimalHolder	BCD::Decimal	decimal	Inout / out
decimal	BCD.Money	BCD::Money	money	In, return
decimal	BCD.MoneyHolder	BCD::Money	money	Inout / out
date	MJD.Date	MJD::Date	date	In, return
date	MJD.DateHolder	MJD::Date	date	Inout / out
time	MJD.Time	MJD::Time	time	In, return
time	MJD.TimeHolder	MJD::Time	time	Inout / out
datetime	MJD.Timestamp	MJD::Timestamp	timestamp	In, return
datetime	MJD.TimestampHolder	MJD::Timestamp	timestamp	Inout / out
resultset	TabularResults.ResultSet	Tabular-Results::ResultSet	ResultSet	In, return
resultset	TabularResults.ResultSetHolder	Tabular-Results::Result-SetHolder	ResultSet	Inout / out

Table A.1 Mapping Jaguar/CORBA data types to PowerBuilder and Java data types

resultsets	TabularResults.ResultSet[]	Tabular-Results::ResultSet	ResultSets	In, return
resultsets	TabularResults.ResultSetsHolder	Tabular-Results::ResultSet	ResultSets	Inout / out

Table A.2 Mapping Java JDBC data types to CORBA IDL

Java JDBC types	CORBA IDL	Mode
java.math.BigDecimal	BCD::Decimal	In, return
com.sybase.jaguar.util.jdbc11.BigDecimalHolder	BCD::Decimal	Inout / out
java.math.BigDecimal	Bcell Icell	
com.sybase.jaguar.util.jdbc11.BigDecimalHolder	BCD::Money	Inout / out
java.sql.Date	MJD::Date	In, return
com.sybase.jaguar.util.jdbc11.DateHolder	MJD::Date	Inout / out
java.sql.Time	MJD::Time	In, return
com.sybase.jaguar.util.jdbc11.TimeHolder	MJD::Time	Inout / out
java.sql.Timestamp	MJD::Timestamp	In, return
com.sybase.jaguar.util.jdbc11.TimestampHolder	MJD::Timestamp	Inout / out
java.sql.ResultSet	TabularResults::ResultSet	In, return
	TabularResults::ResultSet	Inout / out

B

A look ahead at Jaguar CTS 3.6

Jaguar CTS 3.6 and PowerJ 3.6 went to beta as this book was being published. The release of these products will include several new features that update the capabilities of Jaguar CTS, making it compliant with the J2EE initiative. The feature list for Jaguar CTS 3.6 is extensive for a point release. It includes EJB 1.1 support, which has container-managed persistence, XML deployment descriptors, and new EJB transactional attributes. In addition, Jaguar CTS 3.6 will include JavaMail, JSP 1.1, and JMS. Java Message Service (JMS) provides queues for passing and processing messages. Servlet 2.2 support is added as well, which includes additional packaging and deployment capabilities, failover, and access control lists.

New features/upgrades due out in EAServer 3.6, to be released any day now, are:

- Enterprise Java Beans (EJB)

  EJB is server-side component model for building Java components. The latest EJB specification is 1.1. The 2.0 specification draft is also available. See chapter 3 for more information on EJB components.
  http://www.javasoft.com/products/ejb/

- Java Message Service (JMS)

  JMS is a set of classes that will work with messaging technologies to provide reliable, asynchronous communication between components.
  http://www.javasoft.com/products/jms/

- Java Server Pages (JSP)

  JSP technology is an extension of the Java Servlet API and allows dynamic Web sites to be built using a page-centric development approach with Java. The latest specification is JSP 1.1. See chapter 10 for an overview of JSP.
  http://www.javasoft.com/products/jsp/

- Java servlets

  Java servlets are server-side Java programs that extend Web server capabilities. The latest Servlet API is version 2.2. For more information, see chapter 10.
  http://www.javasoft.com/products/servlet/

- Java Naming and Directory Interface (JNDI)

  JNDI provides a means to access various naming and directory services to locate components in the enterprise, which is used by EJB components and clients. The latest release is JNDI 1.2.
  http://www.javasoft.com/products/jndi/

- Java Transaction API (JTA)

    JTA provides an interface to transaction managers. JTA allows components to interact with a distributed transaction manager or application server, which impacts how the transactions are managed.
    http://www.javasoft.com/products/jta/

- JavaMail

    JavaMail provides a set of abstract classes to interact with a mail system.
    http://www.javasoft.com/products/javamail/

NOTE The Sybase production team has reported that JMS and JavaMail will not be part of the Jaguar CTS 3.6 release. These features will be added later as part of the Jaguar branding initiative.

PowerJ 3.6 will be able to allow a developer to take advantage of the new J2EE features in Jaguar CTS. Some of these features include:

- Migration of EJB 1.0 objects to EJB 1.1, including an update to the deployment descriptors.
- EJB 1.1 target wizard, which is similar to the EJB 1.0 target wizard in PowerJ 3.5
- Capability to deploy EJB 1.1 component to Jaguar with a JAR file
- Java Servlet 2.2 target wizard
- Capability to deploy Servlets with a WAR file
- Capability to debug Java servlets
- Java Server Pages (JSP) 1.1 target wizard
- Capability to deploy JSP files with a WAR file
- Automatic creation of the J2EE deployment descriptor, which is an XML file that tells the application server how to deploy the component and set up its attributes.

EAServer certification

On June 5, 2000, Sybase announced the availability of the EAServer Developer-Associate certification. This certification is designed to help customers identify application developers with qualified Sybase Enterprise Application Server expertise. The EAServer Developer-Associate exam (#510-501) consists of fifty multiple-choice questions that must be completed in seventy-five minutes. A passing score is 70 percent, or 35 questions answered correctly. The initial cost to take the exam is $150. Anyone can take the exam and no prior certifications are required. Sybase allows candidates to retake an exam within a 30-day period if an exam is not passed initially.

The proficiencies that the exam will attempt to measure are taken from the tasks listed on the Sybase Web site and seem very much slated towards Java developers and Java-related technologies. The exam also covers Jaguar administration and configuration issues. PowerBuilder developers without Java experience may have difficulty passing the exam based on the exam topics. In addition, Jaguar CTS 3.6 features appear to make up part of the exam despite the fact that the product is not shipping yet.

Some of the tasks on the exam include:

1 Design and develop reusable enterprise components using both EJB and non-EJB components.

2 Design and develop JSP and Java servlets (Jaguar CTS 3.6).

3 Develop clients that can access EJB components.

4 Understand differences between CORBA and EJB.

5 Create and configure database connection pools.

6 Acquire and release database connection pools from a component.

7 Build EJB components that satisfy transactional requirements.

8 Use JTA to manage transactions.

9 Use Sybase tools to develop and debug components.

10 Deploy and configure JSP, servlets and EJB components into Jaguar (Jaguar CTS 3.6).

11 Modify application server properties.

12 Use Jaguar Manager to analyze performance and tune applications.

13 Explain how application design and implementation impacts resources.

14 Set up security policies.

15 Configure load balancing and clustering.

16 Implement failover mechanisms.

While this book does not directly address taking the exam for EAServer certification, the concepts and tasks that the exam covers as outlined by Sybase are explored in detail and should help readers prepare for the exam.

DISCLAIMER   The authors have not taken the exam at the time of this writing. (We were too busy preparing this book, so all information is based on what we could learn from Sybase.)

For more information check out:

http://slc.sybase.com/certification/index.html

This exam is also part of the Certification Initiative for Enterprise Development, which is promoting standards and skill validation for developers using Java and application servers to develop enterprise applications. Sybase is a sponsoring member along with IBM, BEA, Sun Microsystems, and others.

For more information check out:

http://www.jcert.org

index